ROMAN LITERATURE

BY

MICHAEL GRANT

*Professor of Humanity in the
University of Edinburgh*

CAMBRIDGE
AT THE UNIVERSITY PRESS
1954

PUBLISHED BY
THE SYNDICS OF THE CAMBRIDGE UNIVERSITY PRESS

London Office: Bentley House, N.W. 1
American Branch: New York

Agents for Canada, India, and Pakistan: Macmillan

Printed in Great Britain at the University Press, Cambridge
(Brooke Crutchley, University Printer)

ROMAN LITERATURE

870.9
J770

CONTENTS

ACKNOWLEDGEMENTS   *page* vii

INTRODUCTION

1. General Development: Romans and Greeks   3
2. The First Roman Success: Comedy   14

PART I. PROSE WORKS

CHAPTER I. CICERO

1. Cicero's Speeches   35
2. Attitudes to Public Speaking   50
3. Guides to Behaviour: Cicero and Seneca. Law   65
4. The Roman Letter   76

CHAPTER II. FACT AND FICTION

1. History   84
2. From Caesar to Livy   94
3. Tacitus   108
4. Biography and Fiction   117

PART II. POETRY

CHAPTER III. POETRY: LUCRETIUS AND CATULLUS

1. Attitudes to Poetry   133
2. Poetry of Instruction: Lucretius   152
3. Love Lyric and Love Elegy: Catullus and Propertius   158

41928   v

CONTENTS

CHAPTER IV. VIRGIL

1. Pastoral Poetry: the *Eclogues*   *page* 175

2. Descriptive Poetry: the *Georgics*   184

3. Romantic Epic: the *Aeneid*   190

CHAPTER V. HORACE, OVID AND AFTER

1. Literary Lyric and Satire: Horace   205

2. The New Elegy and the *Metamorphoses*: Ovid   223

3. Post-Augustan Poetry   235

EPILOGUE

The Survival of Roman Literature   255

APPENDICES

1. Greek Philosophy learnt by the Romans   277

2. Metre   280

3. List of Roman Emperors   283

4. Who's Who   285

INDEX   293

MAP OF ROMAN EMPIRE   *Inside front cover*

CHART: SOME PRINCIPAL SURVIVING
        LATIN WRITERS   *Inside back cover*

vi

ACKNOWLEDGEMENTS

I AM very grateful to Professor R. A. B. Mynors, and to my Edinburgh colleagues Mr W. K. Smith, Mr Denys Hay, Mr Kenneth Wellesley and Mr J. H. Bishop, for giving me the benefit of their invaluable criticism and advice in regard to a number of the topics discussed in this book.

Thanks are due to the following for permission to reproduce extracts from copyright works:

Messrs Geoffrey Bles Ltd. (L. P. Wilkinson's *The Letters of Cicero*); Messrs Jonathan Cape Ltd. and Oxford University Press, Inc., U.S.A. (C. Day Lewis' translation of *The Georgics of Virgil*); The Clarendon Press, Oxford (C. Bailey's translation of Lucretius, and A. O. Prickard's translation of *Longinus On the Sublime*); Professor C. Day Lewis and the Hogarth Press Ltd. (C. Day Lewis' translation of Virgil's *Aeneid*); Lord Dunsany and Messrs William Heinemann Ltd. (Lord Dunsany's translation of *The Odes of Horace*); the executors of Mr James Flecker and Messrs Martin Secker and Warburg Ltd. (adaptations of Catullus in *Flecker's Collected Poems*); Mr W. F. Jackson Knight and Messrs Faber and Faber (W. F. J. Knight's *Roman Vergil*); the Editors of the Loeb Classical Library (H. R. Fairclough's translation of the *Satires and Epistles* of Horace, and M. Heseltine's translation of the *Satyricon* of Petronius); Messrs Macmillan and Company Ltd. (Sir Edward Marsh's translation of *The Odes* of Horace); Penguin Books Ltd. (Robert Graves' translation of *The Golden Ass* of Apuleius, E. V. Rieu's translation of *The Eclogues* of Virgil, and my forthcoming translation of *The Annals* of Tacitus); Mr Ezra Pound, and Mr D. Pound on behalf of the Committee for Ezra Pound (adaptations from Propertius and Catullus in Ezra Pound's *Personae*, published by

Messrs Faber and Faber Ltd.); the Society of Authors as the Literary Representative of the Trustees of the estate of Professor A. E. Housman (translation of Horace in A. E. Housman's *More Poems*, published by Messrs Jonathan Cape Ltd.) and Messrs Henry Holt and Company, Inc., U.S.A., for the same extract; Dr Helen Waddell and Messrs Constable and Company Ltd. (Helen Waddell's translation of a poem in *Medieval Latin Lyrics*).

Note. The writer of a book on this subject is faced with the problem of what quotations from Roman writers or from their translations he is to include. I have included no Latin. But I have quoted a number of English translations (giving chapter and verse of their originals), and I have also included looser adaptations when these have seemed to convey some of the spirit or the quality of their models. Certain of the modern versions that I have chosen are indicated by the acknowledgements that are gratefully offered above. But I also quote English renderings from many earlier epochs, with preference for those avoiding what Professor Day Lewis calls 'that peculiar kind of Latin-derived pidgin English'. Moreover, in choosing translations or adaptations of poetry, I have tried to keep clear of that great mass of versified material which travesties the great nineteenth-century poets ('eftsoons, I ween...'), and does not fall freshly on the modern ear. In the case of some Latin authors I have not ventured to quote any 'equivalents' at all.

M. G.

January 1954

INTRODUCTION

INTRODUCTION

I. GENERAL DEVELOPMENT: ROMANS AND GREEKS

ROMAN literature is not only what the Romans wrote. It is what was written in the language of the Romans—and many of the greatest Latin writers were not Romans and not even Italians. Rome had an outstanding capacity for absorbing and incorporating the talents of other peoples.

Almost every part of Roman literature was enormously influenced by Greece. Nevertheless, the Roman writers practically never copied the Greeks. What they did was to adapt Greek literature, and the resulting works were wholly different from their Greek counterparts. Nevertheless, the influence of Greece is explicitly corroborated by many of the Latin writers, including the greatest of them. They freely admitted, and indeed boasted of, the extent to which they were influenced by Greek culture. The Greeks, it was felt, had possessed all the ideas, taught all the essential values—as well as the external forms—and asked all the right questions. So it was widely held that Greek thought was common property, of which any new writer was obliged to make use. Since this attitude was prevalent, it is clear that Roman literature, as we know it, could never have existed at all without the Greeks.

This factor in the Roman achievement is summed up vividly by Horace. In a passage about metre and rhythm he offers what might well have served as a general rule:

> Ye, who seek finished models, never cease,
> By day and night, to read the works of Greece.[1]

This was typical of Roman thought on the subject. The same sentiment reappears in the most voluminous and fundamental

[1] Byron, after Horace, *Ars Poetica*, 268–9.

prose treatise of the post-Augustan epoch, the *Training of the Orator*[1] (in twelve books), of which the author was the great scholar Quintilian. He provides a brief but striking review of his opinions on the principal Greek and Latin writers—set against each other, as though it were the role and destiny of the Romans to be set against their Greek models. Elsewhere he asserts that Roman children should be taught to write Greek even before they were taught to write Latin, since they would pick Latin up anyway. The fact that such an assertion was possible from a moderate man of fine judgement illustrates the Romans' admiring attitude to Greek culture. It was 'a rich common, whereon every person who hath the smallest tenement on Parnassus has a right to fatten his Muse'.[2] This was the attitude of the Romans to the Greeks. Latin writers preferred to rival one another, not in originality, but in the use that they made of Greek writings. In such tasks of adaptation they emulated each other with deliberate pride, tempered with a modest awareness of the superiority of their Greek models.

So no attempt to describe Latin literature can omit all mention of the Greeks. As Dr Johnson put it, 'not to name the school or the masters of men illustrious for literature is a kind of historical fraud by which honest fame is injuriously diminished'. But it would not be right to stress the extent to which educated Rome depended on Greek culture without also stressing the *limitation* of that dependence. This may well sound contradictory; and the situation is in some ways contradictory—or at least complex, not to be painted in crude blacks and whites. Although the Romans had this great admiration for the Greeks and studied them so much, there were definite limits to their borrowing. At the very beginning of Roman literature, it is true, *any* imitation of Greek writings was regarded as justified. But very soon this was altered. There came into being an idea that one must avoid actual 'theft'. This conception of 'theft' was the ancestor of our own

[1] *Institutio Oratoria.*   [2] Henry Fielding on the classics.

opinions about what we call 'plagiarism', but the Roman idea left a good deal wider scope for imitation. Ancient critics tried to define it. You could adopt a similar technique, they said, to your model, but not the actual substance of what he said; or sometimes they said virtually the opposite. But most of them laid stress on the fact that whatever you took over must be employed in such a way that it is made *your own*—by some infusion of novelty and originality, however fixed and firm the convention within which it is displayed.

In this the Romans succeeded. The individuality of their achievement is due to fundamental intellectual differences from the Greeks. The minds of the Romans contained some very un-Greek good qualities. They were more sincerely moral, and more practical. Of their moral writings something will be said elsewhere. Their many *practical* achievements are in a class quite by themselves. It has been observed that, if the Greeks asked the right questions, the Romans found the right answers. Their practical achievements are engineering, architecture, medicine, agriculture, law and government. Moreover, they possessed the capacity (and won for themselves the opportunity) of putting the Greek ideas, which inspired these studies, into effect over vast areas of the globe—an opportunity of which the Greeks had deprived themselves by constant warfare.

It is only because of the Romans, and through them, that Greek thought has survived at all. This is partly because so much Greek thought is admiringly preserved in the Latin writings that have come down to us. It is also because of the actual preserving and copying of Greek manuscripts—an activity which could only take place and bear permanent fruit in the peaceful conditions, and with the widespread educational facilities, of the *Pax Romana*.

The Roman achievement is distinct from that of the Greeks owing to their mental differences—and also owing to fundamental differences of language. The significance of Roman literature remains partly hidden without some comprehension of the Latin language. It is impossible to understand Rome without reading the remarkable and in some ways unequalled Latin literature which has survived; and this cannot be fully appreciated unless it is read in its original tongue. Many of the most characteristic aspects of Roman thought and genius are embodied in the actual Latin language. It is extremely forcible and expressive, very precise and at the same time very compact; capable of saying much and of saying it well in a brief space. (That is one of the reasons for the inclusion in curricula of those traditional feats of ingenuity known as Latin Prose and Latin Unseen. Whatever they may or may not do, they are valuable exercises in clear thinking and expression.)

Owing to the extraordinary powers and qualities of the Latin language, large parts of Roman literature constitute an achievement which is very far indeed from being merely a servile imitation. This is even true, perhaps most of all true, of that unpractical branch of literature, poetry. The Greeks had excelled in this. Yet on occasion, Roman poetry is unsurpassed and unsurpassable in the subtlety of its sound-effects and the satisfying quality of its rhythm, in its expressive and musical terseness.

Roman literature, then, had a vigorous life and character of its own. So it is wrong to think of it only in the somewhat humble role of transmitter. This was a mistake often made in the nineteenth century. In that period the romantics rediscovered Greece and took far too low a view of Latin literature. For example, Mr Gladstone remarked: 'Of the study which goes under the well-deserved name of Humanity, Greek learning is the main part.' This ignores the fact that, unequalled though the merits of Greek literature are, the Latin writers not only incorporated much of it, but added a highly individual series of contributions of their own. 'The more that Rome subjected herself to the formative discipline of Greece, the more clearly the natural energy of national life revealed itself.' 'The Latin mind, as it expressed and recorded itself in

Latin literature, was not only transforming, but constructive and creative.'[1]

Evidence for this independent and durable life of the Roman masterpieces is amply provided by modern literature. Our own, for example, shows innumerable debts to classical writings—and the models are Latin authors much more often than Greeks. It is obvious that this applies not only to modern literatures but also to the modern languages themselves. These contain huge numbers of words from the classical languages; the greater part of them come from Latin. This indebtedness of our modern languages and literatures is so profound that very large parts of them are virtually impossible to understand and appreciate without a knowledge of Latin. We owe to the Romans scarcely less than the Romans owed to the Greeks. What Greek literature was to Roman literature, the latter is to our own. English prose goes straight back to Cicero; and the descent of poetry, it has been said, is from Greece to Italy and from Italy to Britain.

This is just one aspect, the literary aspect, of a wider question. The classics form a large part of the basis of our whole civilisation. Without them there would be no civilisation, as we understand the term. And the classical element is not just Greek culture, but what the Romans made of it. So Gladstone's view that the tremendous greatness of Greece makes Rome unimportant is obsolete. The fact that Rome was preceded by the Greeks is no reason why it should be ignored or underrated. On the other hand, Latin studies remain seriously incomplete if no effort is made to find out what had happened in Greece. This mistake needs to be avoided with particular deliberation today. For the Greek language is no longer widely known; so there is not, in general, a direct approach to its most significant thinkers and writers.

The word 'classical' is used with various different meanings. The Latin *classis*, from which it is derived, usually means 'fleet'.

[1] These are the comments of E. Fraenkel and J. W. Mackail.

7

But it originally meant a land-army as well. In very early times it referred especially to the Roman army's foremost ranks, which consisted of men rich enough to provide their own arms and armour. These formed the nucleus of the army; so the term *classici* was used to designate the leading citizens in general. Then, in the imperial epoch, its use was extended to other fields of distinction. Thus the phrase *classicus scriptor* was used to mean 'first-class writer'. When the Renaissance brought ancient literature into even greater prominence than hitherto, the writers considered 'first-class' were automatically those of Greece and Rome. Then, when people's standards widened and varied, the term 'classical' likewise came to be used of matters not strictly applicable to Greece and Rome; and so it is used today. But its primary reference is still to Greece and Rome.

A large proportion of Roman literature is lost. But even the part that has survived comprises very many writers, of whom the best known are listed in Appendix 4 at the end of this book. The branches of literature, and approximate dates, of thirty-three of these are indicated on a Table inside the back cover. For ease of reference, the Table is divided into seven periods. Every classification of this kind is obliged to ignore overlaps; but it can be said that each of these periods roughly corresponds to certain distinct tendencies.

(1) *Late third–early second century* B.C. *The Age of the Dramatists*. This is the epoch of the decisive Second Punic War (218–201 B.C.), and of the further successful wars and conquests which followed it and converted Rome into an international and imperial power. In the first part of this period, Roman literature was firmly establishing itself as a vigorous growth. This was the age of the great Comedy, of Plautus and Terence. By means of their genius, assisted by Greek influences which were now present in ever-increasing force, the language of Latin literature was

converted into a dignified medium, with a new flexibility and range, but—after Plautus—increasingly remote from the spoken tongue. Play-writing was in the hands of slaves and freedmen. Indeed literature as a whole was not yet considered an appropriate occupation for the fairly small group which constituted the Roman governing class. But a step forward was made when a leading statesman of the second century B.C. (Scipio Aemilianus), himself one of those who were thoroughly versed in Greek culture, became the friend and one of the patrons of the dramatist Terence, the 'father of Roman poetry' Ennius, the satirist Lucilius, and the Greek Stoic philosopher Panaetius.

After the early part of the second century B.C., there came a decline in the production of great drama. This was due partly to the difficulty of rivalling Plautus and Terence—and partly perhaps to a new concentration of literary pursuits in the hands of a small upper-class group of men, who still disdained however to enter the dramatic field themselves. The decline was also probably not unconnected with Rome's great conquests. By the last third of the century, Greece and a large part of Asia Minor were in its grasp. Much of their wealth passed into the hands of an emergent Italian upper and upper-middle class, which was alien to the Greek influences apparent in Plautus and Terence and represented by circles such as that of Scipio Aemilianus.

(2) *Mid-first century* B.C. *The Late Republic (Ciceronian Age)*. Rome was now a great imperial power. But under the initial impulse of democratic would-be reformers—the Gracchi—the government had cracked, and was breaking down. First, in the eighties B.C. there was the terrible Social (Marsian) War between Rome and her Italian allies. Civil wars followed. The cliques which had hitherto controlled state affairs were proving unable to handle their vast new responsibilities. There was a long series of revolutions and disputes—Marius opposed by Sulla, Pompey and Caesar by Cato, Pompey by Caesar. Disputes meant biography

and autobiography—and also oratory; and this was the age of great oratory, which reached perfection in the hands of Cicero. That and other branches of literature were in the hands of trained statesmen with an elaborate education.

This education, like the inspiration of the previous period, came from Greece; Greek culture had now permeated the Roman governing class. Under this influence, poetry took its place as part of higher education. Roman poetry set itself to learn Greek forms and to forge original achievement from them. It enjoyed its first efflorescence in the hands of Lucretius and Catullus. Philosophy, too, became a matter of widespread interest; the temperament of the Romans was well adapted to moralising, and now they were acquiring from Greece the habit of abstract thought. This subject now bore two different fruits, the prose works of Cicero and the poem of Lucretius. Roman historical writing also developed. These great achievements were all the products of a tormented epoch of civil war and misery.

(3) *Late first century* B.C. *and beginning of first century* A.D. *The Augustan Age.* The great writers of this period were possibly inferior to those of the Ciceronian Age in vigour and boldness. But they were superior in artistic ability, technical finish, delicacy of human sympathy, and beauty of expression. This was a period of extraordinary productiveness. The Augustan masterpieces show a perfect harmony between language and subject-matter—and also between the native Italian genius and the Greek influences which fertilised it.

In particular, this period witnessed the culmination of Latin poetry in the hands of Virgil, Horace and (slightly later) Ovid. These and other writers, for example Livy, were not statesmen. They were also not Romans, but Italians. They worked with the encouragement and support of Augustus and of his leading advisers, particularly Maecenas. Wonder has often been expressed at this simultaneous occurrence of literary geniuses. Why were there so many of them just at this time? Partly, perhaps, through mere chance; partly because linguistic evolution had reached a certain stage; but perhaps also the personality of Augustus, and the peace that he brought to the long-tortured world, had something to do with it. These great works were stimulated by peace and patronage; and the patronage was cleverly and discreetly exercised.

(4) *First century* A.D. *The Post-Augustans.* The century which followed the death of Augustus (A.D. 14) is often known as the Silver Age of Latin. This implies a deterioration from Gold to Silver. It is true that the Augustans had been so good that it was hard to follow them, impossible to rival them in their own spheres. Also, the imperial regime, when in the hands of suspicious rulers, tended to limit freedom of speech, though this tendency must not be exaggerated, since it was not always apparent.

But it is more useful to think of a shift in emphasis than simply of a deterioration. Roman education had changed, and this change exercised a profound effect on literature. Rhetoric now predominated; education increasingly consisted of school exercises in oratory and debating. Everything was written from the point of view of recitation and declamation; and the great fashion for Stoic philosophy led to concentration on terse, impressive statement, such as the Stoics favoured. Literature was greatly admired—it had never been admired more—but the circle in which this admiration existed was a narrow one, and often laid much stress on artificial expression.

The symbol and central figure of this period is Seneca the Younger. He wrote under Claudius (A.D. 41–54) and Nero (54–68). His brilliance is nowadays, in this country at least, regarded as second-rate. But it exerted enormous influence on English and French literature in the sixteenth and seventeenth centuries. A contemporary of Seneca the Younger was the founder of the European novel, Petronius.

Later in the century, under the Flavian emperors (Vespasian and his two sons Titus and Domitian), there lived and wrote the greatest of Roman educationalists, Quintilian.

(5) *Early second century* A.D. *The climax of the Silver Age*. In the first part of the second century, during the reigns of Trajan (A.D. 98–117) and Hadrian (117–38), the supreme exponents of the Silver Age, the satirist Juvenal and the historian Tacitus, wrote their greatest works. By these men the peculiar rhetorical tendencies of the day—resulting from the changes in education—were worked out in the most vivid and dramatic way possible. Neither was followed by any school; both were inimitable.

These were among the greatest writers of the *Pax Romana*—when the greater part of the Mediterranean world, and of Europe, was at peace. This peace was secured by an imperial rule that was not, indeed, perfect, but was nevertheless enlightened to an unprecedented degree.

(6) *Later second and third centuries* A.D. *The 'New Speech': the Africans*. Tacitus had pushed Ciceronian syntax into strange and striking forms; he had almost created a new literary language. After him, the grammar of Cicero was almost completely abandoned by many writers. Colloquialism, the language of uneducated people, was breaking through into literature and asserting its own standards; and with it came archaism, since many forms of colloquial speech were archaic. The combination was developed into a literary style known as the 'New Speech'. In the hands of one of its exponents this work took on a remarkably rich colouring. This was Apuleius, the only ancient novelist of whom we have a complete work.

Very many non-Italians were now prominent in Roman life. Trajan and Hadrian had been Spaniards. The last two great emperors of the *Pax Romana*, Antoninus Pius (A.D. 138–61) and Marcus Aurelius (A.D. 161–80), who ruled during Apuleius' lifetime, were of Gallic and Spanish origin respectively. Apuleius was a North African; so he was subject to Greek and oriental as well as to Roman influence. His African origin is suggestive of the epoch that was to come.

For North Africa, a little later, produced important Christian writers. Minucius Felix was probably African; Tertullian certainly was. Both wrote at a time when Christianity was not yet the state religion, but was persecuted and 'underground'. A further group of third-century writers consists of the greatest codifiers of Roman Law, Papinian and Ulpian (again neither of them was Italian). It is remarkable that this great constructive activity coincided with a terrible crisis. The prosperous *Pax Romana* was now sinking into a war-ridden totalitarian regime, in which the standard of living fell continually and catastrophically. The first emperor of the 'military monarchy', formidable victor of civil wars, was Septimius Severus (A.D. 193–211). After him, the third century A.D. proceeded amid deepening chaos, external threats and internal anarchy.

(7) *Fourth and fifth centuries. The Christian Fathers.* Contrary to all apparent probability, the reeling empire, after decades of fighting and distress, succeeded in fighting off its enemies without much permanent loss of territory. This almost superhuman task was performed by a series of emperors from the Illyrian provinces (east and north-east of the Adriatic), including Aurelian (A.D. 270–5), Diocletian (284–305) and Constantine (306–37). But a terrible price was paid in human distress; the cost of protection was totalitarian poverty. Constantine saw that the western parts of the Empire could not be protected indefinitely. So he moved the capital to Byzantium (Constantinople) (*c.* 330); and within a century and a half from then Rome and the West were lost to imperial rule.

Constantine's other decisive step was his pronouncement in favour of Christianity. This was the age of the greatest early Christian writers, St Jerome and St Augustine. These men were as brilliant intellectually as Cicero. But the Latin that they wrote was not the same as his, and their thought was a strange and significant mixture of old and new. They were devoted Christians, yet at the same time profoundly and inextricably immersed in pagan Roman civilisation. Their writings do not usually figure in classical courses, because of their post-classical Latin: they are reserved for students of Divinity. But they are among the greatest ornaments of Roman literature. They form a bridge between Antiquity and the Middle Ages.

So does the greatest of the Christian Latin poets, Prudentius. And a little later, at the turn of the fifth and sixth centuries, a similar part is played in the history of philosophy by Boethius, a Christian with a brilliant mastery of pagan philosophical thought. These two men were both westerners. But by the time of Boethius the West had ceased to be part of the empire; and so, according to most reckonings, the Middle Ages had begun. It is not quite accurate to speak of the 'fall of the empire', since the empire continued to exist in the Eastern Mediterranean, with Asia Minor as its nucleus—and this Byzantine empire lasted for a thousand years. In it, the Latin character of imperial culture quickly receded in favour of Greek civilisation—familiar for centuries in the eastern Aegean, but for a long time modified, with increasing strength, by eastern influences. However, before Latin ceased to be the language of Byzantine coinage, the Byzantine emperor Justinian (527–65)—whose generals brought Italy into the Empire for a time—organised the greatest of all codifications of Roman Law.

2. THE FIRST ROMAN SUCCESS: COMEDY

The Romans did not themselves invent any important kind of drama, or semi-dramatic entertainment. But the Italians, outside Rome, did; and long before Latin literature took a definite shape, various primitive forms of entertainment had come from Italy to Rome. These were gradually blended together with Greek influence; and the result was the Roman drama which we know, and which has been used (consciously and unconsciously) as the model and basis of our European theatre.

Several of these primitive forms of entertainment can be dimly distinguished. Two of them seem to have come to Rome from its northern neighbour Etruria. These two kinds of entertainment, elementary forerunners of drama, are the following:

(1) *Fescennine verses*, perhaps named after a town in Etruria called Fescennium, though certain ancient writers believed instead in a derivation from *fascinum*, meaning here an 'incantation' against witchcraft, which these verses, it is said, were intended to avert. They were 'apotropaic', that is to say their intention was to avert the 'evil eye', a familiar conception even today in many parts of Europe as well as of the East. These spells against witchcraft were chanted at important occasions such as harvest-festivals and weddings, their religious or superstitious purpose being combined with an atmosphere of revelry.

Here, then, was singing or chanting without dancing.

(2) The other early sort of entertainment which we find in central Italy consisted of dancing without singing. There are representations of dancing scenes on the tombs of great personages which excavations at the Etruscan cities have revealed. And the first professional dancers known to us came from the same region. So in all probability the dancing was of Etruscan origin, as the Fescennine chants may have been. These dancers did not at first sing or speak. They danced, with a flute accompaniment, and with increasingly elaborate conventional gestures and poses, which might perhaps produce on the modern western mind something of the same effect as the Indian ballet. This Etruscan dancing, like that of the Greeks and other early peoples, was not limited to the motions of the feet which are the main aspect of European-American dances today; it included every kind of rhythmical

movement. Like the Fescennine verses, it combined entertainment with solemn ritual, and, as among other primitive peoples, it was an activity in which the whole community took part, either watching or imitating the professional dancers. This kind of activity may well have occurred at a very early date at Rome itself.

In the fourth century B.C., before any Latin literature that has come down to us, there are signs of the combination of these two primitive institutions of singing and dancing. And the place, or one of the places, where this combination seems to have been effected was Rome. The historian Livy tells us that on the occasion of an outbreak of plague (in 364 B.C.) the Roman authorities, as always deeply concerned with their relations with the supernatural, decided to hold a ceremony of expiation. For such a ceremony, the purpose of which was akin to protection from the 'evil eye', the Fescennine chanting was appropriate. However, it was now further developed. For, from this time on, according to Livy, the singing was combined with displays of dancing. Apparently the fashion was started by an exhibition of ballet by Etruscan professionals imported for this occasion; and their performances were imitated by Roman amateurs. Gradually, increased skill came to be shown in the blending of words, music and gestures. So there was an advance towards an elementary form of drama, perhaps bearing some faint resemblance to our music-hall. It seems at first to have been called a *satura*, or 'mixture', though the word later came to be applied to something quite different.

Livy's accounts of literary origins are often suspected of being unreliable and imaginative, owing to a manifest desire to glorify Rome by endowing its literature with beginnings like those of its Greek counterpart. But in this particular account he may not be far from the real story of the vital development leading to the Roman drama as we know it. This may well have evolved through a combination of dancing and singing on the lines which he indicates—though possibly he has 'telescoped' a long, gradual process into a briefer series of events.

It must not be thought that such combinations of singing and dancing killed the separate performances of each; they continued. Revivals of the 'Fescennine verses' are occasionally heard of centuries later—for example, Caesar's soldiers returning from the wars sang ribald songs modelled on them. And the rhythmical gesturing dance had a long future, under the name of the 'mime'. The mime reached Rome from Italy at least as early as 211 B.C.; and, later on, its 'stars' enjoyed the patronage of the Republican war-lords and then of the emperors. Two developments occurred. The mime became vocal and semi-literary; its most famous name was Publilius Syrus, of the first century B.C. The second development was a new form of dancing, with scenes in dumb show, and singing by a chorus. This was the 'pantomime'. It was extremely popular among many generations, and some believe it led directly to the wandering *jongleurs* of the Middle Ages. But, even in its vocal form, the mime never quite attained literary status, and does not altogether belong to this book.

The future of literary drama lay rather with the successors of the song-and-dance performers ascribed to 364 B.C. Before long we hear of a rather more developed type of entertainment, a simple sort of sketch on the way to becoming a play. These sketches were known as the Atellan Fables, after Atella, a town in Campania—the rich district south of Rome, round the Bay of Naples. These Fables were rustic farces performed on a rough stage. They possessed stock types, characters, not unlike those of a Punch and Judy show; these included the foolish old gentleman ('Pappus'), the cunning swindler ('Dossennus'), the clown ('Maccus'), and the glutton 'Bucco'—who may also on occasion have been called 'Manducus', the word from which the French *manger* is derived.

The Atellan Fables seem to have been imported by Rome from the Italian peoples inhabiting Campania, who spoke the Oscan language (Indo-European but distinct from Latin). It also seems probable that these Oscan-speaking people had first borrowed much in these Fables from the Greeks. Large parts of South Italy and Sicily, especially in the coastal areas, were populated by Greeks, living in colonies planted centuries earlier from various parts of the Greek homeland. Several of the greatest of these colonies were in Campania. One was at Naples itself (Neapolis); and the earliest of all the western colonies was at Cumae, on the coast just north of the Bay of Naples. The Atellan Fables acted by the Oscan-speaking Italians were very similar to sketches which enjoyed great popularity among their Greek neighbours. These Greek sketches (known as 'Phlyax' farces) were given a literary form early in the third century B.C. The Romans derived a number of features of their life, directly or indirectly, from the Greek colonists of Cumae and other centres, and the Atellan Fables seem to owe a good deal to the same origin; but in this case the Oscan-speaking peoples were intermediaries.

Very soon Greek influence is more clearly detectable. In 282 B.C., a Roman envoy to the Greek city of Tarentum in South Italy could speak Greek. Then came the First Punic War, in which Rome had an important Greek ally, Syracuse. That city was a great literary centre, particularly famous for its performances of Greek tragedies and comedies. The Romans looked at these, and by this and other means a new consciousness of literature gradually arose among them.

In 240 B.C., the Roman government requested a Greek or half-Greek from Tarentum, named Livius Andronicus, to produce Latin versions of Greek tragedy, and also perhaps comedy, for dramatic performances. These plays were commissioned for Victory Games on the successful termination of the First Punic War. Games (*ludi*), though they now took on something of a Greek character, were nothing new at Rome; the Circus Maximus, in which they were sometimes performed, was reputed to go back in date to the royal Tarquins, ascribed to the sixth century B.C. To us, Games might seem a strange occasion for a theatrical performance; but the Romans considered them quite as appropriate for this as for chariot-racing, boxing, animal-shows—or displays by gladiators. That last feature had been imported to Rome, from Etruria, only twenty-three years before the first performance of Livius Andronicus' plays. So in these years the Games were augmented by two institutions, both characteristic—in their contrasted ways—of later Rome: the brutal gladiatorial shows, and the literary plays which are the forerunners of our own drama.

The works of Livius Andronicus have not survived; but we know something of them. His comedies, being closely adapted from their Greek originals, are about Greek subjects; as the Romans put it, they are *palliatae*—they 'wear the Greek cloak', the *pallium*. The other (later) type of early Roman comedy concerned itself with Roman themes, so it 'wore the *toga*'. None of those *togatae* have survived. But a number of *palliatae* are intact; and with these we have reached the first name on our list of surviving Latin writers.

The first great Latin dramatist is Plautus. This means 'flat-foot', and may be a nickname related to the 'mime'-actors, who were sometimes known by a term meaning much the same thing. Plautus was born in *c*. 254 B.C. in Umbria, the mountainous country north-east of Etruria. The story goes that he was a handyman on the stage who lost his savings in an unwise commercial venture and had to operate a tread-mill. In his spare time he took to play-writing, thus providing an early example of that familiar modern phenomenon, the literary man who writes while earning his living at quite another job. But his plays became very popular and lucrative. Their reputation was so great that in later times

2-2

many comedies written by other people were claimed as his, and as many as 130 were attributed to him. But the scholar of the Ciceronian age, Varro, made up a list of only twenty-one plays for which the authorship of Plautus was generally acceptable; and, of these, twenty and a bit have survived today.

Plautus provides one of the most striking illustrations of the contention (outlined in the last section) that, though Latin writers borrow from Greece, the result is far from being slavish imitation and is, indeed, highly original. The Greeks from whom Plautus borrowed are the Athenian writers of what is known as the 'New Comedy'. The best known of them was Menander (c. 342–291 B.C.). The fifth-century 'Old Comedy' (of Aristophanes) had been rowdy, hearty, political, and tied in subject-matter to Athens and its neighbourhood. It had also contained fine poetry in the grand style. Greek 'New Comedy' was entirely different. In the spirit of the Hellenistic Age which was now beginning, it dealt with the inner life, with love, with tender sentiment. So it shows us some of the personal preoccupations of ordinary people. Its plots, however, were complicated feats of imagination. The parochial politics of the Old Comedy were left out; the New Comedy possessed a cosmopolitan atmosphere which readily lent itself to adaptation to a different country and language.

Menander's Greek was highly rhetorical. He was himself a skilled orator, and was regarded as a master of rhetorical art. Roman educationalists recommended the study of Menander to those studying oratory. The ancients often held the view—strange to us—that comedy (concerning the nature of which there were many theories) was largely a matter of oratory; and oratory was a subject which played an exceptional part in Roman public life and estimation. Plautus himself possessed an amazing talent for his own language, and was no doubt encouraged by this aspect of Menander's skill—though his style is far more racy and less introspective than Menander's, and he often (though not always) preferred as actual models the latter's less refined Greek contemporaries. When Plautus started to write, the Latin tongue was still primitive. Though he was still far from the refinement of the Augustan Age (and so seemed crude to Horace), he converted the language into a vivid, pliant instrument, which he handles with a superb rapidity.

Plautus played a decisive part in adapting Latin literature to the Greek institution of metre. In other words he admits to his verses scansion according to the *quantity* (long or short) of syllables. This concept of metre was characteristic of Greek poetry. It is not characteristic of our own language, which scans its verses instead according to the natural *stress-accent* of the words, i.e. the accentuation of the words as we pronounce them—and we do not always pronounce them according to quantity.

Latin verse, however, was not originally quantitative, any more than English is. But Plautus took over the extraordinarily difficult and delicate task of writing his poetry as if, to some extent, this was its character. That is to say, each of his lines has a quantitative basis—like Greek verses, and like the whole of classical Latin poetry which was to come afterwards. Nevertheless, remembering his Latin forerunners (whose works have not survived), he *sometimes* scanned by stress-accent instead of quantity—sometimes subordinated the latter to the former (often both this and the reverse process occur in the same line). His poetical successors in Latin never did this. It makes his metres a difficult and advanced subject of study. But it needs to be just mentioned here, since it is impossible to have any idea of Plautus' achievement without realising the metrical revolution to which he prominently contributed. He went far towards making Roman poetry quantitative. It is arguable that in the end this proved unfortunate, since it divorced poetry from the spoken language. On the other hand, it is responsible for the glories of Roman poetry. It introduced much needed Greek discipline and grace into the still crude Latin language; and so it paved the way to the far more subtle metrical accomplishment of Virgil.

The rhythms which Plautus preferred are listed at the end of this book.[1] To him, as to all Latin poets, his sound-effects were vitally important. Indeed, considerable portions of his plays were intended for intonation—perhaps they were something like the recitatives, chanted speeches, which we know from Handel's oratorios. These passages of Plautus (called *cantica*) were intoned to musical accompaniment, provided by a piper, who had his pipes bound to his mouth so that both hands were free to manipulate the stops. Such passages were long and—unlike the short songs in Shakespeare's plays—formed an integral part of the comedies. Their metres are varied, but generally based on one of three combinations of quantities ($- \cup, - \cup -, \cup - -$).

But the fundamental metre of Plautus was that which had likewise been the basis of the great Athenian tragedy of Aeschylus, Sophocles and Euripides, and the Athenian comedy of Aristophanes and Menander—the iambic, based on a 'foot' consisting of a short followed by a long syllable ($\cup -$). Plautus used this for a very large part of the spoken passages of his plays—i.e. the passages which are not *cantica*. The iambic metre was said by the ancients to 'imitate conversation'. The commonest line is constructed of six consecutive *iambi*—the line favoured by the Greek dramatists also.

Most of these metres owed a good deal to Greek precedents. But Plautus performed the great task of adapting them from Greek to his own very different language. In so doing, he utilised the various rhythms for dramatic effect in ways unparalleled in Menander or any other Greek poet. As recent studies of Roman comedy have rightly judged, the greatest achievement of Plautus lies in the fact that he exploited the dramatic possibilities of *rhythm* as no writer before or after him has done.

Here then he exceeded and differed from Menander; and there

[1] Appendix 2.

were many other differences too. For example, their audiences were not at all the same. Menander's were sophisticated Athenians of a disillusioned epoch. Menander mirrors their disillusionment; he is sentimental and tender, but not vigorous. Plautus took his plots from Menander, or Menander's contemporaries; but his treatment of these themes is quite new. His Roman audience wanted farce, action, puns, quick repartee—and Plautus' talents could give them what they wanted. He introduced topical Roman references so that the Greek themes should not be too unfamiliar. And his best plays have 'a complicated plot, plenty of trickery, some remarkable turns of fortune, vigorous dialogue, metrical variety, heartiness, cynicism'.[1] Clever slaves play a prominent part; and this 'low life' increased the audience's happy laughter by giving them a pleasant feeling of superiority—which was heightened by their being 'in the know' about the numerous confusions, incongruities and misunderstandings of which the plots largely consist. Shakespeare's *Comedy of Errors* is a good example; it is largely modelled on Plautus' *Menaechmi*, with borrowings from his *Amphitryo*.

Plautus was versatile and resourceful. Many modern writers have much to learn from him. But they have already learnt a very great deal from him—whether they know it or not (and perhaps Charles Dickens and P. G. Wodehouse, for example, did not know it). 'No ancient writer has thus served as a model so generally, or has had so many successful imitators, as Plautus.'[2] The writer of those words was thinking of poets; but Plautus is also the originator of practically all the forms of modern comedy in prose. The varied types of modern book or play which derive from him have been listed as follows,[3] and the list is pretty comprehensive!

burlesque	comedy of humours
comedy of plot	comedy of domestic life
farce	romantic comedy

[1] W. Beare.   [2] E. P. Lumley.   [3] By J. W. Mackail.

A brief description of one play by Plautus may serve as an example of his plots (I owe it to Mr J. H. Bishop). The *Mostellaria* is a domestic comedy with a ghost-story; its beginning and end are reproduced in Ben Jonson's *Alchemist* (1610).

Theopropides, an elderly Athenian, has been abroad on business. During his absence his son Philolaches has been indulging in a gay life at his father's expense; in this he has been aided and abetted by the old man's slave Tranio. These facts are put before the audience in a lively opening scene between Tranio, who is drawn as the typical smart 'town' slave, and Grumio, an old and loyal servant from Theopropides' country estate. Before the play is far advanced, it is obvious that Philolaches is heavily in debt not only because of his riotous living, but also because he has bought the liberty of his mistress, Philematium. However, he still seems to have funds enough to entertain his friend Callidamates to a drinking party along with Philematium, and Delphium, the other young man's mistress.

The revelry is shattered by the news that Theopropides is back from abroad. The revellers are despatched into the house, and Tranio is left to face the old man, its owner. There follows a series of complications. First, so that the revellers shall not be discovered Tranio invents a story that Theopropides cannot enter his own house; it is haunted and has had to be abandoned. This the superstitious old man accepts with awe, but his suspicions are aroused by the appearance of a money-lender, clearly in search of Philolaches. Tranio saves the situation by explaining that money has indeed been borrowed, but for the worthy object of buying a new house. Where is it? demands Theopropides, still suspicious. Next door, says Tranio. The obvious complications follow. Simo, owner of the neighbouring house, appears, and for a time Tranio manages to keep both the old men in a state of ignorance about the real situation.

But even Tranio cannot lie for ever, and he is fortunate in being able to reach the sanctuary of the stage altar before his master can lay hands on him. Here he manages to temporise until Callidamates appears to intercede for him, and everyone, rather improbably, is forgiven for everything.

So Plautus founded modern Comedy. But the fact that he did so, or even began to write comedies at all, was little short of a miracle. For drama, in the Rome of his day, was gravely handicapped by what, to us, would seem enormous obstacles. Some of these may be summarised as follows:

(1) There was no stone theatre at Rome at this time. Nor, indeed, was there one for nearly two centuries after Plautus' lifetime. A permanent theatre was planned in 155 B.C.; but the project was abandoned owing to objections from the governing class, which still regarded such a degree of devotion to the arts as excessive. It was another hundred years before the capital had a stone theatre (it was given one by Pompey). So, in the time of Plautus, the stage was a temporary wooden affair out of doors. It was low, and broad, and probably (by our standards) unusually long; this helped to make possible the many 'asides'—familiar to us also from Elizabethan drama, of which the conditions were in a number of ways closer to Plautus than to the modern theatre. The 'curtain', in use by Augustan times, was unknown to Plautus. The auditorium was just a semicircle of sloping soil, banked up for the purpose. It is now believed that there were some seats; but most of them were plain wooden benches, and it is not likely that there were enough for all the audience.

(2) To modern taste, another marked disadvantage was the frequently unvarying character of the 'scenery', and its conventional character. It usually consisted of a painted backcloth showing the fronts of two houses, separated by the representation of a niche. The action was all supposed to take place in the street. Modern changes of scene are facilitated by the division of plays

into acts and scenes. But the plays of Plautus and Terence were only divided into acts by later editors—editors first of Terence, in the last years of the Republic. The playwrights themselves had usually written their plays to be acted straight through without a break. Scene after scene, and play after play, had the same permanent background. It is true that in Italy and Greece a greater part of life was (and is) lived in the street than is practicable in our northern climate. Nevertheless, to us, such conventions would still seem to make natural effects hard to achieve. (For example, in one play there is a scene in which a woman 'makes up' and performs her toilet in the street.)

(3) Another handicap, it would appear to us, was the absence of programmes. Without them, it was necessary to resort to a number of devices so that audiences should have some idea what was going on. One such device was the Prologue, by which—in some comedies—the initial situation was explained, the characters introduced, and the play itself advertised. And conventional significance was attached to the two side-exits; one was habitually regarded as leading to the Forum and town, and the other to the sea-coast.

Various methods were also used to help the audience to recognise the people on the stage. It used to be thought that they even wore conventional clothes, in accordance with the characters of their parts; but there is no definite evidence for this from the Roman comedies that have come down to us. However, the various 'types' were recognisable in other ways. Slaves sometimes wore red wigs; old men wore long white beards (like a certain sort of professor who recurs in modern films). It even seems possible that, as in Greek New Comedy, everyone wore masks adapted to their stage character, that is to say expressing it, not realistically, but by some easily recognised formal convention.

Conventional, again, was the music. We have to suspect, with some surprise, that each part had its special music. So if one knew a little about the theatre (Cicero evidently did not, for we find him expressing surprise about this), one could receive an additional hint about the characters by this means. But what is perhaps hardest of all for us to appreciate today is that the gestures of the actors were likewise conventional. This or that gesture was regarded as suitable to this or that emotion, and the text-books classified them accordingly. So this, too, was an aid to what was going on—but again one which, in modern conditions, we should regard as unnecessary and very strange.

(4) By modern standards, acting conditions were unfavourable. Casts were small, not exceeding five actors. These actors 'doubled' the various parts, perhaps with the assistance of their masks, which enabled men to take women's parts. Crowds seem to have been represented by a single actor accompanied by 'mutes'. The playwright himself often had to act a part. We hear that Livius Andronicus, who was in this situation, was a poor speaker; so, at least on one occasion—when he had strained his voice taking encores—he had to have an understudy behind him to supply the words, while he himself made the gestures! Nor would the status of ancient actors be at all acceptable today (though it is true that a guild of playwrights and actors was founded in c. 207 B.C., and actors may have been exempted from military service).

Moreover, it will be remembered that the very first Latin plays were produced at Games; and this custom continued. As part of the programme of the Games, the plays were sandwiched among chariot-races and many other non-literary entertainments. We learn that one play failed because of the rival lure of boxing-matches and rope-dancing. Moreover, quite apart from counter-attractions, there was nothing to prevent members of the audience from just climbing over the side of the embankment and going away—or throwing things.

(5) Plautus had to overcome great difficulties caused by the popular taste for slapstick and ridiculous farce. How great, can

only dimly be imagined by the comments of Horace on the Roman theatre of a much more civilised age.

Often even the bold poet is frightened and put to rout, when those who are stronger in number, but weaker in worth and rank, unlearned and stupid and ready to fight it out if the knights dispute with them, call in the middle of a play for a bear or for boxers: 'tis in such things that the rabble delights.[1]

Or, as Alexander Pope put it,

> There still remains, to mortify a Wit,
> The many-headed Monster of the Pit.

Horace adds, ominously, that one advantage of the iambic rhythm ($\smile$ –) was that it could be heard above the clamour of the audience! Conditions must have been bad indeed in the far more primitive days of Plautus. His audiences were very mixed. The wives and children of Roman citizens came to the plays with their husbands and fathers; and the presence of the children, at least, helped to keep intellectual standards down.

Yet Plautus contrived to give his audiences what they wanted— as well as writing masterpieces. That he did the former as well as the latter is fully recorded. He was immensely successful, and brought whole audiences to their feet in enthusiasm; and his plays were revived time after time throughout the 600 subsequent years of ancient Roman history.

(6) Scarcely less of a hindrance than crude popular taste was the vigilance of the ruling class towards any suspicion of implied criticism of Roman traditional institutions; one playwright, Naevius, was broken by this censorship. For example, no bad woman, and no man who belonged to an unworthy profession, must be described on the stage as a free-born Roman; and no social criticisms or reflections on the rulers, or on the class to

---

[1] Horace, *Epistles*, II, i, 182–6, tr. H. R. Fairclough.

which they belonged, were tolerated. Yet Plautus did not lose official goodwill. Indeed, he actually obtained Roman citizenship.

These, then, were some of the obstacles which might have prevented Plautus' rise to greatness—no permanent theatres, no variety of staging, the need for many explanatory devices, unfavourable acting conditions, crude popular taste, and vigilant government censorship. Yet in spite of such handicaps he persisted in his work and laid the foundations of all subsequent European comedy. Looking back, we can see that a great deal hung on Plautus' attempts to overcome the difficulties that confronted him. His success was complete.

When Plautus died in c. 184 B.C., Rome's second great Comedian, Terence, was about eleven years old. He, in his different way, is an almost equally conspicuous figure in the history of literature. He was not a Roman or an Italian, but is believed to have been North African (Berber); by this origin he foreshadowed a period three and four centuries later, when many of the greatest writers in the Latin language were Africans. The case of Terence is all the more remarkable since the Latin which he wrote was not colloquial like that of Plautus but very pure—a model for Cicero and Caesar, who praises him as 'lover of pure language'.

Caesar ranks him among the greatest writers, and compares him to the leader of the Greek New Comedy, Menander, calling him 'Menander's double'; or perhaps the phrase means 'half-a-Menander', for Caesar also finds Terence deficient in something. But the aim of Terence was very different from that of Plautus. Not only does he lack his predecessor's vivid wit, but he is much less vigorous and rowdy. He is far closer to the contemplative, sentimental 'criticism of life' of Menander himself. His differences from Plautus represent a fundamental distinction: Terence was writing for a much more cultured audience.

For this audience, in the thirty-six years of his short life, he wrote six plays. Despite his alien origin, he achieved admission to one of the most exclusive and highly educated Roman circles of the day. This centred round the great nobleman Scipio Aemilianus, who was thoroughly learned in Greek culture. With this backing, Terence was able to appeal to a more select audience than Plautus, and this suited his less robust talent.

Nevertheless, Terence evidently encountered considerable opposition. This is clear from his Prologues, in which he defends himself from his critics, thus providing us with an early example of Roman literary discussion. He admits that everything has been said before, by the Greek dramatists. But one criticism directed against him was that he borrowed too much from earlier *Latin* adaptations of Greek plays. It was also hinted that the real authors of his plays—written in so highly cultivated a language—were his aristocratic supporters. We cannot tell how far this is true. He is certainly closer than Plautus to his Greek originals; but nevertheless he was accused of 'spoiling' these originals by combining them, in his own plays, with extraneous matter from other sources (he claimed that Plautus had done the same). Terence may be said to stand somewhere between an original creator and a translator.

But Horace lays his finger on a more essential matter when he asserts that Terence 'conquered *by his art*'. It is this artistry, showing a polish that is quite new in Latin literature, which makes all such criticism seem irrelevant. It is displayed not only in his language, but in his narrative power and in the fluency and grace of his dialogue. It is Terence, too, not Menander or even Plautus, through whom people came to understand the art of constructing a play; and in this respect also he has exerted a mighty influence on modern European drama.

Terence is more literary than dramatic; and, from the end of the classical period onwards, his plays were used everywhere as school-books. In the nineteenth century, however, they lost this doubtful privilege, because they were regarded as immoral. In general, however, they are not immoral; they are, rather, amoral: they do not regard morality as their sphere—except when occasionally they reflect the humaneness of the Stoic ethics which were now beginning to become fashionable in Rome. When one of Terence's characters asserts—and this is only one of many 'tags' which the world has inherited from him—'I am a man; I regard nothing human as beyond my scope',[1] Seneca later thought, perhaps unjustifiably, that the dramatist was speaking of the Stoic Brotherhood of Man.

After Plautus and Terence, there were no more great comedies 'in Greek dress'. These plays had been the product of an epoch of spiritual expansion under Greek influences. The future lay with other sorts of literature. Plautus and Terence were, indeed, inimitable. But the change may also have been due to the increasing part played by the rulers of Rome in cultural matters, since by their social standards it hardly seemed proper that one of them should be a playwright. And Rome's conquests had put wealth and power into the hands of an anti-literary class. However, if the age of great play-writing ended with Terence, the most brilliant epoch of theatrical performances was the age of Cicero, a century after Terence's death. By then, there were great theatres, great actors, ingenious stage-devices. But the plays produced were still those of Plautus and Terence; and it is they which have influenced the world.

[1] Terence, *Heautontimorumenus*, 77.

PART I
PROSE WORKS

CHAPTER I

CICERO

I. CICERO'S SPEECHES

PUBLIC speaking was much more important to educated Romans than it is to most people today. It is true that certain respected careers still depend on oratory. But we should not necessarily give them primacy over the numerous other civilian occupations which do not depend on it. Most educated Romans of the Republic thought otherwise. 'The Roman citizen took as naturally to rhetoric as to fighting; to defend a client in the courts was as honourable in peace as to fight for the state in war. Because of the relation of patron and client, honour was at first a sufficient reward; but in the last century of the Republic enormous fortunes were made at the Bar. So careful training was essential.'[1] Oratory possessed an urgency which it rarely possesses today. Gigantic issues depended on the outcome of speeches in the senate or Assembly. The 'art of persuasion'—Cicero's definition of rhetoric—had already been the key to great achievements at Athens. The greatest Athenian master was Demosthenes (384–322 B.C.); and oratory had been much discussed and analysed by the Greeks. In Roman politics the prizes were greater still, and the Romans, like the Greeks, possessed a strong native talent for public speaking.

For such reasons, after studying the Greeks, they ranked oratory exceptionally high as a subject and a profession. Cicero stressed its unparalleled potential *usefulness*. He also made even more exalted claims for it. For he regarded public life—in which

[1] W. A. Laidlaw.

oratory played so great a part—as far more important even than philosophical study, the latter being merely a consolation when evil times made public life impossible:

I only wish we could pursue our studies in a time of peace and under a government stable if not good. Though in that case there would be other considerations which would provide us with responsibilities and duties not without honour....[1]

When the choice had existed, Cicero had ranked those 'responsibilities and duties'—public life and oratory—above philosophy. Indeed, 'I have always thought', he said, 'that to be able to speak copiously and elegantly on the most important subjects *is* the most perfect philosophy'. And this high opinion was often reinforced by an appeal to history. It was argued that oratory was the greatest of the agencies which had induced man to move ahead from barbarism to civilisation; and it was also regarded (as it is hardly regarded today) as a highly significant branch of literature.

These are theoretical reinforcements and enlargements of the great practical appeal which the subject of oratory exercised over the Romans. And this double primacy was not only apparent in adult life; it was strongly reflected in education. The character of Latin literature and culture cannot be understood unless it is appreciated how far this tendency went. Most Romans who thought at all believed that the main aim of education was to produce talented public speakers. This is indeed a profound difference from the present day, in which education often does not comprise any training whatever in public speaking.

The Romans went far in the other direction. Even at a very early age, a boy of the Roman Republic would accompany his father to the Senate House or Forum and listen to what was going on. In this sense 'every child', it was said, 'had his father for schoolmaster'. If his family was well off, a boy went to a junior

---

[1] Cicero to Varro, *Ad Fam.* IX. 8 (45 B.C.), tr. L. P. Wilkinson.

school; then he passed into the hands of the secondary school teacher. Emphasis was continually laid on public speaking. Passages were learnt by heart, and texts read aloud with particular attention to pronunciation and delivery. Our own modern custom usually regards the pupil who can *write* the best as the best pupil; in a Roman school he would have needed to *speak* the best as well—or instead.

The first fee-paying school was opened on the initiative of a certain Spurius Carvilius (mid-third century B.C.). In the second century B.C., interest in public speaking steadily rose. This was partly due to the visits and lectures of distinguished Greeks. Many Romans resisted their indoctrination, but its effects gradually increased. In *c.* 90 B.C. the first centre of higher education came into existence, headed by one Plotius Gallus. Under the influence of Hellenistic Greek treatises, it devoted itself primarily to instruction in public speaking. And so, henceforward, did the whole of Roman higher education. A professor in such an institution was actually called a *rhetor*.

Thus the native capacity and social structure of the Romans, and the educational system which they evolved under Greek influences, all contributed to the idea that public speaking was the supreme civilian accomplishment. So the greatest public speaker whom they ever produced was also regarded—with the possible exception of certain soldiers—as the greatest man in their history.

This was Cicero. Over a hundred of his speeches are recorded; of these fifty-eight (not all complete) survive. A word will be said here about those delivered at some of the critical moments of his life.

Cicero was not actually a Roman. He was born near Arpinum (sixty-five miles south-east of Rome), in 106 B.C. His family had never held office or senatorial rank at Rome, and this was still, at that epoch, a grave and rarely surmounted obstacle to a public

career. However, Cicero studied at Rome under the best professors of philosophy and law, and made his public début at the
age of twenty-five, in 81 B.C. In the following year he took an
important step. At this time the dictator Sulla possessed autocratic power at Rome. Cicero accepted the defence of a certain
Sextus Roscius—himself also from a small town (Ameria)—
against a powerful agent of Sulla, the freedman Chrysogonus. The
father of Roscius had been murdered at Rome, and Chrysogonus
had tried to lay hands on his property as though the dead man
had been condemned as a public enemy (as had not been the case).
To anticipate protests, Chrysogonus also had the son charged
with his father's death.

Cicero took on the young man's defence (*Pro Sexto Roscio
Amerino*), thus apparently braving the anger of Sulla—whom he
cleverly flattered, while pointing out that no man is so great that
he knows what all his supporters are doing all the time. Cicero
successfully attributed the crime to a relative of Roscius who had
stood to gain from it. But the most significant part of the speech
is a passage in which the young orator hints at his own political
position. He belonged by birth to the Italian middle class, who
formed part of the 'knights'. The knights possessed great financial
interests which often conflicted with those of the senate. C. Grac-
chus (123–122 B.C.) had multiplied the wealth of the knights by
giving them the highly lucrative right to farm taxes in Asia
(W. Asia Minor). He had also increased their patronage by
giving them seats on the juries, until then held by the senate.
Sulla returned these seats to the senate, thus acting against the
knights. Cicero, on the other hand, was to defend the interests
of the knights all his life, and rely on them for his most solid
backing.

In the *Pro Roscio Amerino*, he duly praises Sulla, as he must—
despite sympathy for his own fellow-townsman Marius, Sulla's
defeated enemy. But Cicero implies strongly that he himself, and

men like him, will only support the government if it ceases to behave with high-handed cruelty. 'If the brutality which has lately prevailed in the state has made your hearts sour and callous, gentlemen of the jury—and I refuse to believe that it has—then the end has come: better to live with wild beasts than to go on living among people of such inhumanity.'

Cicero remained proud of this plain speaking and its success. But, soon afterwards, his health broke down from overwork; and he retired for two years to Athens and Rhodes. There, he greatly widened his knowledge of philosophy and rhetoric, and in particular learnt to adopt a less flamboyant style of speech. On his return (Sulla now being dead) he was enrolled in the senate. Then, in 70 B.C., he delivered a violent and successful attack on political reaction as represented by the rapacious governor of Sicily, Verres. The closed ranks of the right-wing—and the most distinguished orator of the day, Hortensius—failed to save this man from Cicero's eloquence.

Cicero was to be seen supporting many popular causes, with a special preference for those in which the interests of his friends the financiers were involved. Three years after the triumph over Verres, he became praetor, and after four more years (63 B.C.) consul—'that consulship', as Seneca was to put it, 'which he, not unjustifiably but unceasingly, praised'. The great event of Cicero's consulship was his resolute action against a threatened *coup d'état* by the wild aristocratic demagogue Catiline. Catiline's failure to secure a consulship had increased anarchistic tendencies in his policy. His proposal for a 'clean slate', the cancellation of all debts, particularly alarmed the knights. But Cicero seems to have been justified in also attributing to him plans for a massacre and the forcible overthrow of the government. Cicero's four speeches *In Catilinam* show him at the height of his power. But the first of these torrents of invective was enough to force Catiline to show his hand and revolt openly. He fell. First, however, his associates were executed—with a legality which was, and has been subsequently, disputed.

Cicero claimed that he had succeeded against the conspirators because he had reconciled the senate and the financiers (knights) in a 'Harmony of the Orders'. He had moved nearer to traditional senatorial interests. But Cicero's idealistic 'Harmony' never came to life. His consulship was eclipsed by the return from the East of the greatest soldier of the day, Pompey, with unprecedented victories and funds to his credit. Pompey, resentful of Cicero's proclamations of his own 'triumph', proceeded to a private understanding with Caesar and the millionaire Crassus, which we know as the 'First Triumvirate' (60 B.C.). Cicero could not stomach this power-politics, and so was driven into the arms of conservative, partly aristocratic elements with similar views to his own.

However, he was not able to oppose the Triumvirate openly, as a severe blow soon revealed to him. The senatorial leaders did not, or could not, save him from a year's exile (58–57 B.C.), inflicted at the instigation of one of the Triumvirs' henchmen Clodius—as a penalty for his part in the execution of the Catilinarians. Later, a year's provincial governorship in Cilicia (Asia Minor) (51–50 B.C.) seemed to Cicero a further period of exile. In the intervals between these enforced absences he continued to undertake an extensive series of briefs, but his speeches at this time did not show much political independence.

The Civil War between Pompey and Caesar (50–48 B.C.) afflicted him with harrowing and despairing doubts. He joined Pompey, but when Caesar had won he grudgingly submitted to the dictatorship. While it continued, and again shortly after Caesar's death, the opportunities for an active public life were so limited that Cicero had time to give the world an incomparable series of philosophical works. He was delighted with the murder of Caesar. But he was overcome with disappointment when the only result was the dictator's virtual replacement by a much inferior character, Antony, whereas Cicero's friends, Brutus and Cassius, were forced to retire from the scene.

After a period of absence from Rome in his numerous country-houses—a period of miserable indecisiveness, conveyed to us with painful clarity in his correspondence—Cicero made his decision. He began to attack Antony violently and repeatedly in public. These attacks are preserved for us in the fourteen *Philippics*, speeches of unprecedented vigour and brilliance, composed between September 44 and April 43 B.C. The most famous, virulent and elaborate of these orations, the *Second Philippic*, was never delivered. But it was published, and the ferocity of its invective played a considerable part in arousing opinion against Antony—who had now left Rome. During these months the forces of the Republic broke with Antony. They fought him with some success at Mutina (Modena), and Antony withdrew into Gaul; but in the battle both consuls, the commanders of the Republican army, received mortal wounds.

Throughout this period Cicero—despite the contemptuous protests of Brutus—had relied on the twenty-year-old Octavian (the future Augustus), grand-nephew of Caesar and heir, by the latter's will, to his millions and his patronage. Octavian, fighting with the consuls at Mutina, was left by their death the sole victor. The senate now made the fatal mistake of acknowledging his success and his position in too lukewarm a fashion. So Octavian went over to Antony; with Lepidus as the third party, the dictatorial 'Second Triumvirate' was formed; and Cicero's hopes were at an end. Antony and Octavian destroyed Brutus and Cassius at Philippi in Macedonia (42 B.C.). But before they did so a ruthless purge condemned many senators and knights to execution. Among them, lingering in wretched retirement outside Rome, was Cicero. He met his death composedly on 7 December 43 B.C.

41

In this brief account, mention has only been made of a few speeches bearing a relation to politics. But some of his speeches have little connection with politics, or none at all, being concerned with legal cases of a personal character. Most of them are defences—Cicero did not like the idea of being a prosecutor too often. Out of many such speeches the *Pro Cluentio* (66 B.C.) may serve as an example. It is concerned with a highly complex poisoning case, which throws a lurid light on life in an Italian country town (Larinum) during this disturbed, transitional epoch. Cicero was defending A. Cluentius on several charges of poisoning brought against him by the latter's half-brother Oppianicus (the younger). But, eight years previously, the same Cluentius had successfully prosecuted his own stepfather, the elder Oppianicus, for poisoning. The earlier case had retained its sensational character during the intervening period, owing to persistent rumours that bribery had played a part in the result. So Cicero has to devote a lot of his attention to the earlier case, and he has to destroy a strong prejudice against his client—a prejudice which he even admits that he has formerly shared.

This is one of the most remarkable of the ancient law-suits known to us, and many have felt that it shows Cicero at his most skilful. He takes the bold line of admitting that bribery had occurred in the former case. But he suggests that the man responsible for the bribery had been, not Cluentius, but the man whom Cluentius had prosecuted, the elder Oppianicus. Why, then, had the latter lost his case? Merely, says Cicero, because he had quarrelled with his own satellites, so that the money had gone the wrong way. Oppianicus the elder is represented as a murderer many times over (he was a Sullan partisan, so here, in Cicero's virulence, there is a sign of politics). Moreover, Cicero depicts the wife of the elder Oppianicus, Sassia—the mother of Cluentius—as a fiendish accomplice, torturer and crucifier. Cicero 'piles it on', but we feel that at least some of the mud sticks.

Indeed, reflection induces doubts as to whether Cicero's client, too, did not form part of the same corrupt world. But the speech was intended to be heard, not read, and its oratory is sure to have been highly persuasive; it is a model of the speeches which gained for Cicero his overwhelming success and renown—and a considerable income. It is true that, in his day, advocates were allowed to receive no pay. But an advocate as successful as Cicero made vast gains in thank-offerings of money, books—even libraries and whole houses, not to speak of friends for the future.

It was on these gains that Cicero depended for his large-scale political efforts. He had not a huge capital behind him, like his friend and backer Atticus—who did not risk it in a public career. Cicero inherited a property that was merely respectable, and not equal to the conduct of late Republican politics. He lived on what he received. But he felt it incumbent, as a glorious ex-consul, to live in state—the more so since he was a 'new man' with no senatorial background. That is why we find, from the letters, that Cicero possessed an almost bewildering number of country-houses and financial interests; and why he is intensely concerned to marry his daughter Tullia to a succession of wealthy noblemen. In the exclusive world of late Republican politics, even brilliance as great as his would have been of no avail without such aids. Indeed Cicero, whose wit was sharp and famous, often had occasion to regret jokes which reached the ears of statesmen and noblemen at whose expense they had been made.

It is clear from the foregoing remarks that there were occasions in Cicero's political life when he made up his own mind, and struck bravely for what he believed—and often rightly believed—to be the cause least likely to bring crime and disaster. But he lived in desperately difficult times, and like most people who aspire to political importance in such times he was—though well above the average in honesty—more than once induced, or forced, to trim his sails. Even more often his acute brain, summing up both sides, could not decide (until too late) what it was best to do—as his *Letters*, those unique monuments of a highly articulate man's day-to-day thoughts, reveal with pitiless clarity. The politics in Cicero's speeches naturally do not always stand the test of time—very few speeches written by any man do. The permanently admirable feature of Cicero's addresses is their language, their outstanding brilliance as oratory and as literature.

Their pre-eminence rouses the greatest of Roman educationalists, Quintilian, writing some 138 years after his death, to a vivid and heartfelt passage.

It is our public speakers, above all, who enable us to rival the Greeks in the style of our prose literature. For I would emphatically set Cicero against any one of their orators. I know perfectly well what an outcry this assertion will raise.... I regard the excellences of Demosthenes and Cicero as being for the most part similar, though their styles are not the same....With regard to wit and the power to excite pity, the two most potent weapons in respect of the feelings, the advantage is ours....On the other hand there is one aspect in which the Greek is superior: he came first, and it was he, to a large extent, who made Cicero as great as he is. Cicero was a man who devoted himself wholeheartedly to the reproduction of Greek achievements. In my opinion he succeeded in concentrating in himself the forcefulness of Demosthenes, the abundance of Plato, and the attractiveness of Isocrates. But it was not only by careful study that he reproduced the best qualities of each of these writers. Most of his excellences, or rather all of them, came out of himself, springing from the outstandingly abundant fertility of his superhuman genius...so that he appears to obtain as a favour what he is really extracting by force, and the juryman, in reality forcibly carried away by Cicero, does not know that he is being swept away but thinks he is following (by his own free will).[1]

In equally superlative terms wrote a Greek literary critic—perhaps a contemporary of Quintilian—who composed a treatise

[1] *Inst. Or.* x, i, 105–10.

44

which we call *On the Sublime*. Of the two supreme orators, the Athenian and Roman, he writes as follows:

Demosthenes' strength is in sheer height of sublimity, that of Cicero in its diffusion.... Cicero, like a spreading conflagration, ranges and rolls over the whole field; the fire which burns is within him, plentiful and constant, distributed at his will now in one part, now in another, and fed with fuel in relays.[1]

Quintilian analyses in technical terms this comprehensive character of Cicero's talent. There are three achievements, he repeated from earlier writers, of which a public speaker must be capable—instruction, the arousing of emotion, and the giving of pleasure and entertainment. He felt that Cicero uniquely excelled at all of them.

And so he did. We need not judge by our own impressions, but by the results which he obtained. There was evidently something peculiarly compelling about his oratory. Audiences were profoundly affected by it—and were persuaded. Cicero was to an unparalleled extent master of this 'art of persuasion'—his own definition of rhetoric. Quintilian and the author of *On the Sublime* both follow a convention of Roman literary criticism by which a Latin writer is assessed by comparison with a Greek writer. This is in itself a somewhat cramping custom. But it does not prevent either critic from conveying his veneration of Cicero's oratorical achievement.

Quintilian, indeed, attributes to him the supreme qualities of no less than three of the greatest Attic prose-writers of the fourth century B.C.—forcefulness or fire, abundance or fulness, and attractiveness or charm. The *force* of Cicero's oratory, so vividly described by 'Longinus', was strengthened by countless devices of word-order, emphases, contrasts, repetitions, questions and exclamations. His *abundance*, too, is a quality of great importance to

---

[1] 'Longinus', *On the Sublime*, XII, tr. A. O. Prickard.

our understanding of his style. It was he who played the decisive part in moulding the Latin sentence into the 'period', the multiple unit into which several subordinate clauses are woven. Periods assume a variety of forms and sometimes an elaborate balance, in which a triple structure often predominates. These clauses are built up into an integrated organic whole. It is very different from the shorter sentences of our own language, as everyone who tries his hand at Latin prose-writing soon finds out. To assess Cicero's periods it is necessary to read them aloud, and to dismiss the modern anti-rhetorical idea that a good deal of Cicero's 'abundance' approaches redundancy and verbosity. It is also necessary to recall the great part played by oratory in the life of the Romans, and to remember that they were more emotional than some of their grimmer portrait-busts lead one to suppose. They were intensely susceptible to just the sort of effects which Cicero could exert over them better than anyone else before or since.

Quintilian compares the *attractiveness* of Cicero's style with that of the Attic orator Isocrates (436–338 B.C.). Isocrates had not indeed discovered, but had elaborated and greatly stressed, the technique of endowing prose with a rhythm. And Cicero's far-reaching application of the same idea to the Latin language is what Quintilian here has in mind. To us, this sometimes seems a surprising and alien procedure. We have nothing in our own experience with which to compare Cicero's practice. In part deliberately—following the ideas of Hellenistic text-books—and in part unconsciously, he ends a vast proportion of all his sentences with one or other of a few stock rhythms, actually expressed in the quantitatively long or short syllables of ancient metre (and usually based on the 'cretic', $-\cup-$).

But his attention to rhythm is much more far-reaching. It pervades the entire sound and structure of his speeches, through a multitude of different effects carefully adapted (or unconsciously felt to be suitable) to a variety of subjects and emotions. 'Rhythm, which is the musical flow of language, depends on a well-balanced recurrence of accents and pauses, strong and weak beats which affect the ear, not the eye.... Rhythm in Latin prose was marked in various ways: by balance of clauses, repetition of words, alliteration (a form of repetition).... Short syllables were used in vivid descriptions or to express pathos. Long syllables were used for serious warning, or passionate denunciation....'[1] Cicero thoroughly illustrates the outstanding importance of sound in the Latin language. Rhythm is, of course, more strongly marked in speeches than in other branches of prose literature; and Cicero, who complained that even Demosthenes himself did not always 'fill the ear', is its model.

His fifty-eight surviving speeches are of pre-eminent importance. This is not only due to their remarkable intrinsic qualities. It is also because these qualities have made a tremendous impact upon century after century of subsequent western thought. Much of the incalculably vast influence which Cicero has exerted on posterity is due to his speeches. He regarded oratory as his most important activity; and a considerable proportion of posterity has felt the same. This does not, it is true, apply to the Middle Ages—which preferred his rhetorical and ethical treatises—but it is true of many other periods. Literary criticism in the Roman world was permanently based on the style of Cicero as it is found in his speeches. The profound admiration of men who agreed with Quintilian was, at times, countered by attacks. But, more often, Cicero's supremacy was recognised. For a millennium and a half, his language was the language of western civilisation.

The Renaissance could hardly have come into existence without Cicero. One of its decisive preliminary moments was Petrarch's discovery of a speech of Cicero at Liége (1333). Italian scholars were quick to recognise that this language of his was unequalled

[1] J. A. Nairn.

as a vehicle for speech and thought. In the Renaissance, the writing of Latin was held to be the chief criterion of culture; and very soon there was prolonged discussion and controversy about the style of Cicero. There was not so much argument about whether Cicero deserved to be imitated; for this seemed beyond question. But it was disputed whether men should imitate him word for word or merely attempt to follow him in spirit.

His periods and rhythms were adopted for the pronouncements of the Papal Chancery, of ambassadors, of Universities, of scientists. At the age of sixteen, Queen Elizabeth I with her tutor Roger Ascham had read nearly all his works. A letter by Ascham (asking her for money!) has been described as the most successful attempt to reproduce Cicero's diction in the English language; and later in the sixteenth century, the great preacher Richard Hooker had a truly Ciceronian style which 'was long and pithy, driving on a whole flock of several clauses before he came to the close of a sentence'.[1] John Milton was another convinced Ciceronian, and a master of great rolling periods; but their structure was looser, as better befitted the far less inflected English language.

There were inevitable reactions towards the more compact and abrupt style of Seneca; but the eighteenth century no less than the seventeenth was a great epoch for Ciceronian English:

> O come, that easy Ciceronian style,
> So Latin, yet so English all the while....[2]

It has been suggested that a modern reader, if he is to appreciate the effect of Cicero's rhythmical structure on our language, should turn not to an orator but to an eighteenth-century historian—Edward Gibbon. Gibbon was steeped in the Ciceronian period, in which 'every word seems to reflect part of its meaning on every other'.

[1] T. Fuller.   [2] Alexander Pope.

Gibbon represented the old order. But it was in his lifetime, too, that interest in Cicero was stimulated by two sorts of democratic activity—trial by jury, and free debating in the House of Commons. Both these institutions were enriched by the oratory of Cicero, which was various enough to supply a host of analogies and precedents. Edmund Burke, the greatest orator of his day, owed much of his balance and symmetry, abundance and sonority, to Cicero.

In France and America, in the same later years of the eighteenth century, interest was stimulated by another element in Cicero—his Republicanism. Many of his speeches, especially the *Philippics* directed against Antony, were eloquent of his attempts—vain but at times heroic—to prevent the Roman Republic from totally foundering into an autocracy. This was exciting to the men of the French Revolution who were trying to convert a monarchy into a stable Republic. Cicero also had a profound effect on that great educator of the American Revolution, Thomas Jefferson. He was moved by Cicero as moral philosopher, but he was also moved by him as Republican orator; indeed the ideals attributed to the Roman Republic were often in the minds of the early leaders of the United States.

Those who have studied Cicero's speeches for their substance have often fallen under the fascination of their style. Or perhaps it should be rather said that the technique which Cicero had used for persuading his audiences seemed to later orators best, even down to details, for persuading their own audiences as well. To us, the effect is artificial. It is true that, in the court-scenes of films, the jury invariably succumbs to a 'purple patch' delivered by the 'star'. Elsewhere, however, we do not—in Britain—hear such rhetorical diction today, for it would not prove effective. So it is hard for us to put ourselves in the place of the Roman audiences who were so susceptible to Cicero's rotund vigour. Indeed, we have a feeling that those of our writers in past centuries who most scrupulously imitated his periods accomplished a difficult and unnatural *tour de force*.

But in this respect our twentieth-century view is not typical. 'I think', said Sir Arthur Quiller-Couch, 'that, upon examination, literature—which, after all, is memorable speech—will be found in practice very much more on the side of the purple patch than the generality supposes nowadays.' And naturally this applies in a particular degree to actual speech-making, which is the parent of the rhetorical element in literature.

2. ATTITUDES TO PUBLIC SPEAKING

In the Ciceronian Age oratory was of unrivalled importance in Roman public life and in Roman education. At the beginning of the preceding section it was suggested briefly why this was, and how it came about. In view of the peculiar significance attached to oratory, it was only natural that it should be carefully studied. In this process, as in the practice of oratory itself, Cicero was pre-eminent.

For so outstanding a subject, Greek and Roman thinkers regarded it as essential to formulate classifications, and to lay down rules. Indeed not to do so would have seemed to them, with their passion for order and categories, wrong and incomprehensible. It is the essence of classicism to believe that certain guiding principles, based on the highest possible ideals, can be laid down in any significant field of activity. And it was inevitable that no pains should be spared to find what these principles were in so very significant a field as, to the ancients, was oratory. The principles thus established comprised the Art or Science (opinions differed as to which it was) of Rhetoric.

Indeed, so important was this topic in the late Republic that it tended not only to monopolise higher education, but to absorb the greater part of literary criticism. That development, like so many others, was the result of a combination of Roman practical requirements and imported Greek ideas. The Romans needed to know about rhetoric because of the immense importance of public speaking in their daily lives. And in the second and first centuries B.C. they gradually learned to understand, echo, and apply to their own circumstances, the vigorous controversies about rhetoric which had for several centuries (at intervals) been raging among the Greeks.

In the fourth century B.C., Aristotle had written about rhetoric, classifying it as a part of philosophy; and Isocrates had exalted it as an education in itself, a sort of training for life. He regarded rhetoric as a great study aiming not only at fine expression, but at the expression of the finest thoughts. That is to say, he attributed to this 'art' the vital task of communicating virtue—vital because, without the communication, virtue would not be practised. To the ethically minded Romans this idea, when they heard of it, was attractive. It was in the second century B.C. that they began to give attention to such theories. The circle of Scipio Aemilianus was prominent in this movement. But it was his more austere and conservative contemporary, Cato the Censor, who wrote the earliest known Roman text-book on rhetoric (now lost); and it echoed the lofty sentiment of Isocrates: 'An orator is a good man trained in speaking.'

This view that the public speaker, if he is to deserve the name of 'orator', must be a good man as well as a good speaker, is of vast importance in the Roman theory of rhetoric. For it is the basis of Cicero's own interpretation. He expresses the same view urgently and repeatedly. Cicero's expression of this idea is to be found in a series of treatises discussing very many aspects of oratory in theory and practice. These treatises, and particularly the *De Oratore*, the *Orator* and the *Brutus*, are a treasure house of facts concerning the history of ancient oratory. They give us the opinions and arguments of the man who was its master. They also give us insight into the Middle Ages. For in many of its centuries

Cicero's rhetorical treatises were more highly esteemed than his speeches themselves.

The scope of these treatises is exceptionally wide. They are not wholly original, for they owe technical debts to earlier studies in both Latin and Greek. In Latin, one earlier rhetorical treatise (*Rhetorica*) has survived. It is addressed to a certain Herennius (*Ad Herennium*). We do not know who wrote it—Cicero was not its author; it seems to belong to the time when he was a boy or young man. It makes a threefold distinction, borrowed from Greek literary critics of the third and second centuries B.C., between the branches of oratory: forensic (judicial cases); deliberative (assemblies, the Senate, etc.); epideictic (for purposes of display). We are also introduced by this treatise to some of the 'rules' of public speaking. Style is divided into three categories, *the grand*, *the plain* and *the middle*; and these correspond with the three qualities of *exciting the emotions*, *instructing* and *entertaining*— a triple division later accepted by Cicero (who was said, as has been mentioned, to excel at all three).

The principal bequest of Greek rhetorical theory to Rome was a division between two sharply differentiated schools or movements, a 'grand' and a 'plain' school, which concentrated on *exciting the emotions* and *instructing* respectively.

(1) The *Asianic* movement. This was a product of Hellenistic culture dating from the third century B.C. It favoured an emotional, 'grand' delivery. This comprised a rapid, high-flown, highly rhythmical torrent of Greek speech, depending for its effects either on a florid, lush vocabulary and style, or on a constant series of 'pointed' conceits and figures of speech.

(2) The *Atticist* movement. This too originated among the Hellenistic Greeks, but it did not take effect until the first century B.C. It favoured a severe, plain style. The aim of this movement was not to excite the emotions, but merely to provide information, to instruct. Such a movement was clearly a reaction

against the artificial, excitable Asianic style. But Atticism was rather more than this. It also represented an attempt by the Greeks, now under Roman rule, to revert to their glorious past—to the classic simplicity for which Athens and her art had been famous at the height of her power. The oratorical model of the Atticists was the stylistically austere Athenian speaker of the fifth and fourth centuries B.C., Lysias.

This controversy about the way to use the Greek language in public speaking adapted itself very rapidly to Latin. In Cicero's lifetime the dispute was at its height. His most illustrious predecessor in the immediately preceding generation, Hortensius, was the greatest Asianist of his day. Among Cicero's own contemporaries and juniors, Julius Caesar and Brutus were particularly distinguished Atticist orators.

In rhetoric, as in philosophy, Cicero refused to associate himself too closely with the contending schools. After beginning his youthful years under Asianist influence, he attended a course in rhetoric at a famous school at Rhodes, where his Asianic tendencies were considerably modified by simpler styles. Cicero's professor there was Molon, who exercised a decisive effect on his thought, and so on the thought of the world. Henceforward Cicero decided to be an adherent of neither of the main schools. Asianism now appeared to him to be undignified and exaggerated; it wore badly. But he could not accept Atticism as suitable to the exalted purpose for which oratory seemed to be designed. It was too bare and plain. At times, Cicero felt that its deliberate refusal to excite the emotions was catastrophic. For example, he deplored its failure when, just after the murder of Caesar (of which Cicero approved), the cold, bare oratory of Brutus proved unable to win over the Roman crowd.

Cicero was convinced that a first-class speaker must be capable of both styles, the grand, emotional Asianic, and the simple, informative Attic—as well as the 'middle' style, which was held to be that which sought merely to entertain. The perfect orator, thought Cicero, must speak in whatever style the circumstances of his speech may require. And it is satisfactory to read his further comment, a caution against excessively rigorous definition: the three styles are not watertight compartments, but there are many overflows from one to another—indeed, 'there are as many styles as there are speakers'. This is only one of the many ways in which Cicero rises above the rules, and is not bound by them. But he goes back to recognised systems of classification when he holds that the good speaker needs five qualities: he must possess capacity to choose his material rightly, skill in arranging it, power of expression, good memory and good delivery.

These and countless other matters are discussed in the *De Oratore*, the *Orator* and the *Brutus*. They are highly polished works of art, and there are many reasons why they are admirable. His revolt against the idea that mere rules are enough is attractive. But this also means that one must not expect to find in Cicero any adequate theoretical discussion of general principles. The Greeks were able to conduct theoretical discussion; the Romans were bad at it, and we find little of it even in Cicero. But he does something else of great value. He keeps us in close touch with the practical questions of the orator's training, needs and methods. He gives us insight into successful public speaking and its secrets—which no one has ever known better than he.

Not everybody can write well and cleverly about what they do well. Cicero, however, writes about oratory with the utmost skill, and with a superlatively able judgement. Perhaps his greatest contribution to Roman literary criticism is his application of the historical method. He is not content to discuss the art of public speaking as he found it. He accompanies his discussion with a survey of the past history of that activity. His survey shows a thorough understanding of historical perspective. Cicero is well aware that the achievements of earlier orators have to be assessed in the light of the times in which they lived. Moreover, he regards the acquisition of such historical knowledge as a necessary quali-fication of the modern orator. He often tells us that the perfect orator not only needs to be a man of virtue; he must also possess a wide and liberal culture. These two qualifications together make up the *humanitas* that was his great contribution to education. It is this *breadth* which puts his oratorical works in a separate category from a mere rhetorical treatise or *Rhetorica* (of his sur-viving works on oratory, only the earliest—the *De Inventione*—was a conventional rhetorical treatise).

Cicero's historical method is not restricted to the famous orators of Greece. He holds that the Roman speaker's experience must be based not only on the great Greek models but on the earlier glories of Roman civilisation itself. His survey of Roman oratorical history is a priceless source of information for us. Indeed, it is largely due to him that many of the names of earlier orators are known to us at all. And this is as he would have wished it. For throughout the whole of Cicero's rhetorical works, like his philosophical works, runs a national, patriotic motive. This is 'history' of a patriotic kind. In rhetoric as in philosophy, his deliberate aim was to place Roman culture on a level with that of the Greeks—above it if and when this was possible; but Cicero was too reverent to the Greek cultural tradition to have many illusions on this point. Yet his patriotic aim had a further and, it might seem, paradoxical quality. For the only way, he felt, in which he could give Romans the opportunity to rival Greece was by rendering into Latin the best products of Greek thought. Therein lies one of his greatest talents—and, since the Greek originals are mostly lost, one of his most valuable gifts to posterity.

From the time of Cicero onwards, there occurred two important developments which, at a preliminary view, seem contradictory.

In the first place, the rhetorical element in education strikingly increased; secondly, the quality of adult oratory was almost universally considered to diminish.

In education, the decisive factor was the concentration of professors on training their pupils to declaim. The instruction of students was, as ever, directed towards making them good public speakers. This was now effected, to an increasing extent, by the main recognised sorts of declamation or spoken exercise. In the imperial epoch the terms for these declamations are *controversia* and *suasoria*—respectively, fictitious declamatory themes closely modelled on actual law-court cases ('the imaginary case on some disputable point of law'[1]), and exercises in persuasion or dissuasion—advice to some historical character, or group of characters, as to their action in some emergency. Both these forms of declamation—the former the less elementary and more popular—have roots traceable to the Greeks of the fourth century B.C.; both were developed and unprecedentedly stressed in Roman education under the Principate. It is now, too, that schools began to have speech-days. Their headmasters formed the habit of giving displays to parents and others—sometimes as often as half-a-dozen times in a year. These displays consisted—as was only to be expected—of declamations, at first by the teachers themselves, and later by the boys.

So education became more oratorical still; and prose style naturally took on very many oratorical, declamatory, features. Moreover, the custom of declamation was enthusiastically adopted by adults also. Cicero and his friends had entertained and edified each other by declaiming to private audiences, and perhaps even a century earlier speeches had been privately rehearsed in the same way. Augustus encouraged the practice and attended declamations himself. From that time onwards, recitations to large audiences became a popular occupation among educated Romans—a re-

[1] M. L. Clarke.

fined pastime with set rules of extraordinary elaborateness. Adult declamations for purpose of entertainment were sometimes described as *scholastica*. This term aptly stresses the remoteness of such speeches from the 'real' oratory of public life.

So declamations enjoyed great social popularity in the early Principate—as well as becoming the staple feature of Roman education. Yet it does not seem that, in the public life of this period, oratory flourished nearly as much as it had in the great days of Cicero. Our evidence on this subject does not come from any speeches of the early imperial epoch. We hear of the names of leading speakers; we even hear a little about them. But we cannot judge them by their speeches, for these have not survived. We also hear that Seneca and Tacitus were first-class orators. Again—most unfortunately—their speeches have not come down to us. Only very few Latin speeches of the first three centuries of the Principate are now extant. With the exception of certain fragments of imperial oratory, the first hundred years of imperial rule have bequeathed to us none at all.

Our judgement, then, of Roman public speakers of this period depends wholly upon the literary critics. And, if we allow for varying tastes, we can learn from them a good deal about the subject. The early Principate was an epoch which produced some of the greatest literary critics of all time. These included both Greeks and Romans. The Romans were Seneca the Elder, from Spain, Tacitus—more famous as a historian—and Quintilian, a compatriot of the Senecas, who wrote in the last decade of the first century after Christ.

Seneca the Elder wrote under Tiberius (A.D. 14–37) or Caligula (37–41). Though greatly admired by Ben Jonson, he is much less known than his versatile son of the same name (to whom, in this book as elsewhere, the plain designation 'Seneca' refers). But the father was one of the outstanding Roman critics. His writings that have survived comprise collections of excerpts from school declamations, *controversiae* and *suasoriae*. The excerpts are accompanied by comments and criticisms which show a keen appreciation of the past history, and contemporary position, of public speaking. Seneca the Elder wrote at a time when interest in oratory was very vigorous. In addition to the educational and social attention which it now received, it enjoyed special prominence among the literary critics of the day. In the Augustan Age the most keenly debated subject had been poetry; the creation of a national poetry had been the aim of the greatest literary artists of the epoch. From the later years of Augustus onwards, the centre of critical attention shifted to oratory.

This was partly because of a widespread conviction that public speaking had disastrously decayed since the time of Cicero. Seneca the Elder is one of the first and best of those who tried to determine the causes for this decline. He discussed three possible causes. One, he says, is just 'natural law'—the fact that, in the very nature of things, a time of great achievement is bound to be succeeded by a less distinguished epoch. A second factor which he proposes for consideration is the moral decline which had accompanied the vast increase of luxury in the early Principate. This decline, he said, had caused sight to be lost of the *humanitas* which had been Cicero's ideal, the conception that no one could be a good orator unless he was a good man. Seneca the Elder also touches lightly on a third point—the decay of political speaking. The settled condition of politics under the emperors had almost completely eliminated the need for the political oratory which had fulfilled so mighty a role in the life and letters of the Ciceronian Age. Public speaking had become less spectacular and lucrative, and this naturally had a discouraging effect on the development of oratory. These three points are not original. But they show the sort of discussion on oratory which played a leading part in the literary criticism of the first century A.D.

A particularly important period for such discussions was that of the Flavian dynasty (A.D. 69–96). In this epoch the influence of rhetoric was at its highest point. Also, the interest in education and its problems was intensified and encouraged by the imperial court; so literary criticism flourished. There were three distinguished critics of this age. One, the most brilliant of them, wrote in Greek. We do not know what his name was; we call him 'Longinus', but that arose from a false association. His treatise *On the Sublime* has come down to us, and it contains some of the most exalted and incisive literary criticism ever written. It has a number of comments on the decline of oratory and the causes for it suggested by Seneca the Elder. But they are incidental to his real aim, which is the definition of what constitutes literary distinction and proper literary standards in general.

More directly concerned with the decline of public speaking is an approximately contemporary work, generally regarded as the earliest surviving publication of the historian Tacitus. This is his *Dialogue on Orators (Dialogus de Oratoribus)*. The discussion is presented in the dialogue form made famous by Plato. Much of the ground covered by Seneca the Elder is traversed again here, with the slightly different approach of the 'Silver Age'. But several of the speakers in Tacitus' *Dialogue* also present interesting points of view which are new to us, or at any rate more cleverly and forcibly put here than in other writings which we possess. One of the participants, a self-made Gallic advocate named Aper, is made to depart from contemporary convention by denying that any decline in oratory had occurred at all—it was only, he said, that fashions had changed. Aper added the opinion that there was no justification for setting up the 'classics' as sole and unattainable models and standards: on the contrary, many esteemed classics were now quite out of date and had long been superseded.

Another speaker in the *Dialogue*, a literary figure of the time called Maternus, is made to present a different opinion. He does not agree with Aper that modern oratory is better than that of the 'Golden Age'. Maternus adopts the habitual view that public speaking *has* declined. His analysis of this decline dwells on the third of the causes suggested by Seneca the Elder—the political cause. But he gives a fresh twist to the discussions on this point. Granted, he says, that political stability has caused the eclipse of oratory, but is the exchange not worth while? Great oratory is the offspring of troubled times; let us be grateful for an untroubled age—and less exciting oratory. 'That famous, conspicuous eloquence is the product of disorderliness—which foolish people used to call "freedom"; the companion of riots and revolts, the spur to a hysterical public....Eloquence does not arise under well-ordered governments.'[1]

But perhaps the most valuable message which emerges from the *Dialogue* is that of a modified classicism. Tacitus knows that the oratory of the Ciceronian Golden Age is irreplaceable as a general model. But he suggests that it cannot, in a different epoch, be reproduced without modification. This is significant because it illustrates a departure from dogmatic methods of criticism. The whole matter is held to be relative. The great classics are seen to set a splendid standard, but it is no longer thought that they must be imitated slavishly. The whole argument of classics versus moderns has often been repeated; we may compare the English *Battle of the Books* (the title of a work written by Jonathan Swift in 1704, when the 'battle' in England had already been hotly fought for some years). A century before Tacitus, Horace, writing of poetry, had strongly put forward the same plea for a modified classicism.

A similar attitude is to be seen in the writings of the most famous critic of the Flavian Age, Quintilian. A Spaniard by origin (like the Senecas), he came early to Rome and played a great part in the Flavian educational revival. He was the first man to hold a Chair of Rhetoric subsidised by the government

[1] Tacitus, *Dial. de Or.* 40.

itself. Vespasian granted him this influential post, which he continued to hold for some twenty years, under that emperor and
his sons Titus and Domitian. For a time Quintilian was also tutor
to Domitian's prospective heirs. On retirement from his main
teaching activity, Quintilian wrote *The Training of the Orator*
(*Institutio Oratoria*, in twelve books), which incorporates the
fruit of his teaching experience.

His admiration for Cicero is very great. But, in the same spirit
as Tacitus in the *Dialogue*, he points out that Cicero himself did
not owe everything to tradition: he owed a great deal more to
his own genius. The implication is that there is hope for Quintilian's own contemporaries. They must, he knows, be steeped in
the tradition. But they must not limit themselves to imitating it
slavishly. With Quintilian the doctrine of modified classicism,
outlined by Tacitus, achieves its fullest and most authoritative
expression.

Guided sensibly, he says, the youth of his time will go far. Yet he
shares the widespread belief that oratory has declined disastrously.
This is not a contradiction. For Quintilian explains at length—or
rather in a series of incidental comments—what he means. He
does not attribute the deterioration primarily to any of the causes
suggested by Seneca the Elder, though he is prepared to allow
them a part in the general process. Quintilian is an educationalist,
and the fault to which he ascribes the decline is an educational one.
He ascribes it to the degradation of style current among the youth
of his day—and in particular to exaggeration of the rhetorical
tricks and devices characteristic of the pointed, epigrammatical
style so fashionable in the Silver Age.

For these faults he blames his compatriot Seneca the Younger,
the tutor of Nero and writer of numerous philosophical treatises
(and much else) in the preceding generation. Seneca, he admits,
was a clever writer himself. But he was a bad model for immature
writers and speakers, who reproduce not his good qualities but

his 'attractive faults'. These, remarks Quintilian, are not only praised, but—what is worse—are praised precisely for their bad qualities. Quintilian does not recommend a complete return to Ciceronian oratory. That was impossible nearly a century and a half after Cicero's death; and indeed Quintilian himself writes in the Silver Latin characteristic of his own day. But he holds up Cicero as an ultimate model—at the expense of the more recent and fashionable Seneca the Younger. Quintilian disclaims positive animosity against Seneca the Younger. But there were special reasons why he was not likely to favour his memory. One such reason was, as has been said, stylistic; and Seneca the Younger—despite lip-service to Cicero—had even made the observation, shocking even to a moderate classic: 'There are no fixed rules of prose style.'[1]

But there was more in Quintilian's antipathy than met the eye. One relevant factor was the recrudescence of a four-century-old dispute between Rhetors and Philosophers. Here the two men held diametrically opposed views. Seneca the Younger had minimised the 'liberal arts', stressing that philosophy was the supreme human activity. Quintilian strongly dissented. He was prepared to concede that his pupils should read philosophy; but he felt that, in the educational sphere, the philosopher had attained altogether more prominence than was good for society. He has severe criticism for contemporary philosophers. Many of them were charlatans, he says, failing abysmally to live up to their professions; oratory was a much better education.

Here we may detect an echo of contemporary events. The reigning emperor Domitian also had become deeply suspicious of philosophers as politically 'unreliable'; and, at the very time when Quintilian's work was being written and published, the members of this profession had become the objects of a formidable persecution. Quintilian (unlike other writers) writes admiringly

[1] Seneca, *Ep.* CXIV, 13.

of Domitian, whose young cousins he taught and whose salary he had received. So his views on philosophers, though they contain cogent material, are not altogether unconnected with contemporary political events. Quintilian calls the philosophers 'bad citizens'. The good citizen, he asserts, is traditionally and properly the orator—the man who has guided cities aright. Here is a revival of the doctrine that the good orator must first be a good man—the very basis of Cicero's educational *humanitas*. Quintilian's whole work is aimed at reviving that conception in the more practical terms suitable for his own time and for his educational profession. Like Cicero, he invests this exalted conception of the orator both with a moral and with an intellectual significance. Not only must the orator be a good man, he must be well educated too. He must have a broad intellectual background, and some mastery of the liberal arts; Seneca the Younger, he says, was wrong to minimise these at the expense of philosophy.

This 'Ciceronianism for today' is reflected in the scope of Quintilian's whole work, and also in its title. A common form of literature still was the rhetorical treatise, the *Rhetorica*. Quintilian's book is something more. It is not only a *Rhetorica* but a 'Training of the Orator'; that is to say, it deals not only with the technicalities of rhetoric, but with the orator's whole education. Herein it resembles Cicero's *De Oratore* and *Orator*, which were likewise much more than conventional rhetorical treatises. It is true that some $8\frac{3}{4}$ of Quintilian's 12 books are cast in the traditional form of such a treatise. But the first two books, and the last, deal with the whole broad conception of the orator. And a quarter of the tenth book is devoted to a famous sketch of the general reading with which preparation for this career should be accompanied. As one might expect, Cicero is the general model. However, he is not followed slavishly. Quintilian has been criticised for a lower standard and a lesser idealism than Cicero's. But it must be remembered that Quintilian is thinking in terms of practical possibilities, in terms of the actual process of education, of which his experience was unrivalled.

In ancient and medieval times, Quintilian seems to have been less famous for his *Training of the Orator* than for certain *Declamations*—not unlike those published by Seneca the Elder; but the attribution of these to Quintilian was probably mistaken. His *Training of the Orator* came into its own in the Renaissance, and for this reason he has exercised immense influence on our modern educational systems. The herald of the Renaissance, Petrarch, possessed only a torn and fragmentary Quintilian. The decisive moment came in 1416, when Petrarch's Florentine compatriot Poggio Bracciolini profited from a diplomatic mission to disinter from a filthy, disused tower at St Gallen (in Switzerland) a complete manuscript of Quintilian's work. This discovery, and that of a Greek treatise owing much to it, opened the way to one of the great educational movements of history.

For, to the fifteenth and sixteenth centuries, Quintilian's humanist conception of mental and moral education was irresistible. Educators repeatedly turned to it. Moreover, it is easy to trace how, since then, his ideas have passed down the centuries to our present time. Quintilian's system did not include physical training or instruction in the fine arts, both of which come to us from Greece. But, without him, many other features in our education would be lacking. It is a curious fact that these features owe their existence ultimately to the ancient idea that the aim of education was public speaking. This idea is now long obsolete. But it was the basis of the humane definitions attempted by Cicero and Quintilian, which have so vastly influenced the modern world.

3. GUIDES TO BEHAVIOUR: CICERO AND
SENECA. LAW

The influence of Roman philosophical treatises on the world has been enormous. But, for the original thinking on which they are based, we have to go back to the Greeks. There is nothing unusual about this. But it applies more strongly to philosophy than to any other field. In this branch of thought and of literature the Romans were less original than in any other. Roman philosophical writings echo four great 'schools' of the age following Aristotle (later fourth century B.C.), the age of the Hellenistic Greeks—the 'schools' of the Epicureans, Stoics, Peripatetics and Academy (their doctrines are briefly described in a Note at the end of this book).[1] The Greeks of the Hellenistic Age had lost their earlier compatriots' guiding-star, the independent city-state. They needed a whole new Way of Life; and that is what these post-Aristotelian philosophers aspired to give them.

When in due course the Romans came to be aware of this sort of thinking, it interested them deeply. For it suited their serious, ethical temperaments very well; indeed, it has been said that, whereas the Greeks were a people of intellectual values, the Romans substituted moral values. In the course of the second century B.C., a series of Greek visitors and residents enabled Rome to become thoroughly acquainted with the main philosophical schools, and with the various 'eclectic' views (that is to say combinations of the doctrines of more than one school) which prevailed at that time.

In the first century B.C. this enrichment of the Roman genius by Greek ideas found expression. Indeed, it so happens that Hellenistic philosophy receives its finest literary illustrations, not from Greeks, but from Latin writers. Epicureanism is represented by Lucretius—who was also one of the great poets, and will here

[1] Appendix 1.

CICERO

be discussed among them (Ch. III). Cicero combines an 'eclectic' liking for the undogmatic approach of the Academy with an ethical system which (like most Graeco-Roman ethics) is mainly Stoic. Finally there is another 'eclectic'—though in him Stoicism is even stronger—in Seneca the Younger. These are the three great Roman philosophical writers.

The Roman philosophical works which have had most influence on the thought of the world are those of Cicero, and especially the *De Officiis* (*On Duties*) and the *Tusculan Disputations* (so called because they are said to have taken place at Cicero's villa at Tusculum near Rome). By way of contrast to Lucretius, these are in prose; and they lack his fanaticism. On the whole Cicero favours the Academy, and particularly the Academy of his time. Its chief, Antiochus of Ascalon, was his teacher, and to this fact owes much of his influence and fame. Like him— and this was a special feature of the Academics—Cicero did not feel dogmatic about claims to certain knowledge. But he also resembled many of them in his Stoic adherence to virtue as the best practical guide to conduct. So, in deliberately 'eclectic' fashion, he imported Stoic ethics almost unchanged into his philosophical system.

This Stoic morality was soon to become the common background of most educated Romans. Cicero's presentation of it, in his undogmatic fashion, was to attract and fascinate, in certain cases against their will, the early Christian thinkers. Throughout the subsequent ages, too, the influence of Cicero's philosophical writings has been enormous. It is not that they are original. On the contrary, they were, to a large extent, transcripts and compilations. Cicero disarmingly admits this. 'They are just copies', he says, 'and so all the easier to write: I supply nothing but words, and of those I have plenty.' But the words were put together with an unsurpassed attractiveness which has had an immense effect on the language of posterity.

The substance of these treatises has exerted an equally great effect: for the doctrines which they described were the most enlightened which the world had known. Those doctrines can be summed up by Cicero's own word, *humanitas*—the quality of mind and character of a man who is civilised. One of the most important elements in this *humanitas* is kindliness. A man should treat his fellow-men with kindliness because Man himself is worthy of respect—he has some inherent value in himself. This was a logical deduction from the Stoic Brotherhood of Man, in which by the universal Law of Nature—under the guidance of Providence—human beings counted for something and deserved well of each other regardless of state, race or caste. This preoccupation with the *human* is characteristic of the best thought of Greece and Rome alike.

Cicero was the interpreter of this Greek idea to the world. His philosophical writings were the inspiration of the Italian Renaissance in its task of freeing western mankind, with the aid of Greek and Roman precedents, from the shackles of the Middle Ages. Cicero seemed to Renaissance scholars 'the champion of free thought, free will and individualism'—the very essences of their movement. This was partly because of his active life, of which much was spent in opposition to autocracy. But it was also very largely because of the enlightened spirit of his philosophical treatises. From the eighteenth century, again, these had a further period of intense influence. This is reflected in the American Declaration of Independence and Declaration of Rights, and in the programme of the first French National Assembly. Voltaire and the British philosophers, Locke and Hume, bear constant witness to their debt to Cicero: Hume declared that he had the *De Officiis* before him in all his thoughts.

Already in Cicero's lifetime, and soon afterwards, his philosophical writings enjoyed a wide reputation. They had been composed with the patriotic aim of making the contents of philosophy accessible and known to Romans in their own language. This aim was amply fulfilled. For these treatises played a great part in the extension of Stoic morality. They helped it to become part of the moral and cultural stock-in-trade of most educated men. Many emperors were Stoic—at least in their protestations. Augustus was one of the foremost in this respect; for his official pronouncements were heavily imbued with Stoic terms. His successors continued in the same vein.

So did their followers, and also their ministers. For the third leading Latin writer on philosophical subjects was the tutor and then chief minister of Nero (A.D. 54–68), Seneca the Younger (he will henceforward be described as plain 'Seneca'). His philosophical writings are voluminous. They consist mostly of essays of comparatively brief compass, many of them cast into the artificial form of letters to friends. Seneca, like most other Romans, was not a profound philosopher. That was recognised in the generation just following his own, by Quintilian. This critic felt not only that Seneca's prose style was a bad influence on the young, but that his thought was superficial: 'He was not conscientious enough as a philosopher, though he was excellent as a castigator of moral failings.'[1]

The second part of this comment is as noteworthy as the first. Seneca was unsurpassed as a practical guide to conduct—to the *virtue* which Stoics believed to be the supreme Good. He was a brilliant expounder, to the educated Roman world in general, of the most advanced and humane doctrines of contemporary Stoicism—deliberately extending his discussion to slaves, whose human qualities, i.e. fundamental equality to other men, he explicitly recognises as part of the Brotherhood of Man established by Natural Law and Providence. The humaneness of Stoic ethics, as thus presented, was helping to prepare the ground for

[1] Quintilian, *Inst. Or.* x, 1, 129.

Christianity: the universal, moral Law of Nature, ruled by Providence, was helping to prepare for a belief in the universal Will of God and its concern with man.

Seneca particularly reminds us of this link between Stoicism and Christianity. For the early Christian Fathers were to respect him for having, in part, anticipated their beliefs. So strongly was this held that there came into circulation a collection of letters purporting to be Seneca's correspondence with his contemporary St Paul. This has, for a long time now, been regarded as a forgery. But its existence is a testimonial to the resemblance which was found to exist—despite many fundamental differences of theology—between Roman Stoicism and Christianity.

In modern times, too (though nowadays less in Britain than in continental countries), Seneca's treatises have been found inspiring. William Wordsworth was moved by his belief in the Unity of God and man, and his assumption that moral obligations are imposed by inescapable Natural Law. Here is a strange freak of literary influence. Wordsworth would not have liked Seneca as a man. Seneca's life and career seem at times neurotic and unbalanced; but it was not easy to be a minister of Claudius and Nero, and in any case he must be judged not only by his discordant personality, but by his writings.

These were remarkable for their style as well as for their subject-matter. They represent most completely the Latin prose of the Silver Age. Reference has been made to the overwhelming influence of declamations and reading aloud on Roman education and oratory. This caused the gradual development of a new, highly rhetorical style which would arrest at all costs the attention of hearers, in an age to which boredom came easily. Seneca sparkles: his is the Pointed Style. It aims at vividness, ingenuity and neatness. It achieves these by every sort of verbal trick and device—including many varieties of word-play, alliteration and jingle, emphatic paradox and antithesis. This Silver prose 'glittered iridescent like intermittent jets shot into sunlight from a cleverly contrived fountain...eloquence no longer flowed in a full broad stream'.[1]

The full broad stream of Cicero's copiousness was a thing of the past—the period, typical of his prose, was abandoned. This is the real importance of Seneca's style. Brevity is preferred to rotundity, abrupt vividness to continuity. The emperor Caligula, worthily of Seneca himself, compared this style to sand without the lime which good plaster needs; and Quintilian deplored the influence of this laxity on the young. Under the influence of the brevity favoured by Stoicism—'short, acute, spinous...most worthy of philosophy'[2]—every phrase is a pointed epigram (*sententia*). That is why Macaulay observed that 'to read Seneca straightforward is like dining on nothing but anchovy sauce'. Seneca's Tragedies possess similar qualities; of his extant works, only a cruel and brilliant prose satire on the deification of his patron Claudius avoided them.

In the Renaissance, however, Seneca was admired with a fervour which is surprising to modern taste. His Tragedies enormously influenced Tudor and Jacobean dramatists, including Shakespeare. His prose, too, was found as attractive for its style as for its substance. In the late sixteenth and early seventeenth centuries there was a reaction against the various ornate, formal styles— modelled on Cicero's full-blown periods—towards the brevity and point of Seneca's philosophical essays. Their fluency was also admired: he was the model for a 'loose' as well as a 'curt' style among the Elizabethans.

Francis Bacon—though he criticised Seneca's excessive word-play, which makes 'every passage seem more witty and weighty than it is'—owed a great debt to him; and Queen Elizabeth 'did much admire Seneca's wholesome advisings'.[3] But the role of

[1] J. W. Duff. [2] Thomas Stanley.
[3] Sir John Harington.

intermediary was most emphatically claimed by the 'English Seneca' Bishop Hall (1608), with special reference to the moralising letter. His Senecan style, however, was severely condemned by the Ciceronian John Milton, who describes Hall as 'hopping short in the measure of convulsion-fits'. These English Senecans were much influenced by the Flemish Latinist Lipsius, and he too is castigated by Milton as a 'tormentor of semicolons'. But the Senecan style flourished and left a permanent mark, for it was associated in men's minds with a smart, advanced intellectual independence and escape from conventional orthodoxy.

In the centuries between the Hellenistic epoch and the end of the Roman Empire, Graeco-Roman philosophical thought was exercising great influence in a special field—that of the Law. Roman Law, it is true, goes back to a dim past before the impact of this philosophy was felt. Its relatively early history is represented for us by ancient quotations from the 'Twelve Tables', of which parts at least are believed to belong to the fifth century B.C. But the steady development which followed was given profundity by the influence of Greek thought—and especially by great ideas such as the Stoic Law of Nature. However, long before they had heard of this, the Romans had begun to adjust their legal thought to the need for taking into consideration the practices of non-Romans. The 'reforming influence' or 'universal element' which was thus at work was known as the 'right of peoples' (*ius gentium*). The Stoic Law of Nature and Brotherhood of Man fertilised this conception. The lawyers did not need to be trained philosophers to feel the impact of such doctrines, which were—as has been seen—almost the common property of the more enlightened Romans of the late Republic and early Principate.

The expression of these ideas in Latin was the work of Cicero, and it is by his means that they achieved much of their influence. So the effect of the Law of Nature and kindred doctrines on Roman legal studies was, in the long run, partly due to him. Moreover, his work as advocate naturally gave him a keen interest in law. It may be true that Cicero had not a legal mind; but there is, nevertheless, a close link between his oratory and legal developments. For a great deal of the finest speech-making took place in the law courts or, even when it did not, was closely concerned with legal points. Cicero's formulation of these had its effect.

Moreover, he deliberately devoted himself to what is called, in many countries, the 'Philosophy of Law'. He wrote a philosophical treatise, the *De Legibus—On the Laws* that would be found in a perfect State. It is not altogether unjustifiable that he should have modelled these on the traditional legal system of Rome itself. The Romans had a genius for law. And when first-class oratory had come to an end, some of the greatest names in the whole of ancient civilisation were still to occur; and they were the names of lawyers.

Progress in this field was steady and continuous. Stoic philosophical thought continued to merge with Roman legal acumen. So the law of the Romans became increasingly humane. With their profound interest in moral matters, they early came to exceed the Greeks in attention to the moral, unwritten law. But it was not until the second century A.D., and later still, that the greatest names in Roman Law appeared. The law that these writers hand down is probably the greatest single gift made by Rome to civilisation. In spite of all Greek and especially philosophical influences, it is a Roman gift. This is not only because it was Cicero who had interpreted Greek philosophy, but because the Greeks had never been very well suited to legal formulas. The Romans, on the other hand, had quite early, well before the time of Cicero, successfully applied systematic thinking to law. Yet for a long time, like the English, they were disinclined for codification; they preferred to work from practical matters and single decisions. But then, and particularly from about the second century A.D., came codification; and so it is from this time that the most important surviving legal writings date.

That is to say, they begin at a time when the histories of Latin literature often stop. The legal treatises are not usually included in accounts of this literature. But they should at least be mentioned, for two reasons. First, it is in such legal writings, dry as they are, that the special qualities of Latin, its clarity and precision, show most conspicuously. Secondly, of all Latin writings these have perhaps been the most influential on the medieval and modern world. It would therefore be a mistake, not only for a law student to ignore Latin, but for a student of Roman literature to ignore law.

The earliest of the great names of this epoch is Salvius Julianus (c. A.D. 100–69). Like many other thinkers and writers of this and the following century, he was a North African. He was entrusted with codifying duties of great importance by the emperor Hadrian (117–38). We know of his writings from numerous quotations. His pithy formulations were unequalled; his powers of exposition comprised all the traditional virtues of the concise, lapidary language of Rome, and all the magisterial clarity of her lawyers. Salvius may well be said to represent the culmination of their work.

His younger contemporary Gaius, on the other hand, was not a great lawyer in himself. He began to gain fame in the later empire, owing to the authorship of a highly convenient elementary text-book, the *Institutes* (*Institutiones*). In the Middle Ages this work was lost; it only came to light, in substantial part, in 1816, when a manuscript was discovered at Verona; then in 1933 the soil of Egypt yielded some important additional fragments.

Salvius Julianus and Gaius belong to the great period of Roman peace and prosperity in the second century A.D. It is remarkable that the next epoch of conspicuous progress and of famous legal names coincides with a later and much less happy period, the totalitarian military monarchy imposed on the war-impoverished empire by the African Septimius Severus (A.D. 193–211) and his successors. This epoch witnessed striking legal advances. Prominent in these was the jurist Papinian. His immense reputation is illustrated by a law passed two centuries after his lifetime. This stipulated that, if ever there was a difference of opinion between lawyers on a committee and neither side obtained a majority, then the view of Papinian should be decisive. This compliment was warranted by the brilliant logicality of his mind. And this was accompanied by a high degree of fairness. That, the famous Roman *aequitas*, was not content with the letter of the law; it also left room for the ethical considerations which the Romans were accustomed to respect, and which had been given added profundity through the influence of Stoic education. From the point of view of sheer clarity and legal exposition Papinian is actually exceeded by his younger contemporary Ulpian, who—like the imperial family of his day—was a Syrian (from Tyre).

Roman Law continued to develop in these epochs of which the ordinary classical curriculum knows nothing. Even in as brief a study as this, room must be found for the name of a man who lived after the fall of Rome itself—three centuries after the jurists who have just been mentioned. This was Tribonian, who was born in southern Asia Minor and became the closest adviser of the Byzantine emperor Justinian (A.D. 527–65) in a mighty Latin codification of Roman Law. This included extracts from lawyers extending over more than 300 years. According to the emperor, 3,000,000 lines—of 2,000 books—were read for the purpose of selection, but only 5 per cent of this material was chosen for publication.

It is a matter of prolonged controversy whether the most important part of this codification, known as the *Digest*, should be regarded as mainly classical and Roman, with minor adjustments to bring it up to date in the very different conditions of the

Greek and Christian Empire of Byzantium, or whether it is mainly post-classical, with only minor employment of old materials. At all events, it seems that the man responsible for the vast project was Tribonian. It was probably he who chose the team of writers, and it may even have been he who originated the whole idea. In the result, Roman Law and fairness, and Christian charity, are seen together, and exert an influence one upon the other.

This monumental achievement came at the end of more than a millennium of steady evolution. Just a thousand years had passed since the traditional date of the Twelve Tables. These were centuries of gradual, continual advance in law, even at times when political and social conditions fluctuated disastrously. Tribonian's work is the basis of modern European law. In the early Middle Ages its effects were already present in the West. At first they were latent; but then the Church began to systematise what it knew. In the twelfth century A.D. Roman Law came to the fore again, when a manuscript of the *Digest* was discovered at Florence, and 'Canon Law' was codified at Bologna. The old Stoic Law of Nature, in a contemporary guise, was actually held to be fully represented and exemplified by Roman Law.

We do not, today, give Roman Law this overriding position. But our society has accepted many of the most important legal institutions which Rome had evolved. We accept, for example, in very much the same way as Roman Law, the concepts of family, of private property, of the sanctity of contracts. But this sort of list by no means exhausts the Roman legal ideas which have had vast effects at different epochs of history—ideas including that of International Law, with its obvious debts to the Law of Nature and the Roman 'right of peoples'.

We tend to take these things for granted. But the reason why we are able to do so is because the Romans, with the impact of Greek thought—largely introduced by Cicero and Seneca—

operating on their native environment and mentality, developed them as workable ideas. Those ideas, at different stages of their development, were recorded by Salvius Julianus, Papinian, Tribonian and the rest. That is why these must be ranked among the most influential writers in the Latin language.

4. THE ROMAN LETTER

Through his speeches, and his literary and philosophical works, Cicero reveals to us various aspects of his manifold personality. But these indications are nothing to the intimate disclosures in his 900 surviving letters, and in nearly 100 replies to them which have likewise come down to us. Owing to the fact that Cicero's letters have survived in large numbers, we know more about him as an individual than about almost any other person of comparable significance, ancient or modern.

We have sixteen books of letters to his closest friend the wealthy financier Atticus (*Ad Atticum*), three books of letters addressed to his own brother Quintus, two to Brutus, and sixteen to other friends (*Ad Familiares*). Far and away the greater number of these letters were not written with an eye to publication. It was only at the end of his life that Cicero began to yield to suggestions of publication, and even then he only thought in terms of a much more rigorous selection than we possess. But no publication whatever took place until after Cicero's death (43 B.C.). We owe the survival of the letters *Ad Familiares* to their preservation by Cicero's secretary, Tiro. The others were preserved by their recipients. (The circumstances in which, after Cicero's death, his letters were published constitute a difficult and still not fully elucidated question.)

The letters provide a revelation of social life in the days of the failing Republic. They give many unforgettable pictures of the personalities of this troubled epoch. Naturally the personality which they reveal most clearly is that of Cicero. As his brother wrote to him, 'I have seen the whole of you in your letters'.[1] Cicero emerges as a vain, vacillating, snobbish man who nevertheless possessed and pursued a permanent aversion to autocracies. His vanity was distressingly shown after Caesar's death when he was captivated by a little flattery from one of those who very soon afterwards were to decide upon his death—the twenty-year-old youth who already called himself Caesar, but whom we know as Octavian during these years preceding his assumption of the solemn name Augustus. 'Although he may call Cicero "father", consult him in everything, praise him and thank him', observed Brutus with acid accuracy, 'yet it will become clear that his acts do not tally with his words.'[2]

For Octavian's fellow-triumvir, Antony, Cicero had nothing but hatred. This abundantly colours the *Philippics*, and is also apparent from many letters:

How I wish you had invited me to that splendid banquet on the Ides of March: there would then have been no leavings! As it is they are causing us such trouble that we feel your immortal service to your country left something to be desired. The fact that you, good man as you are, took Antony aside that day, and that your kindness was instrumental in keeping this pest alive, makes me sometimes feel almost angry with you (though I have hardly the right).[3]

Cicero had opposed Caesar in the Civil War; however, he had sought to reach an understanding with him before the Ides. The conspirators did not let Cicero into the secret, though afterwards he claimed to have been morally one of their number. He writes amusingly to Atticus of a visit that the dictator—with a large

[1] *Ad Fam.* XVI, 16, 2.
[2] [Cicero], *Ad Brut.* I, 17, 5; 43 B.C. The translations of all these excerpts from Cicero's letters, except the last, are by L. P. Wilkinson.
[3] Cicero to his friend Trebonius (43 B.C.), *Ad Fam.* X, 28, 1.

retinue—had paid to him (at a time when the plot was already under way):

...His *entourage* was entertained in three rooms on a generous scale. His humbler freedmen and slaves lacked for nothing: the superior ones I entertained in style.

Need I say more? We behaved like human beings together. However, he wasn't a guest to whom you would say, 'Do please come back again on your way back'. Once is enough. Our talk kept off serious topics and was largely about literature. In short, he was delighted and enjoyed himself....

There you have the story of a visit, or should I say, billeting, which was distasteful to me, as I said, but did not prove embarrassing.[1]

At this time Cleopatra was at Rome, causing offence to Republican feeling—and to Cicero:

I hate the Queen...her insolence, when she was living in Caesar's house in the gardens beyond the Tiber, I cannot recall without indignation. So no dealings with that lot. They seem to think I have not only no spirit, but no feelings at all.[2]

The material in Cicero's letters is vast and varied. His passion for the public life of the capital clearly emerges, most poignantly when he was in exile and when—as seemed to him much the same thing—he was obliged to take on a provincial governorship in Asia Minor (Cilicia):

Would you ever have believed that words could fail *me*, and not merely such words as you orators use, but this homely jargon of ours? But so it is, and the reason is my extraordinary anxiety over what will be decreed about the provinces. I have a strange longing for the capital, an incredible longing for my friends, and for you as much as any; and I am so sick of the province....[3]

[1] Cicero, *Ad Atticum*, XIII, 52; 45 B.C.
[2] Cicero, *Ad Atticum*, XV, 15, 2; 44 B.C.
[3] Cicero to Caelius, *Ad Fam.* II, 11; 50 B.C.

There is much, too, in Cicero's letters about his chequered family life and its political and financial complications:

I am worn out and worried to death by the infatuation of my poor, poor daughter [with her deplorable but aristocratic husband Dolabella, about whom Cicero—once complimentary—had experienced a sharp revulsion of feeling]. Was there ever such a creature? If there is any way in which I can help her, I wish you would tell me. I can see you will have the same difficulty as before in advising me, but there is nothing that gives me more anxiety than this. I was blind to pay the second instalment of her dowry, I wish I hadn't; but that's all past history.[1]

In the fourteenth century, Petrarch first knew—and venerated—Cicero as orator and philosopher. When, in 1345, he discovered a manuscript of his letters to his brother, to Atticus and to Brutus, their disclosures of weakness at first shocked Petrarch profoundly. Gradually, however, he came to modify this judgement, doubtless reflecting that few leading politicians, living in difficult times, would come out wholly unscathed from the publication of their intimate correspondence.

The language of Cicero's letters is generally very different from that of his speeches or treatises. The letters are much closer to the ordinary daily speech of educated men. Vocabulary and syntax obey less stringent rules, and Greek words and phrases are often introduced. But Cicero by no means uses the same style for every letter. He adapts his manner to his subject; and, to that extent, his letters are self-conscious. As he writes himself, to his friend Curio:

As you know, there are many kinds of letter, but there is one very definite kind, for the sake of which the whole institution of letter-writing was invented—namely to tell people, who are not with us, if

[1] Cicero, *Ad Atticum*, XI, 25, 3; 47 B.C.

there is anything which it is important for us or for them that they should know...there remain two other sorts of letter which I like very much, one intimate and jocular, the other serious and solemn.[1]

Of the first of Cicero's three kinds of letter, the 'news-letter', his own numerous and incomparably vivid examples and the (much fewer) surviving replies almost form the sum-total of what ancient Roman literature has given to us. But the other two sorts of letter that he mentions were to have an important future. However, there was henceforward a significant difference. Cicero's letters, though to some extent they reflect the self-consciousness almost inevitable to a great stylist, were, as has been said, not written for publication. The letters of later Romans which we possess were written for publication; they are literary letters.

Horace and Ovid wrote poetic 'letters' for moralising and philosophising purposes. The next important collection of prose letters that we possess is likewise of a philosophical character. This consists of the 124 'Moral Letters' (*Epistulae Morales*) of Seneca the Younger (*c.* A.D. 63–4). In these—a variant of his philosophical essays—the letter-form is a framework for the 'pointed' Stoic exhortations of the Silver Age. Here there is a debt to Greek philosophers such as Plato and particularly (though Seneca's Stoic morals were remote from his views) Epicurus, who had used this sort of framework as the medium for philosophical discussion. It is quite possible that Seneca's letters were actually despatched to their recipients. Nevertheless they are essentially epistles of a philosophical and literary character. (The 'English Seneca', Bishop Hall, adapted the style and matter of these letters in 1608 so as to 'introduce into English new fashion of discourse by Epistles. Thus, we do but talk with our friends by our pen.')

But the master of the Roman literary letter is Pliny the Younger, who was born two or three years before the publication

[1] Cicero, *Ad Fam.* II, 4, 1.

of Seneca's epistles. Pliny wrote under the emperors Nerva
(A.D. 96–8) and Trajan (A.D. 98–117). Pliny was the friend of
a genius, the historian Tacitus; but he was in no way a genius
himself. Yet his letters provide us with a gracious, kindly, vivid
and lavishly varied picture of the literary circles of his day, and
also of much else.

One famous letter describes the great eruption of Vesuvius in
A.D. 79 and the death in it of the writer's uncle, the distinguished
scientist Pliny the Elder, who has left us his monumental *Natural
History*, drawing upon 2,000 books.[1] Pliny the Elder had a naval
command not far from Vesuvius.

He ordered the galleys to put to sea, and...steer'd his direct course
to the point of danger...he was now so nigh the mountain, that the
cinders, which grew thicker and hotter the nearer he approached,
fell into the ships, together with pumice-stones and black pieces of
burning rock: they were likewise in danger not only of being aground
by the sudden retreat of the sea, but also from the vast fragments
which rolled down from the mountain and obstructed all the shore....

In the mean while the eruption from mount Vesuvius flamed out in
several places with much violence, which the darkness of the night
contributed to render still more visible and dreadful. But my uncle...
retired to rest, and it is most certain that he was so little discomposed as
to fall into a deep sleep; for being pretty fat, and breathing hard, those
who attended without actually hear'd him snore.

The court which led to his apartment being now almost filled with
stones and ashes, it was thought proper...to awaken him. He got
up....They went out then, having pillows tied upon their heads with
napkins; and this was their whole defence against the storm of stones
that fell round them. It was now day every where else, but there
a deeper darkness prevailed than in the most obscure night; which
however was in some degree dissipated by torches and other lights

[1] For other Roman scientists, see Celsus (medicine), Frontinus and
Vitruvius, and—for agriculture—Cato the Elder, Varro and Columella,
in Appendix 4.

of various kinds. They thought proper to go down further upon the
shore, to observe if they might safely put out to sea, but they found
the waves still run extremely high and boisterous. There my uncle,
having drank a draught or two of cold water, threw himself down
upon a cloth which was spread for him, when immediately the flames, and
a strong smell of sulphur which was the forerunner of them, dispersed
the rest of the company, and obliged him to arise. He raised himself
up with the assistance of two of his servants, and instantly fell down
dead; suffocated, as I conjecture, by some gross and noxious vapour,
having always had weak lungs, and frequently subject to a difficulty
of breathing.[1]

But perhaps the most noted quality of Pliny the Younger has
proved to be his feeling for nature, and his capacity to describe it.
Virgil had loved nature, and so in his way had Horace. Most
Romans, however, had preferred nature in its 'Riviera' aspects,
or when it was disciplined in formal parks or vegetable gardens.
But Pliny is one of those writers who show that classicism does
not exclude the romantic. For he loved and expressed the more
solitary aspects of nature as aids to meditation and inspiration.
His somewhat florid versions of the Silver Latin style of Seneca
the Younger adapt themselves admirably to such subjects.

Have you ever seen the source of the river Clitumnus? . . . At the foot
of a little hill, covered with venerable and shady cypress-trees, a spring
issues out, which gushing in different and unequal streams forms
itself, after several windings, into a spacious basin, so extremely clear
that you may see the pebbles and the little pieces of money which are
thrown into it, as they lie at the bottom . . . the banks on each side are
shaded with the verdure of great numbers of ash and poplar trees, as
clearly and distinctly seen in the stream as if they were actually sunk
in it.[2]

[1] Pliny, *Letters*, VI, 16, 7–19, tr. Melmoth (1748). Melmoth's translation
is not exact in every particular but gives a fair general impression.

[2] Pliny, *Letters*, VIII, 8, 1–3, tr. Melmoth.

Pliny's letters are collected in ten books. The tenth is of a special character. It contains a remarkably valuable exchange of correspondence between Pliny as governor of Bithynia and Pontus (N. Asia Minor), and the emperor Trajan. Bithynia and Pontus had a large community of Christians, and Pliny sought guidance from the emperor regarding their treatment. This is Trajan's reply, a unique document concerning the imperial attitude to the early Christians.

The method you have pursued, my dear Pliny, in the proceedings against those Christians which were brought before you, is extremely proper; as it is not possible to lay down any fixed plan by which to act in all cases of this nature. But no search should be made for these people. If indeed they should be brought before you, and the crime is proved, they must be punished; with this restriction, however, that where the party denies himself to be a Christian, and shall make it evident that he is not by invoking our gods, let him (notwithstanding any former suspicion) be pardoned upon his repentance. Informations without the accuser's name subscribed ought not to be received in prosecutions of any sort, as it is introducing a very dangerous precedent, and by no means in keeping with the spirit of the age.[1]

In its recorded letters Rome handed down a distinctive gift to the culture of Europe, as Horace Walpole and Alexander Pope testify. Modern distaste for artificiality makes the epistle intended for dispatch and not for publication seem more interesting than its literary counterparts. But the latter form a very distinguished, independent branch of literature. Pliny the Younger showed them to be perfectly adapted to certain sorts of descriptions and discussion, on a not very large scale. During the first four centuries after the Renaissance, this kind of letter exerted a great influence on cultivated expression; it is only comparatively recently that it has gone out of fashion.

[1] [Pliny], *Letters*, x, 97 (Melmoth's translation, amended).

6-2

FACT AND FICTION

1. HISTORY

THE Greeks and Romans founded history, and they are the founders and ancestors of the history-writing of today. What is more, the greatest ancient historians wrote with a brilliance that is unequalled. They also provide anticipations of many of the special attitudes to history, concepts of history, which are prevalent today. Yet they possess features which come as something of a surprise to the modern reader.

These features are to some extent inherent in the origins of the writing of history. In early Greek times, historical prose-writing was at first extremely close to epic poetry. Indeed history owed its technique and its very existence to the epic poets. These, like any other poets, were not primarily concerned with an accurate narrative of events or analysis of trends; and ancient history never quite forgot its early link and debt to poetry. Again, when Greek tragic drama developed at Athens, this too influenced history. Aristotle finds it natural and desirable to compare history with poetry. There *is* a difference, he says. History tells what happened, poetry rather tells what might happen. So, in one sense, poetry is the *more* scientific of the two as being concerned with general truths! However, the comparison is made. Other such comparisons come from Rome. It is true that Cicero and Quintilian both point out, with greater explicitness than Aristotle, the differences between history and poetry—which we take for granted; yet Quintilian comes to the conclusion that 'History is very near to poetry, and may be considered in some sense as poetry in prose'.[1]

[1] *Inst. Or.* x, i, 31.

There was room then in ancient history for more or less fanciful 'philosophies of history'. And they appeared. Nationalism, for example, inspired famous stories of early Roman history which, though inspired in many cases by a patriotic ideal, were not based on any actual events. But this is not only a question of nationalism; the stories have a profoundly moral tone. For to the ancients the phrase 'philosophy of history' is applicable in a special and literal sense. Their histories were strongly affected by contemporary philosophical movements. In Hellenistic and Roman times it was particularly influenced—as was the whole of education—by the Stoics. These laid great stress on ethics. And so did the historians. Among them, too, there is a vigorous atmosphere of moralising.

The aim of a moralist is to persuade, to teach and to guide. The art of persuasion was rhetoric. So it is inevitable that ancient historians, who wanted to exercise the moralist's persuasion, were powerfully affected by rhetoric. This accounts for another ancient observation on the subject, which is as strange to the modern reader as those of Aristotle and Quintilian: 'History is a branch of study which is predominantly the concern of the orator.'[1] This remark is attributed by Cicero to his friend Atticus—and probably mirrors an opinion of Cicero's own. 'Do you see what an asset history is to the public speaker? I think its greatest benefit lies in its flow of prose and its variety. But I do not see it entered anywhere under a heading of its own in the rhetorical handbooks.'[2]

We, on the other hand, should never expect to see a discussion of history in a handbook of the public speaker's art! Cicero is looking at the whole matter from the standpoint of the orator and his words are significant of the general attitude to history. In putting forward this attitude, he was to a large extent echoing the Athenian Isocrates. For Isocrates, trying in the fourth century B.C. to map out rhetoric in systematic terms, had actually thought of history as part of rhetoric. The Romans were able to

[1] Cicero, *De Legibus*, I, 5.   [2] Cicero, *De Oratore*, II, xv, 62.

understand this attitude. 'It is difficult for us, who use words primarily as a means of conveying what we believe to be the truth, to penetrate the mind of Roman writers, who...often used them primarily for effect.'[1] (As a corollary of this, nearly every ancient historian is vague or inaccurate in his use of technical terms—military, constitutional, etc.)

Quintilian seems to rebel against this attitude of Isocrates and Cicero. For his apparently reassuring comment is that history is written to tell a story—not to prove anything. But the words must not be taken out of their context, and his final definition still does not set up truth as the ultimate, or at any rate not as the sole, aim of history. History is written, he says, 'to remind posterity and to win a reputation for its author'. In this context his denial of any aim of 'proving' anything is ominous rather than reassuring. He is contrasting history with oratory, and seems to imply that the former is actually less concerned with demonstrating facts than the latter.

Quintilian continued his discussion by observing that history, being what it is, has to avoid monotony by employing an impressive and spectacular style. And this brings us closer to the attitude of leading Roman thinkers towards history. Cicero, too, had repeatedly stressed that to write history well a man must be not only a scholar but an artist—that is partly what he means by saying it is the orator's concern. Like Quintilian, he felt that every possible device of stylistic attractiveness needed to be lavished on history; and he added that the Roman historians of earlier generations had failed to meet this requirement. From his time onwards, however, though some historians were still bad writers, others produced unequalled works of art. And good and bad historians alike henceforward thought of history as artistic, rhetorical, moral —qualities which do not invariably square with mere objectivity.

Three results of this situation may be quoted.

[1] L. P. Wilkinson.

(1) Many Greek and Roman historians insert in their works a number of speeches attributed to personages. But these are not usually designed to reproduce what was actually said on the occasions in question. They are rather intended to provide what would now be described as 'background'. They illustrate the general points of view of the principal historical figures. They show, not necessarily what was actually said, but what might well have been said. 'I have put into the mouth of each speaker', says Tacitus, 'the sentiments proper to the occasion, expressed as I thought he would be likely to express them.' The Greek historian of the Roman Republic, Polybius, had likewise been opposed to verbatim quotation, since he felt it was the duty of the historian to interpret speeches rather than to quote them. Speeches were an attractive ingredient in artistic and moralising history, since they lend themselves with particular ease to rhetorical treatment. And, as if to stress this purpose, the speeches are often provided in pairs, balancing or contrasting nicely one with the other in sentiments and morals, in the true rhetorical spirit.

(2) Curiously enough, a partial parallel can be drawn between the speeches in ancient historical writings and another of their characteristic features, the battle-scene. Military events play a great part in ancient and particularly in Roman historical writing, and we might at least have expected accounts of fighting to be straightforward attempts to recount what actually happened. But when we try to reconstruct this from them, we are sometimes frustrated and mystified. Like speeches, these accounts of battles often aim not so much at detailed veracity as at a general presentation of 'atmosphere'. Sometimes, it is true, they give a realistic picture. But on other occasions they are, instead, pieces of fine moralistic writing—vivid illustrations of heroism, panic, reversals of fortune and the like. They bear a strong resemblance both to each other and to the narrative portions of the stock rhetorical exercises for schools, the declamations.

(3) Works of historical research today indicate the sources on which they rely. But the careful references, footnotes and appendices in which this is done are a modern invention. Ancient historians were not usually very careful to specify their sources. Some did not do so at all, others did, but in a fragmentary and unsystematic fashion. Sometimes it even seems as if they deliberately prefer, from reasons of pride, to specify only those sources on which they have relied the least. It would be an absurd reversal of propriety to blame the ancients for not observing modern methods. But it is important to our appreciation of their historical reliability that we should be clear when they did not; and they did not feel any obligation regularly to cite their authorities.

So ancient and modern historical methods are different. But ancient thought has handed down to us many interpretations of the function of history which will win approval today. For example, Cicero hails it as 'the witness of the age, the light of truth, the life of the memory, the instructress of life....For who does not appreciate that the first law of history is that its writers should not venture to say anything that is untrue—that their writing should be subject to no suspicion of influence or of partisanship?'[1] This is a splendid ideal. But all the rhetorical, moral and artistic features of ancient history that have been described were, in practice, too much for this theoretical aim. This is even true of Cicero himself. Half playfully, he virtually admits this in one of his oratorical treatises, by saying that 'rhetoricians are allowed to tell lies in their historical writings'.[2]

This is only a half-serious observation, and it might represent not so much Cicero's considered opinion as a 'dig' at the rhetorical historians of Hellenistic Greece and Republican Rome. Again, when in a speech he describes the chief aim of literature as the glorification of the State, he may be mainly reflecting a popular

[1] *De Oratore*, II, 36, 62.   [2] *Brutus*, XI, 42.

view. Nevertheless, there is also a famous passage in a letter of Cicero's to a friend which reveals that he did not, in practice, consider veracity as the final criterion in the recording of his own doings. His friend was Lucceius, a historical writer. Cicero proposes to Lucceius that a subject he might well tackle was the story of Cicero's own consulship, in which the latter had played a leading part in suppressing the conspiracy of the aristocratic revolutionary Catiline. Cicero cannot refrain from inserting in his letter the suggestion that, in writing of this subject, Lucceius should pitch his tone pretty high, even to the point of exaggerating—that is to say, of disregarding strict historical accuracy. This is what he says: 'I ask you most emphatically to bestow on our friendship even just a little more than will be allowed by Truth.'[1]

It would be an over-simplification to regard this as just plain dishonesty on the part of Cicero. The trouble rather was that, despite his own idealistic definitions of history elsewhere, the ancient world as a whole—with a few exceptions—did not firmly place truth in the very forefront of its aims. Poetry had contributed to the origins of history. Tragic drama had left its mark. And Cicero is, in effect, requesting that his consulship should be treated in accordance with the technique of poetic drama—a less startling suggestion for a history then than now, when historical novels, perhaps, could be treated in this way, but hardly respectable histories.

Furthermore, another early influence on Greek and Roman historical writing had been the *encomium*—rhetorical essay in honour of some personage. Such essays were naturally bent on praise above all else. Cicero, in writing to Lucceius, has this kind of literature in mind. He is asking the historian to apply its ways to the story of his consulship. However, any moral superiority that this might tempt us to feel is removed by two further

[1] *Ad Fam.* v, xii, 3.

considerations. In the first place, history in Cicero's day was still a relatively young study—not much more than five hundred years old. Secondly, at no time have there been more flagrant examples of untruthful historical writings than in our own twentieth century—when the profession could have benefited from the additional experience of two millennia.

What is really striking and unusual about Cicero's letter to Lucceius is not so much its sentiments as the frankness with which they are expressed. It would be a disservice to the classics not to appreciate the self-set purposes, and even limitations, of ancient history: the ancient frontier between history and the historical novel was, by our own standards, a little blurred. To claim for ancient history what it did not claim for itself may mean losing sight of its real, superlative, unequalled excellences: which are those of narration, artistry and stylistic brilliance.

Roman historians show the usual paradoxical relation to Greece. The historians of Rome, like its other writers, could not possibly have written what they did and as they did without their Greek forerunners. As usual again, the Romans profited from this Greek influence to such an extent and in such a way that their achievement is in the truest sense original. Furthermore, this Roman achievement has exerted far greater direct influence than that of the Greeks on the historical study of the Middle Ages, the Renaissance and the present day.

Even before the last great Greek historian, Polybius (second century B.C.), Romans too were writing history. The first known Roman historian is Fabius Pictor, of the third century B.C. He wrote in Greek in order that Greeks should learn of the glories and blessings of Roman rule. Soon, Latin was used; and the serious business of politics, which was of supreme importance in the life of educated Romans of the Republic, came to be regarded as including the study and writing of history. So the men who wrote it were often of noble or at least of senatorial rank; they are sometimes known as the 'senatorial historians'. Writers of this status combined a measure of Greek culture, which they possessed in varying degrees, with a reverence for Roman traditions and institutions, and for the records of Roman family and State.

The State was intimately bound up with religion. Indeed, religion was primarily a governmental affair: nothing could be done by the State without first finding out the will of the gods. So it is not surprising that the great priesthoods provide the earliest important repositories of information about the past. A landmark in the history of history is the establishment, perhaps at a date not far from 300 B.C., of the 'Records of the Priests' (*Tabulae Pontificum*). These were annual notices set up by the chief priest at his official residence. They were primarily concerned with events of a religious character, that is to say with the recording of days on which the priests should hold their appropriate ceremonies. But the Records also came to possess a wider importance. For a number of these events were inevitably political—victories, declarations of war and peace, and the like. So the *Tabulae* began to record historical events. And this yearly documentation, of a markedly Roman character, plays its part along with other Roman sources—and along with Greek influences—in the formation of Roman historical writing.

The greatest name in Roman history before the last years of the Republic is that of Cato the Elder (the Censor) (third/second centuries B.C.). Though theoretically opposed to Greek influence, he had—as has been seen—written the first Greek-inspired rhetorical text-book in Latin; and he also did much to blend the Greek and Roman strains of history into a method combining the distinctive features of both. His great historical achievement, now lost, was the *Origines* (in seven books), taking the story of Rome from Aeneas to his own day. Cato's motto was 'look after the subject-matter, and the style will look after itself'. But he does not fail to introduce simple structural and rhetorical devices learnt from the Greeks; and his writings affected Latin prose style. Under the inspiration and encouragement of Cato the Elder, a considerable attempt was made to use the records and traditions that were preserved, in order to reconstruct the whole past of Rome. The historians who were engaged in this task in the second and early first centuries B.C. are often known as the 'Annalists'; this name does not imply that their writings were bare lists of events, but that they more or less followed chronological order.

Before long, in *c.* 123 B.C., an official endeavour was made to provide a comprehensive, authoritative record of the whole of past Roman history. This work filled eighty books; it was known as the *Annales Maximi* ('Greatest Annals'). These 'set out in formal arrangement year by year the official events of the State, viz: elections and commands, civic, provincial and cult business. The composition involved for the regal period legendary and antiquarian speculation, for the early Republic systematic reconstruction from the nucleus of records, and added to the framework of the *tabulae pontificum* from the fuller records in the archives.'[1] Then came a generation of 'Annalists' who expanded this sort of material—in some cases with scant regard for probability—in the light of the rhetorical ideas of history inherited, ultimately, from Isocrates.

In spite of such embroidery, these 'Annalists' and their predecessors were blamed as stylistically inferior in the first century B.C., by Cicero. As was mentioned above, Cicero stressed—even to the exclusion of factors which would now be regarded as of equal importance—that the historian should be an artist and a stylist; and by his standard all earlier Roman history was held to have fallen short. Cicero himself did not write a history book. He wrote a poem—about the stirring events of his consulship—which he regarded as in some sense a historical work, and he toyed

[1] A. H. McDonald.

with the idea of a prose history on the same subject. But he did not write it.

However, he has left us valuable comments on the duties of the historian; and he also wrote two books which, if not actually historical accounts, contain a great deal of Roman history. One of these is the treatise *On the State* (*De Republica*). It is an attempt to define the best sort of constitution and government. Cicero's ideal State is an idealised Rome with an infusion of conceptions derived from various Greek writers. One of these ideas was that the perfect State comprised a mixture between three sorts of constitution—monarchic, aristocratic and democratic: according to Cicero (and Polybius had felt the same) it was Rome which exemplified this ideal threefold mixture most perfectly. Not all of this work of Cicero's has come down to us; and the greater part of what has survived was only rediscovered in 1820. It is not a history; but it is full of important historical material. For example, it contains much-disputed references to 'guides of the State', 'ideal statesmen'. This phrase does not exactly foreshadow the Principate, but it does suggest that Cicero was, at least to some extent, moving—with his times—away from wholly Republican ideas.

Also of great importance is a treatise called *On the Laws* (*De Legibus*), of which about three-fifths survives. It tells us much about Roman legal history. In particular, a whole book (the third) is concerned with the actual machinery of government, and so is a historical document of unusual significance. Yet, despite this work and the *De Republica*, Cicero left the actual writing of Roman history to others.

2. FROM CAESAR TO LIVY

A historian who far outstripped his Roman predecessors in skill
was Cicero's slightly younger contemporary Julius Caesar. His
'Commentaries' (*Commentarii*) include the *Gallic War* (*De Bello
Gallico*) in seven books, and the *Civil War* (*De Bello Civili*) in
three books. (The additional books on the Spanish, African and
Alexandrian wars were evidently not written by Caesar himself,
but by his officers.) Caesar displays the brevity and lucidity
favoured by the Atticist school of oratory. His own speeches
have not survived. They were reputed second only to Cicero's;
and Quintilian said they could have equalled Cicero's if Caesar
had had time. Of the brilliance of Caesar's style, both in his
speeches and in his historical writings, Cicero speaks very highly—
or rather he puts the words in the mouth of the distinguished
Atticist orator, Brutus, Caesar's future murderer:

I like his speeches very much [Brutus is reported as saying]. I have
read a number of them, and also the Commentaries which he wrote
about his activities...they deserve the highest praise; for they are
bare, straightforward and graceful. They are as free of all oratorical
adornment as a naked body is free of clothing....In historical writing
there is nothing more agreeable than pure limpid brevity.[1]

This brilliant brevity of Caesar has at times encouraged the
view that his style is the straight, plain writing of the simple
soldier. But that is by no means true. On the contrary, Caesar
was a supreme exponent of the typically classical maxim 'true art
lies in the concealment of art'. A suspicion of the truth may be
aroused when we read of the quality of Caesar's speeches. Oratory
in the last century B.C. was a systematised art in which success was
only achieved by elaborate training. Caesar was a man of consummate education who was thoroughly imbued with this tradi-

[1] Cicero, *Brutus*, 262.

tion. In ages like our own when no similar tradition exists, it is very easy to misunderstand the appearance of simplicity in the writings of such a Roman. The truth rather is that Caesar's apparent simplicity, and lack of rhetoric, were deliberate artifices based on mastery of the most elaborate rhetorical theory. Caesar's words are simple, not because he chose the first words that came to hand, but because of an Atticist preference for this sort of style.

We have on record his own assertion that a writer ought to avoid unusual or little known words 'like rocks at sea'. Though plain, however, his words are cunningly and brilliantly chosen. Caesar's language shows what the Elizabethan Ascham calls 'unspotted proprietie'. And the resulting style is highly individual—by no means as typical as the prominence of Caesar in elementary curricula might suggest, but crystal clear. Bernard Shaw characteristically observed that he liked Caesar best of Latin authors because 'his remark that all Gaul is divided into three parts, though neither interesting nor true, is at least intelligible'.

Caesar writes of himself, in a self-effacing fashion, in the third person; and the title of these histories, the 'Commentaries', is of modest, simple appearance, suggesting that the work is scarcely a history, but rather its raw material—being based, as it partly is, on the reports of subordinates. However, such displays of simplicity conceal, and have often concealed only too effectively, a propagandist intention. Yet this is propaganda of a subtle kind. Very few facts are actually *falsified*. But Caesar is a master of re-arrangement, emphasis, omission, skilfully directed to his own political aim. The apparent simplicity of his diction is one more device contributing to the general impression of straightforwardness.

In purpose, the *Gallic War* is a defence against Caesar's political enemies. They blamed him—among other things—for wanton aggression, caused by a desire to win personal glory and so political advantage. Some also (especially his political enemy

Cato the Younger) blamed him for cruelty towards the Gauls. The *Gallic War*, written in haste before the breach with Pompey, directs the attention to quite a different picture (and incidentally glosses over military setbacks, such as the inconclusive 'reconnaissances' of Britain in 55 and 54 B.C.). Similarly, the *De Bello Civili*, written shortly before Caesar's death (and never completed by him), is not merely a plain, soldierly account of the civil war between Caesar and Pompey (49–48 B.C.). It is an ingenious attempt to make it appear that the war-guilt rested entirely with the other side.

The measure of Caesar's success, and of the glamour which it has exercised, is the fact that nearly all schoolboys and schoolgirls who study Latin are very soon given the *Commentaries* to read. This is partly due, it is true, to the alleged plainness of his language; but the view has also often been put forward that Caesar is not only 'simple' but 'improving' as well. Some of those who selected Caesar for this reason appear to have mistaken his insidious 'plainness' for simple, soldierly patriotism or Olympian forthrightness. 'Caesar', it was said in 1715, 'writ like a man of Quality;... he possesseth this almost peculiar to himself that you see the Prince and the Gentleman as well as the Scholar and the Soldier in his Memoirs.'[1] This eighteenth-century admiration of Caesar's aristocratic brilliance unduly ignores the grim side. Others however, such as Mommsen, have admired Caesar for the rather different, if not opposite, reason that he suppressed the traditional aristocracy of his own day. Napoleon III, and many more, frankly admired him for his successful autocracy and aggression. But as Trollope remarked (1870), 'we cannot... take the facts as the Emperor of the French gives them to us'; and the same writer often expresses uneasiness at significant omissions from the *Commentaries*.

Yet these very differences of opinion hint at the reasons why

[1] Henry Felton.

Caesar's *Commentaries* are of real and great importance. In the first place, he provides problems for the critical judgement. It is fascinating to try to decide how far what he says represents a fair selection of truthful material. The study of Caesar from such a viewpoint will show how really clever publicity can twist facts without actually falsifying them, and such insight can usefully be applied to modern conditions. Furthermore, the admixture of this grain of salt still leaves the essential greatness of Caesar's *Commentaries* intact. There is first-class interest in the interpretation, by a man of outstanding ability in life and letters, of the times which he dominated. There is also much cause for reflection in this graphic picture of practical efficiency and discipline—the cause of Rome's conquest of the world and retention of its conquests. Other Roman historians do not reveal this machinery nearly so clearly.

The last book of the *Gallic War* was not written by Caesar but by a senior staff officer, Aulus Hirtius. He begins his book by a eulogy of his commander's historical writing. And what he says is true. 'Caesar not only wrote with supreme fluency and elegance. He also knew superlatively well how to describe his plans and policies.'[1]

Yet, in spite of these excellences, Caesar was not very much read by the ancients. This was not usually because of any deviations from objectivity on his part (though one of his officers, the historian Pollio, hinted at deliberate inaccuracies). It was rather because his Attic style was not ornamental enough for most later Roman tastes. For this reason his historical writings were less popular than those of his younger contemporary who will next be discussed.

Sallust was about fifteen years younger than Caesar. We are not in a position to estimate his achievement completely, since his

[1] *De Bell. Gall.* VIII, preface.

Histories, probably the most important of his works, are almost entirely lost. But this was a book which exerted considerable influence on the rhetorical schools that were so greatly to affect post-Augustan literature.

Sallust's surviving works are the *Catiline* and the *Jugurtha*—or, more accurately, the wars against these two men (*Bellum Catilinae* and *Bellum Jugurthinum*). Catiline was an impoverished, reckless and ferocious nobleman who organised a conspiracy against the established order in 63 B.C., but was detected and overcome. In the *Jugurtha* Sallust gives an account of Rome's war with King Jugurtha of Numidia (North Africa, 111–106 B.C.) who was eventually defeated by Marius and given up to the Romans.

These are the first important Roman historical monographs, i.e. treatises on separate limited themes. To what extent this sort of historical writing was new is a complicated question. But it was Sallust who attracted to it the attention of his compatriots. Moreover, he came to be regarded by many Roman historians as its foremost exponent. The poet Martial, towards the end of the first century A.D., rates him very high indeed. To him, Sallust is 'first of Roman historians, as the feeling of men of learning bears witness'.[1]

But the scholars of modern times mostly do not agree. Nowadays Sallust is under a cloud. But, in considering criticisms of his work, it is necessary to distinguish carefully between his achievement as a historian in any of the senses in which we use the word, and his artistic achievement as a writer. If we consider Sallust as a historian and compare his historical standards with those of serious historians of today, criticism is inevitable. An ominous modern eulogy of Sallust praises him on the grounds that he 'manipulated the evidence in the interests of the higher truth'. This was clear to some ancient readers. For, however much the

[1] Martial, *Epigr.* XIV, cxci.

influence of oratory on history might be admitted, it was felt that a boundary nevertheless existed between the two—and that Sallust overstepped it. In the words of a historical handbook of the second century A.D.: 'People say that Sallust ought to be read not as a historian but as an orator.'[1]

Thus truthfulness is not necessarily the foremost of Sallust's preoccupations. In discussing the times of Jugurtha and Catiline, he is thinking of his own day, and—behind a façade of austere and ethical impartiality—is conducting vigorous party politics. He wrote these two treatises (and his *Histories*) in the years immediately following the death of Caesar. Two surviving letters purporting to be addressed to Caesar in his last years[2] are also attributed to Sallust, but their authorship is uncertain. Sallust wrote as a partisan of his former chief, Caesar, but also as one who was disgusted by the miseries of contemporary public life, and had withdrawn from them (he had retired—with great wealth—from a public career of dubious distinction). The implication is that Caesar's great gifts had been even more conspicuous amid the sordid contemporary scene.

The *Jugurtha* was written to glorify Jugurtha's conqueror Marius. The memory of Marius was favoured by the Caesarians as it had been by Caesar himself, whose aunt Marius had married; so Marius is shown as much preferable to his enemy Sulla, and better too than Marius' predecessor in the African command, the arrogant (but not wholly unsuccessful) aristocrat Metellus. In Sallust's version of the Catilinarian conspiracy the hero is not Cicero, who is represented as mediocre and ineffective, but Caesar—together with Cato, who (though Caesar's enemy) was recognised by all parties alike as an incarnation of the Republican and Stoic virtues. Sallust compares and contrasts the qualities of the two men: the impression emerges that Caesar's talents were

[1] Granius Licinianus, XXXVI.
[2] *Epistulae ad Caesarem senem De Re Publica.*

the more useful, since Cato's were barren and unpractical. Both are contrasted with the villain of the story, Catiline:

> From his youth addicted to civil dissensions, to quarrelling, to cheating and discord: these were merely the humours of his youth. His body could well inure itself to undergo want, watching and cold, more than human. Bold of spirit, subtle, wayward, a deep dissembler, greedy of another man's thrift, prodigal of his own: talkative enough, void of wisdom, of a high mind, accompanied with desires unsatiable, incredible, too, too ambitious.[1]

So Sallust adopts a strongly moral tone; he stresses the decline of the old-world virtues, and the growth of corruption and other evil forces. This won his writings popularity among moralists such as John Milton—as it had in the Middle Ages also. In a French work of the twelfth century,[2] he was treated as a principal source for the life of Caesar.

Sallust's characters are adapted to this moralising purpose. They are 'types', showing clearly the influence of the Athenian tragic drama. Such a treatment does not always leave room for careful chronology or a judicious weighing of causes. But this powerful delineation of the anti-Republican Catiline, and of his fall, impressed many generations of readers. In the eighteenth century, especially, it was read avidly by French revolutionaries. Thus, paradoxically, Sallust—himself an anti-Republican of the Caesarian persuasion—was admired for his denunciation of another sort of anti-Republican, Catiline.

These repercussions of his work recall the distinction that has to be made between Sallust as a historian and Sallust as a story-teller and a stylist. For it is by his superb artistry that he has earned this admiration. Nobody has presented action and debate with greater vigour and dramatic power than Sallust. The word

---

[1] Sallust, *Cat.* ii, tr. T. Heywood (seventeenth century).
[2] *Les Faits des Romains.*

which his writing suggested to the ancient critics was 'rapidity'. Quintilian speaks of 'that superhuman rapidity of his style'.[1] But this is very far from the cool Attic directness of Caesar. Sallust is vivid, abrupt and spectacular, and loves the strange and archaic words which Caesar would not admit. Sallust is a professed admirer of the Greek historian Thucydides, whose style was likewise highly individual and sometimes even tortuous.

Yet Sallust and Caesar have brevity in common. And they share something else as well. Sallust's abrupt brevity is no more unpolished and spontaneous than is the lucid brevity of his patron. However, the styles of both men are calculated to possess just such an appearance. Sallust's style has a superficial air of ruggedness which, like Caesar's apparent simplicity, conceals an elaborate and calculated rhetorical technique. This has deceived many of his readers. But it did not deceive Quintilian, who recognised his carefulness—and regarded it with approval. After emphasising how important it is that a writer should revise what he has written—especially in any passage which seems to have gone too easily—Quintilian comments: 'That, we are told, is how Sallust wrote; and certainly the manner of his writings shows clear evidence of the pains which he expended.'[2] The result was impressive. Indeed, it was widely held that by Sallust, for the first time, history in Latin was treated with the eloquence, and the beauty of language and style, which the subject deserved. That, rather than any unusual gift of historical accuracy, is his distinction.

Like most other ancient historians, Sallust wanted to teach and persuade. What he wanted to teach and persuade was that Caesar was always right. So had Caesar himself. In the next period another of Sallust's heroes, Augustus, carried on this tradition by writing or inspiring a document which showed that Augustus was always right. This was published in inscriptional form after

[1] *Inst. Or.* x, i, 102.   [2] *Inst. Or.* x, iii, 8.

his death as the *Summary of the acts of the deified Augustus*, generally known as the *Res Gestae*. Being an inscription, and not a very long one at that, perhaps it ought not to be included in a sketch of Roman historical writings. But it deserves attention since it throws light on certain of the Roman traditions which affected biographical and autobiographical composition. It is modelled to some extent on the autobiographies of earlier statesmen; and links with the style of Caesar's *Commentaries* have been traced. But it also possesses some of the monumental terseness which had for long been associated with inscriptional eulogies of consuls and victorious generals, whether set up in their lifetimes or after their deaths.

The *Res Gestae*, however, is a complex work in which Augustus (or his chancery) draws on a variety of Roman customs to achieve his ends. The subject is dealt with under four headings, each of partially traditional character:

(1) the honours received by Augustus;
(2) a statement of the personal funds which he claimed to have expended in the public interest;
(3) an account of the victories and conquests which he claimed;
(4) a final summing-up of his position in the State.

Practically the whole document was prepared during his lifetime; after his death only a brief epilogue was added.

The document was designed for Romans and Italians. But when Augustus died, at least one copy was set up in the chief temple of Ancyra (Ankara), then the capital of the province of Galatia. For that is the copy which has come down to us— the *Monumentum Ancyranum*. Some of its textual imperfections have been checked by fragments of further copies found at two other cities in a southern district of the same Galatian province.[1] Copies were no doubt distributed by the Roman government itself.

[1] Antioch and Apollonia-Mordiaeum, both in Pisidia.

In these circumstances absolute impartiality is of course not to be expected. At any epoch it is hard for anyone to be impartial about himself. And this was, and is, particularly hard in a lifetime which had begun with violent events arousing the strongest partisan feeling. Augustus achieves his effect by subtle and skilful use of official phraseology and especially of the good old traditional, ostensibly simple, Republican terms. This cleverly used traditional language was the velvet glove in which the iron hand was effectively concealed. At first sight the Latin of the *Res Gestae* looks quite easy and direct. But the more one studies it (using critical means which were not available to contemporaries), the more elusive the actual events of his reign become. These seemingly straightforward, concise Latin sentences do not quite reveal them—or the personality of Augustus himself.

Augustus was also honoured by historians other than himself, among whom was Livy. He wrote a history of Rome from the earliest times down to his own day. It took him forty years, and consisted of 142 books—the equivalent of twenty or thirty modern volumes of average size. Of these 142 books, nearly 107 are lost. This is one of the most lamentable of all our vast losses from Latin literature, and one which forgers have sometimes tried to make good.

Livy's work is a mighty historical feat; indeed there is no parallel to it. As a historian in the modern sense, he is much better than Sallust. He seeks to tell the truth. He has the true antiquarian spirit. He quotes his sources more often than most other ancient historians do; he often qualifies assertions so that they should not be too sweeping. He distrusts dubious evidence. Indeed, he often tries to exercise a workmanlike choice in favour of what is plausible, contemporary or appropriate. So excellent is the result that Dante called him 'Livy who errs not'. Yet, despite his efforts at selection, Livy's use of sources is, more often than not, uncritical. Moreover, his conclusions are based on no profound research or knowledge of Roman institutions. This was clear to the waspish emperor Caligula (A.D. 37–41), who called him 'long-winded and careless'.

Moreover, despite Livy's historical talents, or indeed because of their special character, a considerable portion of his work is not history at all, in any recognised sense of the word. For at least his first ten books are myth—a Virgilian evocation of Rome's past. This part of his work has been described as 'not scientifically but artistically and imaginatively true'. It is not mere chance that these books are among the most stimulating of all that Livy has handed down to us. His gifts were essentially of this romantic and poetic character; he was an epic poet in prose.

So, like other writers in this strain, he is a strong adherent of the widespread ancient custom of seeing history through the eyes of a moralist. Indeed, though he aims to tell the truth, his main aim was to draw moral lessons from the past for the needs of the present. It is possible to define this aim of Livy's more closely. For these moral lessons from the past were harnessed to the supreme purpose of the greater glory of Rome, and it is for his glorification of Rome that Livy is most to be remembered. One of the heroes of his work is Rome—and another is Italy. Italian patriotism was something new when Virgil and Livy became its exponents. There were still men living who remembered the disastrous Social (Marsian) War in which Italy had been rent asunder. Moreover, both the poet (from Mantua) and this historian (from Patavium, the modern Padua) belonged to that rich and racially mixed northern region, Cisalpine Gaul, which had been joined formally to Italy only twelve years before Augustus became sole ruler. So theirs is the keen, emotional patriotism of frontiersmen and 'colonials'. It is vigorously displayed in the books of Livy which are most widely read in schools—those about the Second Punic War. Perhaps this emotional attitude may have been the 'Patavinitas' in Livy at which a contemporary, Pollio, sneered; or it may have been a brogue.

Italy and Rome are Livy's heroes, and another hero is Augustus. It is true that those parts of his work which deal with contemporary affairs are lost, together with much else—including everything that he wrote on the years after 167 B.C. (Books 46–142: the large number of books shows that for this later period the scale of treatment had become more detailed). But we can detect a deliberate analogy and foreshadowing of Augustus in Livy's depiction of half-mythical early Romans, like Camillus in the dim fourth century B.C. Yet his sympathies were too wide to exclude all who had, in the troubled past, clashed with Augustus or with his great-uncle, Caesar. Indeed, Augustus himself did not wish to display too narrow a partisanship—which would be unseemly in one who claimed to restore the Republic. So there was no real reproof when Augustus, as an anecdote recounts to us, mockingly described Livy as a 'Pompeian', that is to say a backer of Caesar's enemy Pompey. Indeed, it appears that even those who had fought against Augustus himself were not excluded from honourable allusions. Livy, like Horace, is known to have written with respect even of Brutus and Cassius.

But all this harmonised with the greater patriotism with which Augustus sought to identify his own position and which Livy instils into his account of every century. Despite a considerable attachment to the true story of the past, he is constantly inspired by emotional, patriotic and moral missions. In the early part of his work, which is frankly imaginative, this is no disadvantage. But in the latter parts it causes him to look too favourably on the dealings of the Roman Republican government with other nations. The early Romans had been neither so virtuous nor so civilised as he makes them.

Livy's preface compares them favourably with his own contemporaries. This was written when the Civil Wars were only just over, and the world had not got used to the Augustan peace.

If I succeed in writing the history of the Romans—going right back to the foundation of the city—I am by no means sure that the achievement will be worth the trouble; and if I were sure, I should not venture to say so. For I know how stale and platitudinous such boasts are. Every new writer who appears thinks he is going to provide some original research about the facts, or write cleverly enough to supersede old-fashioned styles. However, whether I am successful or not, it will give me satisfaction to have done my part, to the best of my ability, in contributing to the record of the greatest people in the world. And if I fail to make my mark among the very large number of historical writers, it will be some comfort to think of the importance and distinction of the men by whom my reputation is eclipsed.

Besides, my subject is of formidable dimensions. It goes back more than seven hundred years: from small beginnings it has grown to a vastness which threatens to be its ruin. Now I am well aware that many readers will not be so very interested in Rome's origins and initial stages. They will be impatient to get on to contemporary history, which displays our nation suicidally eating up its own mighty resources. I, on the other hand, will feel rewarded for my labours by the chance to rest my eyes from the miseries which for years have beset this generation of ours—to rest my eyes from them just while I concentrate on reconstructing the remote past. This is a task that I can approach without any of the nervousness felt by the historian who deals with contemporary events; and that, even if it does not cause lapses from truthfulness, can be a worrying thing.[1]

The result was a nobly imaginative achievement—the reconstruction of a national tradition throughout eight centuries, the narration of Rome's greatness by a master of her language. The whole of Rome's past could only have been successfully evoked by a brilliant artist; and that is what Livy was. That, indeed, is his most real and lasting achievement.

[1] Livy, I, preface.

His prose was worthy of Cicero's, though it was not quite like Cicero's—it was more subtle, more malleable, and more poetic. Quintilian talks of its 'milky abundance', 'milky' indicating not only richness but clear purity. Then the same critic, following the habitual custom of comparing Greek and Latin authors, asserts that Livy is not inferior to the 'father of history', Herodotus. Quintilian goes on to add a further eulogy of Livy's style.

In narrative, he has a wonderful attractiveness and natural flow, and the speeches which he inserts are eloquent beyond description. Everything that is said is ideally adapted to the circumstances and the speakers. As regards the emotions, and particularly the more agreeable of them, I can say in a word that no historian has ever represented them more perfectly. So, by fine qualities of quite a different kind, he has equalled in fame that superhuman rapidity of Sallust.[1]

Livy's writings enjoyed an immediate success. But the circulation of the complete history was limited, owing to its size: for example, the poet Martial tells us that he had not room in his library for the whole work. So there came into circulation much-abbreviated versions, skeleton summaries, called *epitomes*. The existence of these epitomes made it easy for large parts of the great work itself to disappear. They also fall utterly short of their original in its specific excellence, style. Francis Bacon called epitomes 'corruptions and moths of history...that have fretted and corroded the sound bodies of many excellent histories, and wrought them into base and unprofitable dregs'. But for historical purposes the epitomes of Livy, though their value is not enormous, are not altogether valueless.

[1] *Inst. Or.* x, i, 101–2.

3. TACITUS

In the three-quarters of a century following the deaths of Augustus (A.D. 14) and Livy (A.D. 17) there were a number of historians; but most of their works are lost. They do not seem to have possessed talents comparable with those of Caesar, Sallust and Livy. On the other hand, it may also be that circumstances were less favourable for them. Certain of the emperors of this period, especially Caligula, Nero and Domitian, were 'touchy'. Their suspicions may have prevented contemporary historians from doing themselves full justice. But there may also have been quite different reasons for the apparent decline of historiography during this period. For one thing, there seems to have been an enlargement, a wider dispersal, of historical interest. To an increased extent, writers and thinkers now devoted themselves to subjects such as geography, science and ethnography.

Such tendencies are apparent in the earliest historical works of the greatest post-Augustan historian, Tacitus. After a work on oratory (*c.* A.D. 80), he began to make it clear to the world that Roman historiography had not died, or become moribund, in the days of Augustus. Within a short time of one another, he published the *Agricola* and the *Germania* (*c.* A.D. 98). Both these works show clearly the widening of historical horizons in the eight decades which had elapsed since the death of Augustus. The *Agricola* is a biography of Tacitus' father-in-law. To a large extent it follows the familiar Greek tradition of the *encomium*, the eulogistic, semi-biographical study, with an ethical bias. But it concerns us because Agricola was a governor of Britain (under Domitian, who, according to Tacitus, failed to appreciate him). Moreover Tacitus, who had absorbed the wider interests characteristic of the time, not only describes Agricola's campaigns but has a good deal to say about the island and its people. He is not at his best as a geographer, but despite many deficiencies and obscurities the information which he provides is indispensable to students of early British history.

The *Germania* contains an even larger proportion of descriptive work: it is an ethnographical study of the peoples of Central Europe. Here too Greek traditions were followed, and their conventions—as well as imperfect knowledge—imposed limitations on the writer. But here too Tacitus had contemporary motives of his own. Yet the character of these motives is disputed; and they were probably varied. But one motive was moral. He does not, it is true, over-simplify the Germans as 'noble savages'. He has a good deal to say to their discredit, and when he compares the Romans it is sometimes the one people and sometimes the other which has the advantage. But Tacitus is insistent on the differences between the two; and from the work as a whole there does emerge a deliberate, though not always explicit, contrast between the decadence of Rome and the crude vigour of the teeming, and potentially threatening, peoples beyond the Rhine. Seventy years later, the danger was to become a very real one; and most scholars have felt that thereafter German invasions contributed—perhaps contributed in a very large degree—to the eventual eclipse of the Roman Empire in the West.

Next followed Tacitus' two main works, telling the story of the emperors from A.D. 14 to 96. The *Histories*, which cover the later part of this epoch (from A.D. 68), were written first. We have about a third of them, describing the civil wars with which the era began. Tacitus' last and greatest creation was his *Annals*, which tell of the Julio-Claudian emperors from just before the death of Augustus to the death of Nero (14–68). He explains why he has chosen this subject:

Famous writers have recorded Rome's early glories and disasters. The Augustan Age, too, had distinguished historians—until the rising tide of flattery had a deterrent effect. The reigns of Tiberius, Caligula, Claudius and Nero were described during their lifetimes in fictitious terms, for fear of the consequences; whereas the accounts written after their deaths were influenced by animosities still unquenched. So I have decided to say a little about Augustus, with special attention to his last period, and then to go on to the principate of Tiberius and what followed.[1]

By far the greatest part of the *Annals* has survived (there is a gap in the middle, and Nero's last two years are lost), though the accuracy of the text that has come down to us is disputed at a good many points. The *Histories* and the *Annals* are so remarkable that at least two critics have tried to prove that they are forgeries. But this is not true. They are unique, but genuine.

Their diction shows a sharp contrast to the flowing, 'milky' style of Livy. The prose of Tacitus, as it reached its climax in these works, has undergone all the influences of Silver Latin and added to them his own intense individuality. Often he writes in short, abrupt sentences, in startlingly staccato phrases, in trenchant epigrams. We are given many surprises and never allowed to sit back: his style varies markedly, from simplicity to extreme individuality, according to the significance which he attaches to each episode. His words can be vivid and often semi-poetical, his syntax forcible and far removed from Ciceronian rotundity. Indeed, his language is far not only from Cicero but—despite debts to Sallust—from any Latin at all, spoken or literary, which has happened to survive. Much of Latin literature is remote from the spoken tongue, but never had it been as remote as this. Yet Tacitus, though he did not apparently go to a rhetorical school, has contrived to convert the rhetoric and point of the Silver Age from the second-rate quality of all too many of its exponents to an unequalled brilliance. This is the only time in the first two centuries A.D. that Latin prose has been transcendently first rate. Tacitus no doubt borrowed much; but he made it his own.

[1] Tacitus, *Annals*, I, I.

Tacitus' treatment of his subject is as vivid as his language. He is the supreme artist and craftsman among ancient historians, 'the greatest painter of antiquity'. Tacitus incorporates and blends into a single framework all the traditional features of historical writing. The antique title *Annals* suggests that Roman traditions are not forgotten. Here, too, are Hellenistic ethnology, biography, stock rhetorical types and situations—and moral purpose, not always the ally of historical objectivity; and emotional effects.

Tacitus himself writes that he was unmoved by indignation or partisanship, since in his case 'the customary incentives to these were lacking'—he had nothing to gain from them or to lose from their absence. But this assertion needs to be regarded in the light of historical custom. Such protestations were traditional, and in this instance they must be regarded as being—in some degree—conventional. Or, if they were not, Tacitus deceived himself. For his attitude shows clearly enough that, when he wrote his major historical works, he had recently lived through the sombre and perhaps terrifying last years of Domitian (A.D. 81–96). And so he was obsessed by the real or imaginary Domitians of past history. For example, Tiberius (A.D. 14–37)—a gloomy but apparently honest ruler—is depicted by Tacitus in the role of the stock tyrant of ancient literature, cunning, suspicious, sensual, unjust and ruthless. Domitian may also have affected Tacitus in another way: he may have been on Tacitus' conscience, since the latter—as praetor—must have been obliged to acquiesce in some of the purges undertaken by the emperor in senatorial circles close to the historian himself.

Tacitus' studies of Domitian's predecessors and their associates are unforgettable, but they do not seem to us to be free of hatred and partiality. Yet Tacitus's narrative is so enthralling that it carries conviction as a work of art, and very nearly carries conviction as history. The actual facts that he narrates are generally accurate. But, whether unconsciously or by deliberate intent, the manner of their presentation is invidious. For our information about the early Principate we have to depend greatly upon Tacitus; there is very rarely a better literary source from which we can check him. But his own employment of his sources is liable to the imperfections characteristic of ancient historical writings as a whole. There is no doubt that he took a great deal of care in composing his narrative. But his display of judicious selection often proves to be another means towards a sinister hint, a damning delineation—and Tacitus, though perhaps not a first-class psychologist, presents unforgettable psychological pictures.

Fairness was subordinated to the combined claims of rhetoric and ethics. Virtues and vices are dramatised and presented with forcible vividness. This moral aim, as often in Greek and Roman history, was predominant. This is no speculative conclusion; Tacitus tells us so himself. 'I regard it as the foremost task of the historian to ensure that virtues are not left unrecorded, and that evil words and deeds are made subject to the fears inspired by posterity's denunciation.' [1] Tacitus was urgently sincere; but his truthfulness, the reliability of his picture, is a much disputed subject.

Rhetoric and moral philosophy were two of the influences on ancient history and on Tacitus; another was Virgilian epic, and another was tragic drama. These influences together inspired Tacitus with an exalted conception of his task. His speeches are lost; but a well-informed contemporary, Pliny the Younger, tells us that they were notable for their quality of elevation. And to Tacitus, history is a conspicuously elevated theme. This means that he avoids undignified words and expressions, and that he avoids subjects which do not seem to him to contribute to the dramatic whole. This principle of selection markedly affects the scope of his tale. For the highest drama appeared to be centred at the all-powerful, glamorous, sinister imperial court. So we

[1] *Annals*, III, 65.

hear much of the emperors and their *entourages*. We also hear
a good deal of the senate—in so far as its powerlessness illustrates
the moral theme of degeneracy from the good old days and throws
into relief the power of the autocrats. But in the huge tracts of the
provinces, Tacitus—heir to the traditional, centrifugal view of
Roman history—often finds comparatively little to serve his
purposes (it was only under Hadrian, A.D. 117–38, that the idea
of a Roman 'commonwealth' began to be familiar). At most, the
faults or fate of an occasional imperial visitor or governor throws
a little light on the lurid central picture. The life of the peoples of
the Empire is often neglected. Military history, again—though
there is a good deal of it, as befitted the Roman tradition—is
sketchy, even unusually sketchy; it consists largely of set battle-
pieces which illustrate dramatic themes of bravery or panic.

What was the purpose of Tacitus? The purpose of Livy had
been patriotism, and the purposes of Caesar and Augustus had
been the glorification of Caesar and Augustus respectively. What
Tacitus wanted is not so easy to say; it remains something of
a mystery. Probably Tacitus did not quite know himself. 'His
views on philosophy and religion have been variously called
agnostic, sceptical, Stoic, fatalist, superstitious, and (as a last
resort) "deeply original".'[1]

He may have possessed what some modern psychologists call
a 'split personality'. His attitude to the political structure of the
State is characteristic of this division. He greatly admired the
traditional virtues of the antique Republic. Yet he realised that
the Republic was a thing of the past and could never be revived;
he even regards political opposition, if it goes beyond passive,
resigned disapproval, as theatrical and immoderate. Again, when
he is talking of post-Augustan tyrants, he seems to admire
Augustus. But his introductory survey of Augustus' own reign
(valuable as a check on the official tradition) is a series of sneers.

[1] B. Walker.

Tacitus himself wrote under enlightened emperors, Nerva, Trajan and Hadrian, and he expresses grateful awareness of this good fortune. Yet he constantly stresses the evils of rule by one man. Perhaps this conviction is the central point of his philosophy. No amount of experience, he makes a speaker say, can stand up against the corrupting effects of autocratic authority. 'Even after his enormous experience of public affairs, Tiberius was ruined and transformed by the violent influence of absolute power'[1]— a hypothesis, incidentally, which is hardly consistent with Tacitus' other suggestion that Tiberius had a radically vicious nature which only became apparent by degrees.

Though Tacitus is a staunch senator, and a supporter of the senatorial view of society, he does not see any help in the senate of imperial times. For he knows that the senate can do nothing against the ruler, and that it is, in the last resort, unnecessary— since the ruler, through his own direct and indirect means of influence, does everything that matters. That is why Tacitus scrutinises so closely the motives and morals of the successive emperors. The results make him embittered and pessimistic. His experience and temperament cause him to be aware that man is unreliable; so that, when the State is unified under an omnipotent ruler, 'human happiness hangs by a thread'. When the emperor is a bad man and rules badly, there is misery.

Oppressive rule, and the moral degeneracy which causes it and comes from it, are the subjects of Tacitus' most vivid writing: a series of continually reiterated themes emphasise their insidious growth. In spite of the excellence of contemporary rulers, time has shown, he feels, that there is no certain safeguard against oppression. So there are moments, and whole epochs, when everything seems to be at the mercy of a fate which is blind—or even malignant. It sometimes appears to Tacitus that events are blighted by anger from the gods. At other times he is not certain

[1] *Annals*, VI, 48.

whether there are any gods at all. Yet his fears that mankind is doomed reflect an attitude which explains why others, later, attached themselves to religion—why they withdrew into an other-worldliness which led to the victory of the Church.

Human fate often looks black to Tacitus; and so does human nature. Yet he is far from sceptical about the potentialities of the human spirit. Even in times of civil war or oppressive government, he discerns human actions of extraordinary virtue, bravery and pertinacity. Indeed he is a humanist. 'Though mistrustful of "civilisation" and its debilitating effects, he never despairs of human nature.... Napoleon called Tacitus a "traducer of humanity"; from one who spent his powers in annihilating humanity this verdict is interesting, but simply untrue.'[1]

These are matters relevant to our estimate of Tacitus as a historian. But his outstanding quality is brilliance as a stylist and an artist. Now ancient readers usually recognised talent, and by no means found that it interfered with their enjoyment when history contained a strong infusion of rhetoric, morality and drama. The *Histories* and *Annals* of Tacitus had all these things. Yet they are written in such unusual Latin that they were almost unappreciated in ancient times, and also in the Middle Ages. They only survived by a narrow chance. In the fourteenth century, Petrarch knew nothing of Tacitus. His rediscovery is veiled in obscurity and mystery. It appears that the earliest Renaissance scholar who read Tacitus was Petrarch's compatriot and younger contemporary, Boccaccio. A part was also played in his preservation by another Florentine, Poggio Braccioolini (1380-1459).

But it was not until the next generation—the latter part of the fifteenth century—that Tacitus, for the first time since his death, began to make his impact strongly felt. At that time ancient history was a favourite field for translation and study; and the fame of Tacitus reached sensational proportions. In the sixteenth

[1] M. P. Charlesworth.

century, Machiavelli and Montaigne were greatly moved by him. Later, a committee of Venetian scholars blamed Tacitus for the attitude of Machiavelli 'who would destroy public virtue'. This may seem an unfair judgement of Tacitus. But, if so, its unexpectedness illustrates a conspicuous feature of his reputation. He was so versatile, and his personality so complex, that he seemed to provide slogans for—and against—every section of political opinion. Everybody saw in him an adherent of something different. Thus, while the Venetians attacked him for political cynicism, a French royalist praised him as a supporter of autocratic law and order; and, in reaction, he was attacked by John Milton as one who had despaired of the Republic. And, once started, controversy about Tacitus, as historian and writer, has never ceased.

Tacitus founded no school; and after him there was only one great Roman historian, Ammianus Marcellinus, who in the fourth century A.D. wrote a balanced account of his own times. Ammianus wrote objectively. But most Roman historians had sought to teach and persuade—and to do so in a comparatively narrow field. When this is so, it is necessary for *us*, in order to satisfy our own different (though varying) conceptions of history, to search for other evidence which can serve as a check on their completeness and accuracy. Against the comparative narrowness of the field which their interests comprise, we have inscriptions showing what went on in the huge areas which he neglects. Against Tacitus' hostile comments on the rulers, we have their own coins. These provide a kaleidoscopic variety of representations illustrating each emperor's own description of his policy. The latter is not necessarily the truth. Nor is the picture painted by Tacitus. He paints it in dark colours; coins display the roseate hues of imperial propaganda. Both pictures are likely to be exaggerated. But each needs to be counteracted by the other, if either is to attain its full value and significance.

We also have *papyri*, wonderfully preserved by the dry sand of Egypt. These, too, provide us with indirect assistance in our evaluation of the literary historians. Papyri have given us texts of ancient authors, some entirely unknown before. They have also revealed official documents of all sorts, from imperial decrees to birth certificates. What is more, they give us something that is rare in the ancient world, a glimpse of what ordinary people were thinking and doing—and ordinary people in an eastern province at that. We have their wills, their business correspondence, their private letters, and even their school exercises.

Out of all these different sources, added to the literary histories, we can build a somewhat shaky reconstruction of the life and history of the Roman Empire. The literary historians are indispensable for this purpose; but they are not enough. However, in another respect, they fulfil every possible expectation. They may not always have written history as we understand the term—and they would probably have been very surprised at our researches in epigraphy and papyrology. But in a significant respect, their achievement was stupendous: the works of art which they created are unequalled, and have exercised an incalculable influence on the world.

4. BIOGRAPHY AND FICTION

Tacitus, despite his outstanding talent—or because of the individual form which it took—had far less influence on the immediately following centuries than his contemporary, Suetonius. The latter was not a historian so much as a biographer. He wrote the *Lives of Distinguished Men* (*De Viris Illustribus*), dealing with writers, and the *Lives of the Caesars* (*De Vita Caesarum*), comprising the biographies of Julius Caesar and the first eleven emperors.

Ancient biography had a pedigree of its own. Works of biographical tendency had appeared in Greece as early as the fifth

FACT AND FICTION

century B.C., when several branches of art began to show an
increased interest in the individual. But the results were often
frankly eulogistic—or the opposite; and biography was often
inextricably mixed with legend and gossip. However, the scientific approach of Aristotle greatly encouraged investigations on
this as on other subjects; and the Alexandrians, with their special
interests in research and psychology, adapted their scholarly
methods to this medium.

At Rome these Greek traditions merged with a strong native
tendency to venerate ancestors, and with a desire—which also led
to autobiography[1]—to express political views. Perhaps the first
Roman to write compositions recognisable as biographies was
the most versatile of Latin writers and scholars, Varro (first
century B.C.). Like most of his works, these have not survived.
We have a number of biographies of Greeks and Romans by
Cicero's friend Nepos. We have the eulogistic biography *Agricola*
of Tacitus. We have a few of the literary *Lives* of Suetonius, in
forms more or less approximating to the originals. We have
almost the whole of his *Lives of the Caesars*, and this is by far the
greatest surviving Roman contribution to this *genre*. (Suetonius
was a contemporary of the best known biographer in the
Greek language, Plutarch—whose influence on Shakespeare was
incalculable.)

Suetonius was for a time, until involved in a scandal, private
secretary to the emperor Hadrian (A.D. 117–38). Consequently,
official files are likely to have been accessible to him. This acces-
sibility may partly account for the wonderfully varied collection
of letters, documents, etc., which he reproduces as they stand,
without the ancient historians' usual attempts to 'integrate' such
material with their style. Much the same applies to Suetonius'
employment of historical writers. Indeed, all this evidence is

[1] The autobiographies of many emperors, and of Nero's mother
Agrippina, are lost.

118

taken indiscriminately from the friends and enemies of the men about whom he is writing. So the pictures which they contribute are naturally somewhat haphazard; they do not necessarily strike a true balance. In each biography, too, the 'facts' are grouped together (with more or less thoroughness) under traditional headings— origin, early life, career, omens, etc. Nevertheless, here at last is a 'historical' writer who makes no effort to present a rhetorically or morally preconceived version.

Here, in the translation of Philemon Holland (1606), are some personal comments of Suetonius about three emperors:

Of stature he [Caligula] was very tall, pale and wan-coloured, of body gross and without all good-making; his neck and shanks exceeding slender; his eyes sunk in his head, and his temples hollow, his forehead broad, and the same furrowed and frowning; the hair of his head growing thin, and none at all about his crown; in all parts else hairy he was and shaggy. It was therefore taken for a heinous and capital offence, either to look upon him as he passed by from a higher place, or once but to name a goat upon any occasion whatsoever. His face and visage, being naturally stern and grim, he made of purpose more crabbed and hideous, composing and dressing it at a looking-glass all manner of ways to seem more terrible and to strike greater fear....[1]

For appetite to meat and drink his [Claudius'] stomach served him passing well always and in every place. Sitting upon a time judicially in Augustus' hall of justice to hear and determine causes, and scenting there the steam of a dinner, that was a-dressing and serving up for the priests Salii in the temple of Mars next adjoining, he forsook the tribunal, went up to the said priests, and there sat down with them to meat....[2]

Of all the liberal sciences, in manner, he [Nero] had a taste when he was but a child; but from the study of philosophy his mother turned his mind, telling him it was repugnant to one who another day was

[1] Suetonius, *Caligula*, 50, tr. Holland.
[2] Suetonius, *Claudius*, 33, tr. Holland.

to be a sovereign; and from the knowledge of ancient orators his master Seneca withdrew him, because he would hold him the longer in admiration of himself. And therefore, being of his own accord readily inclined to poetry, he made verses voluntarily and without pain, neither did he (as some think) set forth other men's poems as his own. There have come into my hands writing-tables and books containing verses very famous and well-known abroad, written with his own hand; so as a man may easily see they were not copied out of other books, nor yet taken from the mouth of any other that indited them, but plainly penned, as a man would say, by one that studied for them and, as they came in his head, so put them down; so many blots and scrapings out, so many dashes and interlinings were in them.[1]

Suetonius' manner of writing appealed to contemporaries and later generations, and it is not very hard to trace the links in a chain which connects him with most subsequent biographical writing. Despite the somewhat modest ambitions of his *Lives*, he is the father of modern biography.

The border between biography and fiction was never very solid, and Greek 'biographers' had already overstepped it near the outset of the Hellenistic epoch and Alexandrian movement. Symbolic of this trend is a certain Clitarchus, who lived at Alexandria in the third century B.C. and, influenced to some extent by a fashion for character sketches, wrote a *Life of Alexander the Great*, which was little more than an inferior historical novel; such unveracious *Lives* soon attained enormous popularity. So Clitarchus and other Greeks who wrote in similar fashion represent a landmark in the development of fiction. Further landmarks were provided by 'travellers' tales', another form of Hellenistic story which was scarcely less popular and again lent itself to fantasy.

[1] Suetonius, *Nero*, 52, tr. Holland.

Such tendencies towards fiction crystallised in the Greek romantic novel. A recent discovery has revealed to us the fragments of one such Greek novel written as early as the first century B.C.; we know it as the 'Ninus Romance'. We have several later examples, too, of this branch of Greek literature. These novels are 'middle-brow' stories of adventure and love, as full of unprofound description and vigorous action (it has been suggested) as a modern film. These novels particularly flourished on the borders between Hellenistic civilisation and the cultures of Persia, Phoenicia and Egypt. The peculiar Greek talent for story-telling, of which the fountain-head had been epic poetry, had now, in this post-classical age, flowed into this less elevated but more abundant channel of prose romance, the novel or 'novelette'.

These novels were not intended to be funny; but, quite early on, this Hellenistic taste for story-telling was also turned into satirical channels. Menippus of Gadara (third century B.C.) wrote Greek sketches in mixed prose and verse, a *genre* which we know, after him, as 'Menippean satire'. Then came a taste for pungent, improper Greek short stories, described as 'Milesian tales' after one of their writers, Aristides of Miletus (*c.* 100 B.C.). Neither 'Menippeans' nor 'Milesians' have survived. Roman adaptations followed before long (but they too are not extant): in the first century B.C., the versatile Varro, whom we have seen earlier in this section described as the 'founder of Roman biography', wrote Latin 'Menippeans'; and his contemporary Sisenna translated the 'Milesians' and achieved best-selling fame and notoriety at Rome.

Most of these threads were woven together in the achievement of the Roman novelist Petronius. He is identified by most critics with a leader of politics and fashion at the court of Nero (A.D. 54–68). A part of his novel, which we know (though probably he did not) as the *Satyricon*, has survived. What has come down to us seems to consist of portions of its fifteenth and sixteenth books. We learn from these of the varied, exciting and often scandalous adventures of three sophisticated but disreputable young men in South Italy and elsewhere. The dialogue changes, according to the speakers, from the daily talk of the educated to the ordinary speech of uneducated people, both forms of utterance which rarely come to us in the largely artificial language of Roman literature.

This is a story of wanderings, and so owes something to the Hellenistic 'traveller's tale'—and in its turn created the modern 'traveller's tale'. It is, however, in some sort a unity, and is much concerned with love; in these respects it is the heir to the Greek novels. But their high-flown heroes and heroines are conspicuously absent from the novel of Petronius. All his characters are shady—this is a 'picaresque novel'.[1] So here the 'novelette' tradition is given a satirical twist by the debasement of its 'heroes'; this is a realistic story. But, in the tradition of Menippean satire, the prose is interlarded with poems in various metres and on various topics, and very elegant some of them are. Yet this is not true satire at all, for a moral is conspicuously lacking. There is an affinity with the amoral stage-shows known as 'mimes'; and there is also, after certain Greek models, a strong element of parody—caricature and exaggeration. The two longest surviving poems in Petronius' novel are probably intended as comments on contemporary work, perhaps by Lucan and Seneca the Younger. In the prose sections, too, there is literary criticism, including attacks on bombast and over-emphasis. It seems possible that, if we had the whole work, we should find that it parodied 'the wrath of the gods'—a traditional theme of the Homeric and Virgilian epic.

Enough of this novel has survived to show us that it contains not only poems but 'Milesian tales', of which the best example is known as *The Widow of Ephesus*. But the most famous of the almost self-contained portions of the work is *The Dinner of Trimalchio (Cena Trimalchionis)*, a riotous account of a vulgar

[1] *Picaro*, Spanish = rascal.

millionaire's dinner-party. This owes its brilliance to the author's original talent. But even here his treatment is based, though loosely, on existing literary kinds. The *Dinner* (*Cena*) was a subject already well known to Greek and Roman literature in three main forms. There is the purely gastronomic account, once attempted by Ennius—an offshoot of the informative sort of poem which we call 'didactic'. There is also the more general description with little or no dialogue, familiar in its 'rustic' variety from short anonymous poems which we know as the *Hostess* (*Copa*) and *Salad* (*Moretum*).[1] Then finally there is the 'symposium', an account which includes dialogue, sometimes in prose—either philosophical, as in Plato's Athenian *Symposium*, or mock-philosophical and burlesque. Petronius borrows what he wants from all earlier accounts of dinner-parties. It is possible that he derived ideas from an obscure Greek writer (Hippolochus); but it is Petronius who has left his lasting mark on the literature of the world.

This is a scene from Trimalchio's dinner-party:

A donkey in Corinthian bronze stood on the sideboard, with panniers holding olives, white in one side, black in the other. Two dishes hid the donkey; Trimalchio's name and their weight in silver were engraved on their edges. There were also dormice rolled in honey and poppy-seed, and supported on little bridges soldered to the plate. Then there were hot sausages laid on a silver grill, and under the grill damsons and seeds of pomegranate.

While we were engaged with these delicacies, Trimalchio was conducted in to the sound of music, propped on the tiniest of pillows. A laugh escaped the unwary. His head was shaven and peered out of a scarlet cloak, and over the heavy clothes on his neck he had put on a napkin with a broad stripe and fringes hanging from it all round.[2]

The millionaire host's reminiscences are of value to students of Roman social history. The guests also have a lot to say, in richly

[1] In the *Virgilian Appendix*.

[2] Petronius, *Satyricon*, 31 f. The translations from Petronius given here are by M. Heseltine (Loeb ed.).

varied idioms. Trimalchio rounds on one for failing to amuse, and the result is a ghost story:

My master happened to have gone to Capua to look after some silly business or other. I seized my opportunity and persuaded a guest in our house to come with me as far as the fifth milestone. He was a soldier, and as brave as Hell. So we trotted off about cockcrow; the moon shone like high noon. We got among the tombstones: my man went aside to look at the epitaphs. I sat down with my heart full of song and began to count the graves. Then when I looked round at my friend, he stripped himself and put all his clothes by the roadside. My heart was in my mouth, but I stood like a dead man. He... suddenly turned into a wolf. Please do not think I am joking; I would not lie about this, for any fortune in the world. But as I was saying, after he had turned into a wolf, he began to howl, and ran off into the woods. At first I hardly knew where I was, then I went up to take his clothes; but they had all turned into stone. No one could be nearer dead with terror than I was. But I drew my sword and went slaying shadows all the way till I came to my love's house. I went in like a corpse, and nearly gave up the ghost, the sweat ran down my legs, my eyes were dull, I could hardly be revived. My dear Melissa was surprised at my being out so late, and said, 'If you had come earlier you might at least have helped us; a wolf got into the house and worried all our sheep and let their blood like a butcher. But he did not make fools of us, even though he got off; for our slave made a hole in his neck with a spear.' When I heard this, I could not keep my eyes shut any longer, but at break of day I rushed back to my master Gaius's house like a defrauded publican, and when I came to the place where the clothes were turned into stone, I found nothing but a pool of blood. But when I reached home, my soldier was lying in bed like an ox, with a doctor looking after his neck. I realized that he was a werewolf, and I never could sit down to a meal with him afterwards, not if you had killed me first. Other people may think what they like about this; but may all your guardian angels punish me if I am lying.[1]

[1] Petronius, *Satyricon*, 61 f.

Petronius plays a great and varied part in the mixed beginnings of modern fiction. But, in its complex pedigree, there is one more important Latin ingredient. This is the *Metamorphoses* of the second-century African writer Apuleius. It is the only Roman novel which has survived complete. It is a fantastic story about a certain Lucius who is accidentally turned into a donkey and has many strange adventures. To this central theme the work owes its usual modern title, *The Golden Ass*. Theme and title recall a shorter Greek story called *Lucius or the Ass*, and it is possible that both versions may go back to an unknown Greek *Metamorphoses*. Perhaps this was by Lucian of Samosata,[1] a brilliant Greek popular philosopher or 'sophist', characteristic of the second century A.D., which ranked such talkers higher than poets, and rewarded them greatly with esteem and cash (as it rewarded Apuleius for similar activities). But the title *Metamorphoses* recalls to memory, as it was intended to, that Ovid had constructed his greatest poem, of the same name, out of a whole collection of such transformation scenes.

The language of Apuleius is startlingly brilliant, florid and extravagant. Its exuberance has been attributed to his African origin. But it is hard to say how far this is true, since comparison with other writers is difficult: for a large proportion of the greatest writers of this and subsequent generations were North Africans. This is perhaps the Latin of an epoch, rather than of a country. It is in part the daily speech of the educated people of the time. But it contains also a rich added decoration, part of which is due to the influence of travelling 'sophists'. Ciceronian grammar is rapidly breaking down, and modern 'Latin' languages are almost in sight. Another feature of this period, and of Apuleius, is a return to archaisms—to the language of Plautus, eclipsed in the intervening centuries by the literary language of Ciceronians, and then Augustans, and then Silver Latin writers.

[1] Or by an unknown Lucius of Patrae.

This second-century movement of colloquialism combined with archaism was known by one of its originators (Marcus Aurelius' tutor, Fronto) as the New Speech: its greatest exponent was Apuleius. 'In him, style celebrates its orgies with the impetuous dizziness of bacchants, launching into the furies of the whirlwind, evaporating into a sea of floating clouds, into a fantastic disorder.'[1] We have come far from the pure classical spirit; but Apuleius justifies his unorthodoxy by his success. One feature of his writing and of his epoch—not found in Petronius—is the ecstatic belief in mystery religions which marked, in some sense, the transition between state-paganism and Christianity. Apuleius seems to record a deeply felt experience of his own when he describes his hero's initiation to the mysteries of the Egyptian Isis: and to her he devotes the riches of his imagination. It is not nearly enough to see such passages from the viewpoint of orthodox classicism. This was not just a bad version of an old age; it was a new age.

It was an age of interest in natural and supernatural phenomena—an age of what St Augustine was to call, in words that do not require translation, *damnabilis curiositas*. The second century A.D. recalls the epoch between our two Great Wars, in its love of sensation and of rapid movement from place to place. Apuleius was a versatile representative of his time. He was novelist and 'sophist', lawyer and lecturer, poet and initiate. It is not surprising that he was accused of magic—a charge from which he defends himself in a dazzling and outrageous speech, the *Apologia*, one of our few surviving Latin speeches apart from those of Cicero.

Just as the novel of Petronius contains its 'inset' *Dinner of Trimalchio*, so Apuleius, too, introduces the even more famous story of *Cupid and Psyche*. This elaborate story of the 'Fairy Bridegroom' contains many features of folk-lore which reappear, as is the mysterious habit of folk-lore, in the tales of widely

[1] E. Norden.

separated lands. It is a masterpiece of narrative and descriptive art. Perhaps the English of the Elizabethan Age, though not a wholly accurate translation of the original, is best fitted to convey its spirit:

Thus poore Psyches being left alone, weeping and trembling on the toppe of the rocke, was blowne by the gentle aire and of shrilling Zephyrus, and carried from the hill with a meek winde, which retained her garments up, and by little and little brought her downe into a deepe valley, where she was laid in a bed of most sweet and fragrant flowers.

Thus faire Psyches being sweetly couched among the soft and tender hearbs, as in a bed of sweet and fragrant floures, and having qualified the thoughts and troubles of her restlesse minde, was now well reposed. And when she had refreshed her selfe sufficiently with sleepe, she rose with a more quiet and pacified minde, and fortuned to espy a pleasant wood invironed with great and mighty trees. She espied likewise a running river as cleare as crystall: in the midst of the wood well nigh at the fall of the river was a princely Edifice, wrought and builded not by the art or hand of man, but by the mighty power of God: and you would judge at the first entry therin, that it were some pleasent and worthy mansion for the powers of heaven. For the embowings above were of Citron and Ivory, propped and undermined with pillars of gold, the walls covered and seeled with silver, divers sorts of beasts were graven and carved, that seemed to encounter with such as entered in.[1]

In the later nineteenth century, Walter Pater evolved an ornamental style which again possesses recognisable affinities with what he called the 'perfumed personality' of Apuleius.

While to Psyche, fearful and trembling and weeping sore upon the mountaintop, comes the gentle Zephyrus. He lifts her mildly, and, with vesture afloat on either side, bears her by his own soft breathing over the windings of the hills, and sets her lightly among the flowers in the bosom of a valley below.

[1] Apuleius, *Metamorphoses*, IV, 35–V, 1, tr. W. Adlington (1566).

Psyche, in those delicate grassy places, lying sweetly on her dewy bed, rested from the agitation of her soul and arose in peace. And lo! a grove of mighty trees, with a fount of water, clear as glass, in the midst; and hard by the water, a dwelling-place, built not by human hands but by some divine cunning. One recognised, even at the entering, the delightful hostelry of a god. Golden pillars sustained the roof, arched most curiously in cedarwood and ivory. The walls were hidden under wrought silver: all tame and woodland creatures leaping forward to the visitor's gaze.[1]

The unfortunate Psyche, in trouble with Venus, appealed to the goddesses Ceres and Juno. They are represented by Apuleius as hard Roman ladies of fashion; and the unsatisfactory replies of these Olympian dowagers require a contemporary translator:

Ceres answered: 'I would dearly love to help you; but the truth is that I can't afford to offend my niece. She has been one of my best friends for ages and ages and really has a very good heart when you get to know her. You'd better leave this temple at once and think yourself lucky that I don't have you placed under arrest.'

Psyche went away, twice as sad as she had come: she had never expected such a rebuff. . . .

My dear (said Juno), I should be only too pleased to help you, but unfortunately divine etiquette forbids. I can't possibly go against the wishes of Venus, who married my son Vulcan, you know. . . .[2]

However, it all came right in the end; by the intervention of a somewhat disreputable Jupiter, the orthodox happy ending is contrived. But how different are these pictures of superficial Olympians from his mystic and heartfelt description of the goddess of his choice, the Egyptian Isis.

Apuleius himself may have adapted his version of the story from that of a quite unknown Greek.[3] Hellenistic art had often represented Cupid torturing Psyche—who denotes the soul, as

[1] Apuleius, *Metamorphoses*, IV, 35–V, 1, tr. Walter Pater, *Marius the Epicurean* (1885).

[2] *Ibid.* VI, 3 f., tr. Robert Graves.   [3] Aristophontes of Athens.

the seat of the passions. When, in the fourth century A.D., the search for such allegories became popular, the hint of allegory in Apuleius' work was magnified into an elaborate construction. So Cupid and Psyche appear on early Christian sarcophagi, with a spiritual significance.

But the Christian Fathers, after long discussion, were disposed to let Apuleius fall from favour. Subsequently, we have one eleventh-century manuscript of his novel, but it was not until the Renaissance that his powers as a story-teller first began to be truly appreciated. In 1427 Poggio Bracciolini discovered a further manuscript, and it was published at Rome in 1469, only four years after printing had been introduced into Italy; and Raphael based a series of twelve pictures on the story. The Renaissance loved the gay spirit of *The Golden Ass*, its quick response to beautiful things, its frank freedom. Most influential of all was the story of Cupid and Psyche. It was translated into English in 1566 and appealed to Elizabethan and Jacobean exuberance.

Here, then, were the forces which contributed to the beginnings of the modern novel. The ingredients occur in varying proportions in the French and English literatures of the seventeenth century, in Racine and Defoe. But Smollett (18 c.) is the English novelist most strongly influenced by Petronius; and Richardson in his novel *Pamela* (1740) took the mixture as he found it (he had no classical or literary knowledge), and converted it to the requirements of the rising English middle-class. Henry Fielding (who had read Petronius) called his *Tom Jones* a 'prose epic'. This takes us back to the beginning again. For it reminds us that the story-tellers who were Fielding's ancient forerunners, Apuleius as well as Petronius, themselves had many debts—through the medium of Menippean satire and Greek romance and historical novels—to the epic poems, Homer's *Iliad* and *Odyssey*, which had been the first stories in the western world to assume a literary form.

PART II
POETRY

CHAPTER III

POETRY: LUCRETIUS AND CATULLUS

1. ATTITUDES TO POETRY

IT is of little use to consider individual Roman (or Greek) poets in any detail without first noting certain general facts about them. For they cannot be understood in the light of the usual modern idea of the position, or lack of position, of poets in society. In certain respects the ancient poet's task, and his reputation, differed a good deal from anything in our own experience.

(1) *In the ancient world, poetry usually played a far more important part in daily life than it does today.* In our own time, most people, even literate people, do not regard poetry as an integral part of their lives, or of life. Most moderns, of most ages or environments, could anticipate an unfavourable reaction if, when asked at a social gathering what their profession was, they replied 'poet'. Except in specialised circles this reply would cause a certain shock. It would not have shocked even reasonably well-educated Greeks, or Romans of the late Republic or Principate.

Today, moreover, the reading of far the greater part of the population is entirely restricted to the 'low-brow'. Bare readability is regarded as good enough; that is to say poetry is entirely excluded. Whether there is a chance of this tendency being arrested, as some believe, is a matter beyond the scope of this book. The tendency itself is stressed here in order to illustrate a profound contrast between modern and ancient feeling in this respect. On the whole, educated Greeks and Romans thought of poetry as playing a much more fundamental part in life. This was true of the Greeks at all periods, and by the late Republic it had become true of cultured Romans; in Rome, at first, poetry had not been considered a suitable occupation for important citizens, but this attitude changed in the second and first centuries B.C.

Among Greeks and Romans alike, poetry had considerably preceded prose-writing in date. In Greece, prose was still unknown for centuries after Homer's *Iliad* and *Odyssey*. So, as Aristotle pointed out, poetry was the first sort of literature to arouse people's interest in questions of style. Under the Roman Empire, too, the importance of poetry was felt so strongly that the greatest authority on education, Quintilian, wanted secondary schools to concentrate on the reading and teaching of poetry, leaving prose writings to what we should now regard as the university stage. His advice was not wholly followed, but at any rate it shows the importance attached to poetry by the ancients. It formed an essential part of Greek and Roman society.

Aristotle suggested an explanation for this importance. He compares poetry with history, and estimates that poetry is the more important of the two because it is concerned with truths of general significance, as opposed to the particular facts which are the subject-matter of history. This point of view would occur to few people now. Aristotle's master, Plato, had gone further still, and paid poetry the compliment of regarding it as dangerous— partly because of the great influence which it exercised on people's emotions. A gulf is fixed between the ancients' valuation of poetry and that of most people, even most educated people, today. (It is true that Horace, in his *Epistle to Augustus* and *Ars Poetica*, strikes a familiar note by complaining that it was hard to induce the public to recognise modern talent. But he shows that this was not because of any lack of interest in poetry; it was because they were such resolute supporters of the *classical* poets!)

(2) Many are likely to be equally surprised by another ancient view about poetry. *Greeks and Romans often had a strong belief that the aim of poetry was not only to please or excite, but to teach*

134

and improve people. Greek and Roman literary critics very often believed that poetry had a mission to instruct. Its purely artistic qualities were regarded as indissolubly merged with moral considerations. The philosophers held that 'the good poet must first be a good man'; so good poetry was what made men good—and thus philosophy added its great influence to an already existing tendency to regard edification as the aim of poetry. This was particularly the view of the Stoics, the school which emphasised ethics most strongly. But it was also true of the rival Epicurean school—including the Roman poet Lucretius. He is a man eager to improve the world, and he describes his poetry as the 'honey at the edge of the cup'—to make it easier for the 'medicine' to be taken.

Other Romans felt the same; and this was to be expected in so morally minded a people. But some of the cleverest judges of Latin literature, sharing the typical Roman distaste for too rigorously abstract theories, adopted the compromise opinion that the function of poetry was twofold—to edify, certainly, but also to please. This attitude is put forward by Horace. It is true that in his *Epistle to Augustus*, echoing a popular view that the chief function of literature is patriotic, he reminds the emperor how useful poets can be to the nation and to the government. But in a further poem of literary criticism, the *Ars Poetica*, he expressed the double aim: 'every vote goes to him who mixes the useful with the agreeable'; or, as Byron paraphrased it,

> That bard for all is fit
> Who mingles well instruction with his wit.[1]

The controversy regarding the two theories, thus neatly combined by Horace, has continued to rage in modern times, with a larger body of opinion than hitherto in favour of the interpretation of poetry as entertainment. Thus, in the eighteenth

---

[1] Byron, after Horace, *Ars Poetica*, 343.

century, Dr Johnson maintained that 'the only end of writing is to enable the reader better to enjoy life, or better to endure it'. So, too, Keats; but Shelley opposed him, repeating the classical view that 'poets are the unacknowledged legislators of mankind'. Therein he follows Milton, who some two centuries earlier had asserted as the purpose of *Paradise Lost* the desire 'to justify the ways of God to men'. Today the idea of didactic poetry is an alien one. But it is important to see the prominence of this idea among the ancients, for through them it has influenced the world for nearly three thousand years.

(3) The poetry of the ancients reflects an *infinitely more careful study of style* than is habitual today. In the field of style, the ancients 'understood a thousand secrets whose existence we do not even suspect, or which we understand with difficulty when they are explained by Cicero or Quintilian'.[1] In particular, *ancient poetry was strongly influenced by rhetoric*. 'Rhetoric', in regard to Greek and Roman literatures, often merely means something like 'the art of speaking so as to persuade'—a vital matter in a society which held effective speech to be the main aim of education itself. In the ancient world even more than our own, every art had its own comprehensive and detailed rules; and so had rhetoric. And this art of persuasion, like other arts, was understood to consist of numerous classifiable devices and technical points, which required to be consistently borne in mind and applied. Some even thought of rhetoric as a science, with immutable rules.

Even in the field of public speaking, in which we might find this attitude most readily comprehensible, we do not today approach the matter in the same systematic fashion. But what seems strangest is the fact that rhetorical rules of equal elaborateness and complexity were applied by the ancients to poetry also. Much poetry was designed to teach and persuade, and rhetoric clearly assisted in this task. And so effectively were these tech-

[1] Leopardi.

niques employed by their poets, and expected in them, that Roman school-children were asked to write essays on subjects such as this: 'Was Virgil an orator or a poet?' And some even thought they could discover a complete system of rhetoric in the *Iliad* and *Odyssey* of Homer, written long before the art or science of rhetoric was invented.

Cicero states the rhetorical character of ancient poetry in general terms. 'The poet is very close to the orator, [the only difference being that the former is] a little more tied down in regard to rhythm.'[1] This attitude is less surprising when we reflect that poetry was widely studied as an aid to the orator—also that the object of poetry was often held to be instructive and uplifting. For in order to teach and 'improve' people, it is necessary to study the methods and techniques of persuasion; and this is just what rhetoric set out to do. So poetry, according to its own needs, did the same.

Ancient thought about the rules and techniques of poetry is preserved for us in several hexameter *Epistles* of Horace. One of these, his Epistle to the Pisos, is known to us by a name which Horace probably did not attach to it, the *Ars Poetica*—literally 'Poetic Art'; but it is really both a 'Treatise on Poetry' and a 'Poet's Manual'. It contains a series of nearly thirty maxims for the guidance of the young poet, based to a large extent on a Greek literary critic of the third century B.C., Neoptolemus of Parium. These maxims are expressed with brilliant pungency and have enjoyed great fame. Yet part of this fame is based on a misconception. For the scholars of the Renaissance believed, erroneously, that this work should be regarded as a complete guide to poetry. So it was translated by Boileau and had a vast influence on classical French drama. This influence is a testimonial to the belief, which still survived in the seventeenth century and later, that poetry was largely a matter of rules.

[1] *De Oratore*, I, 70.

Many of the exponents of that belief carried it to extremes—and that is true of the ancient world as well as the heirs of the Renaissance. Horace, and other enlightened critics, did not do so; indeed they repeatedly tell us not to. But it was logical that they should attach importance to the rules of poetry. For they ascribed rules to rhetoric, and believed that rhetoric and poetry had much in common.

(4) Rhetoric and poetry possessed a further resemblance, which is again alien to modern ideas. *A great deal of Latin poetry was intended primarily for reading aloud.* Now Greek poetry, at first, had been designed for singing aloud; and the poetry of classical Athenian tragedy and comedy was intended for stage performance, consisting partly of a choral accompaniment but chiefly of actors' spoken parts. By *c.* 300 B.C., however, even non-dramatic Greek poetry was written for recitation rather than singing. And in Augustan Rome, silent reading had become an alternative to recitation[1]—or to the witnessing of a play:

> Think of those Authors, Sir, who would rely
> More on a Reader's sense, than Gazer's eye.[2]

Virgil may have envisaged silent reading; but he recited parts of his poems—though apparently with reluctance. The books of the *Aeneid* are perhaps too long to be recited in their entirety; but they include shorter passages which are eminently suited for reading aloud, and were, indeed, intended for such a purpose. This adds significance to the Romans' admiration for Virgil's 'rhetorical' talent. It also helps to explain the very great importance which he and other Latin poets attached to all combinations of vowels and consonants, to rhythm and also to metre—

---

[1] Though, even four centuries later, St Augustine was surprised to come upon St Ambrose reading silently. Sir Walter Scott was nervous about the effect of silent reading on the reception of his novels.

[2] Alexander Pope, after Horace, *Epistles*, II, i, 214–16.

both matters which, though they still play a part today, are not subjected to the meticulous and intricate attention which they received in the ancient world.

(5) A further contrast between the ancient and modern worlds lies in their attitudes to tradition. *Ancient poetry observed a far keener devotion to tradition than is ever the case, at least in the West, today.* It preferred familiar subjects, familiar processes of thought, familiar arguments. There was a persistent idea that thought was largely common property, that a number of ideas are naturally inherent in any situation, and that it is not by abandoning or amending these ideas that the poet must show his skill. With such conviction was this view held that well-known reflections and sentiments were listed by literary and rhetorical experts in their text-books, under the heading of 'commonplaces'. Far from being ashamed of using these, a poet regarded it as legitimate to do so, and indeed highly desirable.

In other words a poet, like any other writer—it was said— must devote himself to unremitting study of his predecessors. The foremost of these predecessors, in time and quality, were Greeks; and Horace's advice may be repeated:

> Ye, who seek finished models, never cease,
> By day and night, to read the works of Greece.[1]

And this was done. When Horace wrote this, he may well have been thinking primarily of metre and rhythm, and not intending a general maxim; but the general maxim too would have been valid in his view.

A new poetic achievement, then, was held to be possible only by working within the conventions which forerunners had established—that is to say, by adopting the characteristically classical view that they had established the highest artistic ideals yet known, and that it was necessary to follow these. This classical idea of

[1] Byron, after Horace, *Ars Poetica*, 268–9.

a *continuous* tradition is rejected by W. H. Auden today, but T. S. Eliot has felt that the western literatures form parts of a single tradition in which the same standards are applicable throughout.

Like him, however, the ancients who held firm to classicism did not condemn themselves to soulless imitation. Their principles did not necessitate mechanical copying. It would be 'theft', or as we should say plagiarism (though our word goes further), to imitate treatment *and* technique *and* thought.

> 'Tis wiser to prefer
> A hackney'd plot, than choose a new, and err;
> Yet copy not too closely, but record,
> More justly, thought for thought than word for word.[1]

The Greeks and Romans held, as others have held since their day, that poetic merit depends not upon what is said, but upon how it is said. They would have rejected scornfully the idea that this respect for antiquity implied a slavish adulation. Indeed, Horace himself spiritedly trounced people who thought that no writer was any good unless he had been dead for a hundred years.

> If Time improve our Wit as well as Wine,
> Say at what age a Poet grows divine?
> Shall we, or shall we not, account him so,
> Who died, perhaps, an hundred years ago?
> End all dispute; and fix the year precise
> When British bards begin t'Immortalize.
> 'Who lasts a Century can have no flaw,
> I hold that Wit a Classic, good in law.'
> Suppose he wants a year, will you compound?
> And shall we deem him Ancient, right and sound,
> Or damn to all Eternity at once
> At ninety-nine, a Modern and a Dunce? . . .

[1] Byron, after Horace, *Ars Poetica*, 128–30, 133–4.

I lose my patience, and I own it too,
When works are censur'd, not as bad, but new;
While if our Elders break all Reason's laws,
These fools demand not Pardon, but Applause.[1]

The excessive conservatism denounced by Horace certainly existed—it is apparent in inferior Roman poets—but it is by no means an inevitable feature of the classical outlook. The modern poet, it was felt, had ample opportunity to display his talent—not indeed in flights of original thought, but in his choice and arrangement (within the established framework) of words, and phrases, and rhythms. And audiences appreciated such variations: 'such is the potency of word-order and word-connection; such is the admiration accorded to what is taken from the common stock.'[2]

(6) This emphasis on the effects of words and sounds and their combinations led to the growth of a *poetic diction* in a much stricter sense than the phrase is understood today. Both the Greek and the Latin literatures, early in their careers, moved a long way from the spoken tongue of the people. Thus in Latin, for example, almost the only well-known authors who write in a language bearing some kinship to the spoken word are the dramatist Plautus and, in parts of his work, the novelist Petronius. Horace's *Satires*, too, show a studied informality and occasional colloquialisms. Nearly all other writers use an artificial language.

Not surprisingly, this particularly applies to the poets: about poetic diction the ancients held clearer and more emphatic ideas than are generally held today. The diction of poetry is, even now, often different from that of the spoken word. But the ancients held much more clearly defined and rigorous views on this subject. Among the Greeks, Aristotle, as so often, reflected (or initiated) this tendency. He observes that, in poetry, diction too near that of daily life should be avoided, since it is liable to sound

[1] Pope, after Horace, *Epistles*, II, i, 34–44, 76–8.
[2] *Ars Poetica*, 242 f.

too humble or prosaic: and Horace, too, criticises the poet who 'crawls on, afraid to fly'.

Poetic diction is partly a question of the choice of words. Some words are, habitually, regarded as more suitable than others. But it is significant that the greatest of the Augustan poets did not generally choose words that were particularly elevated, or unusual, or alien to daily life. Horace frequently warns against 'purple patches' (we owe the term to him):

> One falls while following elegance too fast,
> Another soars, inflated with bombast.[1]

Virgil and Horace were careful to be unassuming in this respect. Yet they are marvellous exponents of poetic diction. At first sight this may seem a paradox; but Horace suggests the means by which poetic diction was achieved—word-order and word-connection. One of the puzzling things about Latin poetry to us is its word-order: the rules of poetry were held to permit greater elasticity in this respect than those of prose.

It is by the use of these means, to create the profoundest effects of sound and sense, that the greatest Latin poetry was achieved. It is true that one or two contemporary critics complained that such methods were artificial. One of these critics—Augustus' chief adviser, general and admiral, Agrippa—saw clearly enough what the special character of the achievement was. But because of it he calls Virgil 'the discoverer of a new affectation, neither florid nor bare in style, but created out of ordinary words and for that reason concealed'. However, Agrippa's description of Virgil's style as 'affected' won little support either in his own time or in later ages: more often it has been thought of as achieving a poetic diction which is authentic and indeed unsurpassable.

Of all English poets it is John Milton who most nearly approaches to classical ideas of poetic diction. Sometimes he uses

[1] Byron, after Horace, *Ars Poetica*, 26 f.

grand words. But sometimes, also, like his Roman predecessors, he produces great effects by the use of ordinary words in splendid rhythms. Perhaps an illustration may be repeated here.[1] Milton writes:

> High on a throne of royal state which far
> Outshone the wealth of Ormuz and of Ind,
> Satan exalted sate.[2]

The following prose version has been facetiously composed: 'His Excellency was on a raised dais, seated on a state chair carved in a style suggestive of the Persian Gulf or India, but far more expensive looking than can be found in the possession of any of the native rulers.'

It will be agreed that the two versions convey somewhat different impressions. Yet, except for a single romantic Proper Name (a device taken from the ancients), Milton's rendering does not use any stranger words than that of its 'journalese' paraphrase. But, like the Roman poets whom he so closely followed, he knew the art of combining these ordinary words in such a way as to produce great poetry. This is the most characteristic method of Roman poetic diction: it is one of the chief ways in which originality was achieved.

(7) However, the ancients' devotion to tradition did not stop here; it did not even limit itself to subject-matter, thoughts, arguments and words. It shows itself most clearly of all in regard to the *forms of poetry*. The Greeks and Romans were convinced that certain forms were appropriate, indeed were indispensable, to certain subjects or 'kinds' (*genera*) of poetry. These forms were thus allocated to 'kinds' according to tradition, and their allocation was only subject to variation within a narrow range. For

[1] It is owed to Gilbert Murray.

[2] C. E. Carrington points out that Milton had in mind Sir Thomas Roe's prose description of the Emperor Jahangir enthroned at Agra: 'High on a gallery, with a canopy over him and a carpet before him, sat in great and barbarous state the Great Mogul.'

example the Epic, Elegiac, etc., were expected to be written according to conventional prescriptions regarding their metre, length, structure, diction and content. In this way the artistic conceptions of Greek and Latin poetry were more clear-cut than our own. The ancients applied to poetry their 'classical' devotion to order, proportion and definiteness.

> Learn hence for ancient rules a just esteem;
> To copy Nature is to copy them.[1]

The conventions thus established were formulated (chiefly by the Alexandrian Greeks) in a classification known as the Doctrine of Kinds. 'It was assumed that there were certain kinds of art-forms into which an artist was bound to cast his material according to the nature of his subject. These forms had been discovered by experiment, by lucky accident, by the instinct of genius.... They must not be confused or inter-mingled.'[2] Yet

> Poets and painters, as all artists know,
> May shoot a little with a lengthen'd bow;
> We claim this mutual mercy for our task,
> And grant in turn the pardon which we ask.[3]

'but not so far'—continues Horace—'that savage should mate with tame, vipers with birds, or lambs with tigers'.

'Kinds' were distinguished by subject, treatment and metre alike. The most obvious basis of their differentiation was metre. This word denotes the 'measure' or 'measurement' (Greek *metron*) of 'feet'—a word which suggests the steps of dancers. From Plautus onwards, Roman metre was based on quantity, on longs and shorts—unlike the poetry of our own language, in which the difference between long and short syllables is largely overlaid by stress-accent. 'It is very doubtful if our ears, ac-

[1] Alexander Pope.   [2] J. A. K. Thomson.
[3] Byron, after Horace, *Ars Poetica*, 9–11.

customed from childhood to stressed verse, are capable of being trained to a full appreciation of quantitative verse.'[1]

Aristotle, writing before the work of classification was far advanced, criticised any suggestion that metre was the only basis on which it should be attempted. For one thing, there were more 'kinds' of poetry than metres. Also metre could sometimes take second place—for purposes of classification—to content. Nevertheless, it was universally held that certain metres were inevitably and indissolubly associated with certain sorts of poem. For example, it was not considered possible, in either Greek or Latin, to write an epic in any metre except the hexameter. Other metres, again, as will be shown elsewhere, were regarded as appropriate to love-poetry; and so on. It is true that the greatest poets adapted these 'rules' to their own requirements. In general, however, the conventions, applied to poetry by respect for ancient tradition, dictated metrical structure no less firmly than they dictated subject-matter and diction.

These ideas are far from the conception of the poet which exists among the vast proportion of educated and semi-educated mankind nowadays. Most people today think vaguely about a poet as a long-haired or otherwise eccentric person who moons about, and beautiful thoughts and words come to him in a flash: he expresses himself without reference to tradition. That is to say, most people (unconsciously) subscribe to a romantic extreme form of the Inspiration Theory. If asked whether they believe that inspiration or thoughtful, effortful knowledge[2] plays the greater part in a poet's achievement, they would unhesitatingly plump for the former; the role of the latter would hardly occur to them. (This does not at all apply to modern *poets*, many of whom lay emphasis on form; but they are not characteristic of the literate community as a whole.)

[1] J. W. Duff.
[2] The Roman terms are *ingenium* and *ars*.

This exaltation of 'self-expression' belongs to the same romantic movement as produced the denial of classic architecture. The earlier, classical view was that effort was necessary as well as inspiration; that poetry would not come without a long period of thought and study; that the poet must have technical skill—that is to say, skill to compose his own original contribution within the strict tradition which had been built up, as the best, throughout the centuries. It must not, however, be thought that the ancients left no place at all for inspiration. When William Morris said, 'there is no such thing—it is a mere matter of craftsmanship', he was not echoing the best classical opinion. From Homer onwards, ancient poets prayed the Gods and the Muses for the 'divine fury'. But it was believed that this needed the backing of effort—careful thought and knowledge—added to native talent and inspiration. The need for these two to be combined is admirably laid down by Horace:

> The question was asked whether a poem became good by nature, or by art. I for my part do not see what is the use of labour without a rich vein [of inspiration], of or native wit [if it is] untrained; so true is it that the one thing requires the help of the other and makes a friendly pact with it.[1]

This is the effortful spirit in which A. E. Housman described one of his own poems: 'I wrote it thirteen times and it was more than a twelvemonth before I got it right.' He was seeking to achieve that compact purity of form, that unencumbered clarity, which, in literature as in architecture and the other arts, we call classical.

This is one legitimate aspect of that famous contrast between the terms 'classical' and 'romantic'. Extreme romantics regard poetry as unmixed 'inspiration' and 'self-expression'; the classical view requires also a background, convention, tradition, sane

[1] *Ars Poetica*, 408 ff., tr. H. R. Fairclough.

clarity, pure form and organic structure—with parts carefully related to the whole and to each other.

> In fine, to whatsoever you aspire,
> Let it at least be simple and entire.[1]

Today classicism, in poetry as in other branches of art and life, is unfamiliar and unwelcome—largely because it is hard to live up to and to maintain.

However, 'classical' and 'romantic' characteristics must not be thought of as mutually exclusive. Much romance, by any definition of the word, is found in Greek and Roman literature. We can trace the development of the romantic spirit, with its imagination, intensity and emotion, in the Athenian dramatist Euripides and later Greek poets, down through the great Latin poets of the Augustan Age, on into the work—heralding the medieval epoch—of the novelist Apuleius. Shelley, too, has shown how a writer can be romantic, while loving Greek and Roman literature. The combination of the classical and romantic conceptions has often produced wonders. Men miss a great deal when they consciously or unconsciously allow all their views of life to be coloured by a romanticism not tempered or counterbalanced by classical elements. Balance is one of the classical virtues; and balance between the classical and romantic is also good. This balance, this manifestation of the classical ideals without the sacrifice of romance, is apparent in the greatest Latin poetry. That is one of the many ways in which the best Latin poets utilised tradition so that the conventions thus imposed, far from crushing all novelty and originality, brought out those very qualities, and showed them to their best advantage.

Although, to the Latin poet, tradition meant Greek tradition, the Latin poetic achievement is something original—something

[1] Byron, after Horace, *Ars Poetica*, 23.

wholly different from that of fifth-century B.C. Athens or of any other Greek community. This is partly because centuries elapsed between these two civilisations which constitute the nuclei of the Graeco-Roman achievement. The interval was filled by a culture which, though Greek, was different from the classical Greek or Hellenic Age which preceded it. This later epoch, which linked Greece to Rome, is known as the Hellenistic Age. Roman poetry is what it is, partly because of Roman and Italian ingredients, but partly also because of Greek writings of this Hellenistic Age.

The dominant literary, and especially poetical, manifestation of the Hellenistic Age was the Alexandrian movement. This does not mean that all the followers of this movement came from Alexandria. But Alexandria was its centre. For, in the period which started at the death of Alexander the Great (323 B.C.), Alexandria supplanted Athens as the cultural centre of the Greek world. The greatest libraries, publishers and patronage were all at Alexandria, and it was from there that poets of widely separated Greek lands took their colouring. This Alexandrian epoch was essentially different from the earlier period of Greek culture. Then, the position of the Athenian city-state had been unrivalled. But the Hellenistic or Alexandrian Age began at a time when the power of the city-states was eclipsed—for ever—by the dominion of Philip of Macedon and his son Alexander. The city-states continued to exist, but they were no longer a political force or even truly independent. Power now rested with the great monarchies which succeeded to the heritage of Alexander.

The psychological effects of this transference of power were enormous. Greeks had hitherto based on the city-state not only their political allegiance, but their strong patriotic feeling, and indeed their fundamental conceptions of human society and of ethics. Their literature had been written on the assumption that the regime of these small independent communities was the normal, the best and the indispensable state of affairs. Now all was changed. The units that mattered were no longer city-states but great monarchies. But the old sentiments of patriotism could hardly be kindled by these new monarchies, which were huge and impersonal and did not absorb the daily existence of the citizen. Moreover, it was not practicable (perhaps not safe) for him to enter into practical affairs. These were perhaps conducted far away, and were in the hands of only a few royal advisers and governors. So the Greek, accustomed to an intense political life, was 'floating in strange seas without chart or pilot'.[1]

These were the circumstances in which, between *c.* 300 and *c.* 260 B.C., the Alexandrian movement of Greek poetry flourished. Its principal characteristics have been defined as follows:

(1) It shows a new *concentration on the individual*. In an age that many found monotonous, the inadequacy of the political unit as a focus for emotion encouraged escape into a richer land of the imagination. There was a new interest in personal psychology and sentiment; an interest in the loves of human beings. Love and psychology were already subjects with a long literary history. But the Alexandrians handled them with a new intimacy and carefulness of observation. This absorption would have appeared strange to classical Greece. But since it was handed on to Latin literature, it has come down to our own day; and it seems to us 'modern'. This emphasis on the individual and his concerns was an attempt to bring poetry into touch with what really mattered to the people of the Hellenistic world—the old concerns of the city-state had had their day. Articulate affection for other human beings gained at the expense of patriotic fervour. Moreover, another successor of the old patriotism was a new romantic attachment to the land, the countryside itself; Alexandrian poetry shows a new appreciation of nature.

To these developments Roman and modern love poetry and nature poetry owe a great debt.

[1] J. W. Mackail, to whom the summary that follows is owed.

(2) The Alexandrian movement was also a movement of *scholarship*. Its leading men were, some of them, the greatest scholars that the ancient world had known. This shows itself in their literature, in two ways. Interest in scientific matters was intensified; and there was a new scholarly self-consciousness about art. This latter tendency stimulated a meticulous attention to language. The language of Greek poetry took on a more self-conscious, highly finished character, in accordance with a new sharpening and fastidiousness of taste. Under the influence of Callimachus, there was a minority movement in favour of small-scale works in which perfection of technique could more nearly be attained.

This scholarly approach to art and letters among the Hellenistic Greeks was accompanied by an even deeper reverence for literary tradition than had been apparent hitherto. The Alexandrians were often antiquarians in their keen study of their predecessors. This, too, is a development which was profoundly to affect the Roman poets. In some, an excessive artificiality was caused by the misplaced cleverness of men who were not stimulated by tradition but deadened by its weight. Others were moved to the final and fullest expression of the classical literary ideal.

(3) Yet the most significant feature of Alexandrianism at its best is its capacity for *experiment*. This experimentation took place within the existing traditions. But, without departing from their essential conventions, many adjustments were attempted. These often consisted of the mixing together of old 'kinds' of poetry. The Doctrine of Kinds was, it is true, never out of mind; but liberties were taken with it. That is to say, metres or linguistic styles hitherto restricted to certain subjects were now employed for other subjects as well or instead. Similarly, the more barren or well-worn topics of mythology were varied by the judicious introduction of local and regional myths. By such means, these Greek poets utilised subject-matter which, though old, was new

to verse or to the particular kind of verse in which they were writing. Often, too, old-fashioned presentations of religious topics were infused with modern, sophisticated rationalism and humanism. There were many subtle touches to give fresh significances to old themes; there were careful surveys and exploitations of the full possibilities inherent in the classical tradition.

Without an appreciation of what the Alexandrians undertook in this field, it would be impossible to have a clear understanding of the achievement of Catullus, Virgil and Horace, and of many other Romans before and after them. For the Roman poets too obtained some of their successes by similar adjustments of form to subject. These were suggested to them by their Alexandrian predecessors. Yet the greatest of the Roman poets utilised Alexandrian *genres* in no slavish fashion, but rather as a framework for true originality within the classical conventions.

The Romans did not receive the full impact of Alexandrianism for two centuries. There was a transitional period at the beginning of the first century B.C., when Q. Lutatius Catulus formed a circle of poets and other writers who took an interest in Alexandrian ideas; and Laevius wrote erotic and mythological poetry. Then Alexandrianism became highly fashionable among the most cultivated young Romans of the day; and this development produced as distinctive results at Rome as it had produced two hundred years earlier in the Eastern Mediterranean. In one respect, the causes of the Romanisation of this movement were similar to those of its original creation in Greek Alexandria. In the Roman Empire of the first century B.C., as in the Successor States of Alexander in the third century B.C., there were political and social disturbances which encouraged retrenchment behind the individual's own spiritual resources. Besides, in both cases a period of literary and poetic creation had given place to an epoch of scholarship, of criticism, and of miniature forms of poetry. Just as the Hellenistic epoch followed upon the age of the Athenian tragic poets and prose-writers of the fifth and fourth centuries B.C., so the Romans of the first century B.C. had behind them the dramatic gifts of Plautus and Terence. Though an age of more refined culture came after these dramatists at Rome, it produced no poetic successors or rivals to them.

Yet, as is always the case in such comparisons, the resemblances between the two epochs and movements, the Hellenistic of the third century B.C. and the Roman of the first century B.C., were by no means exact. The two languages and cultures had not reached comparable stages at the dates when Alexandrianism came upon them. Greek poetry, by the fourth and third centuries B.C., had already attained fabulous excellence and refinement. But the literature and poetry of the Romans, despite the Comedians, was still far from maturity when it received the impact of the Alexandrians in the first century B.C. The consequence was that at Rome, much more than in Hellenistic Greece, it was one of the aims of the Alexandrian movement to revolt against current imperfections, and to promote ideals of technical achievement, which were still unsatisfied by Latin literature.

2. POETRY OF INSTRUCTION: LUCRETIUS

Much of ancient poetry seeks to improve; but the poetry which is known as 'didactic' deliberately instructs and informs, and does so in certain special fields—philosophy, science or some craft or art. To many people today it is a strange idea that great poetry should be written about such subjects. It was not strange to the ancients. This was partly because of the widespread idea that poetry possessed a 'mission'; it was also partly because these topics were not traditionally separated from poetry. There was, in earliest Greece, a strong desire to collect what experience had taught, and to recite it for posterity. The natural medium for recitation was the hexameter, the grandest and most ancient of metres.

So Greek didactic poetry has its origins far in the past. Hesiod, second only to Homer in reputed date, had written the *Works and Days*, moral precepts and descriptions of farm-work, and the *Theogony*, on traditions concerning the gods and the origins of the universe. These represent two different sorts of didactic poetry[1]—the former aiming at *right action*, and the latter at *right information*. The next great name in the Greek didactic poetry of pre-Alexandrian times is that of Empedocles of Acragas (Agrigento in Sicily) (*c.* 493–*c.* 433 B.C.). He was a man whose versatility passed into legend. But less than 500 lines of his poems on natural science, metaphysics and religion have survived.

It was natural that the Alexandrian movement of the Hellenistic Greeks should pay much attention to this sort of poetry. For one of its principal features was scholarship, and one of its keenest interests was science. There was a particular desire to aid in the systematising of knowledge, and this was felt to be a proper role of poetry—even when the subject was a technical one such as physics or astronomy.

When influences of Hellenistic and Alexandrian thought became strong at Rome, the same habit took root there also. It was suited to the seriousness of the Roman character. The 'father of Roman poetry', Ennius, wrote several didactic poems, now lost except for fragments. In the first century B.C. this approach led to one of the greatest successes in the whole field of Roman poetry and literature. This is the poem *On the Nature of Things* (*De Rerum Natura*) of Lucretius (*c.* 94–55 B.C.). We do not know who Lucretius was; it has been suggested that he was a Roman aristocrat, but this is quite uncertain.

In many respects he seems alien to the Alexandrian movement; his fire and passion and rapidity are out of keeping with it.

[1] As R. A. B. Mynors points out.

Nevertheless, he should not be thought of as exempt from the influences of his time. In the first place, his subject-matter is drawn from a Hellenistic philosophy, that of Epicurus. Secondly, the idea of expounding such matters in verse, though pre-Alexandrian in origin, was fashionable in Alexandrian times. Thirdly, the grandeur and pathos of many passages of Lucretius not only owe much (nobly acknowledged by him) to earlier, cruder Roman poets such as Ennius, but are conveyed by means of a poetic technique which would not have been possible in Latin but for the advances initiated by the Alexandrians.

The Epicurean philosophy is outlined elsewhere (Appendix 1); but its treatment by Lucretius requires a special word here. Curiously enough, he is the most fanatical of Roman philosophical writers; this is curious because his Greek master, Epicurus, had been mild. The greater part of the *De Rerum Natura* is concerned with a demonstration of the material nature of the universe. Lucretius expounds the teaching of Epicurus—derived from earlier physicists Leucippus and Democritus, but also strangely anticipatory of modern science—that every concrete object is constituted of ceaselessly moving material atoms, that there is no such thing as the immaterial, and that the one and only basis for knowledge is sense-perception. He contrives to present material-ism, and reliance on the senses, in the most dramatic fashion, and in verse which is an amazing descriptive achievement. Epicurus, in view of his beliefs regarding the structure of the universe, had pointed out that fears of death, and of the gods, must be baseless. His arguments on these topics are converted by Lucretius into onslaughts, sometimes violent sometimes highly poetical, on those who have such fears, or encourage them. There are gods, he says, but they have no interest in the world:

> The Gods, who haunt
> The lucid interspace of world and world,
> Where never creeps a cloud, or moves a wind,

> Nor ever falls the least white star of snow,
> Nor ever lowest roll of thunder moans,
> Nor sound of human sorrow mounts to mar
> Their sacred everlasting calm . . . .[1]

And death is as irrelevant as the gods; for it brings no pain, but is eternal sleep.

> Then star nor sun shall waken,
>   Nor any change of light:
> Nor any sound of waters shaken,
>   Nor any sound or sight:
> Nor wintry leaves nor vernal,
> Nor days nor things diurnal;
> Only the sleep eternal
>   In an eternal night.[2]

It might seem that this was a grim, unfeeling doctrine. But Lucretius expressed the pathos of death in a passage which has awakened many later echoes.

> For them no more the blazing hearth shall burn,
>   Or busy housewife ply her evening care:
> No children run to lisp their sire's return,
>   Or climb his knees the envied kiss to share.[3]

Elsewhere, Lucretius uses pathos as a powerful aid to his arguments; and it rescues his doctrine from grimness. But it is pointless, he says, to be afraid either of death or the gods; and it seems to him to be the duty of philosophy to remove such fears—for nothing else can.

Without Reason, that is to say without the philosophy of the Epicureans, Lucretius feels that all human activity and bustle is useless.

[1] Tennyson, *Lucretius*, after Lucretius, III, 17–22.
[2] Swinburne, *The Garden of Persephone*.
[3] Thomas Gray, after Lucretius, III, 894–6.

> In his cool hall, with haggard eyes,
>   The Roman noble lay;
> He drove abroad, in furious guise,
>   Along the Appian Way.
>
> He made a feast, drank fierce and fast,
>   And crowned his head with flowers—
> No easier nor no happier passed
>   The impracticable hours.[1]

But Lucretius is far from contemptuous of man and his poten-tialities. Indeed, it is with a superb exaltation that he expresses the confidence of Epicurus and himself in the destiny and achieve-ments of man. Lucretius asserts the master's belief in the 'oc-casional unpredictable "swerve of the atoms" from the absolutely straight line'; and this means a measure of Free Will—it is an assertion of freedom in a world of necessity. Lucretius also presents an unforgettable reconstruction of the early history of the world, told in terms of human achievement, of the humanism which had been inherent in the doctrines of his master Epicurus.

But instead of writing bad prose like his Greek master, Lucretius attracts attention to what he has to say by saying it in wonderful Latin verse. Though he shows real intellectual profundity, he omits careful philosophical argumentation in favour of vivid pictures, concrete and not abstract. He is a violent, inspired poet, an unexpected disciple of the retiring man who gave him his inspiration.

Yet like the Hebrew prophets, he pities as well as denounces. His poem ranges from anger to irony, from irony to tenderness. Lucretius is universal. He is also persuasive. Tennyson tells us of readings at which all present were 'carried away and over-whelmed...by the poignant force'. 'Few minds, perhaps,' it has also been said, 'that were not stiffly cased in foregone con-

---

[1] Matthew Arnold, after Lucretius, III, 1060–4, 1068.

clusions have ever met the storm of his passionate eloquence without bending before the blast.'[1]

So although Lucretius faithfully reflects the doctrines of Epicurus, he also illustrates the capacity of Romans to receive a tradition and stamp on it their own individual and national imprint. This is true of his poetic technique as well as his thought. Although he profited by living in an age when Hellenistic techniques were transforming the Latin language, he was far from Alexandrianism—a much greater poet than any Greek didactic writer of the Hellenistic Age. He was also a Roman poet; he strikes a patriotic note again and again.

Yet, in spite of his many qualities, we do not hear much about Lucretius from his contemporaries. There is an isolated reference to him in a letter written by his younger contemporary Cicero to his brother: 'the poetry of Lucretius is just as you say in your letter—it has the highlights of genius, and it also shows superb artistry'.[2]

This attribution of both the traditional kinds of merit ranked high among the compliments which a Roman could pay. To many readers today the genius of Lucretius is more apparent than his artistry. For Lucretius wrote before the Augustan poets had added the final polish to Latin versification, and—in particular—before Virgil had invested the hexameter with its ultimate refinement. But Virgil's debt to him was great; it may be acknowledged in a fine tribute in the *Georgics*. Another poet, Statius, writes in the first century A.D. of 'the towering frenzy of learned Lucretius'. Yet in ancient times, on the whole, Lucretius made little mark.

Since then, however, the scientific aspects of his philosophy, as well as the epic grandeur of his poetry, have attained far wider fame. Although he seems to have followed Epicurus scrupulously, it is Lucretius, not Epicurus, who has handed down to the world the atomic theories of the Greek precursors of Isaac Newton—

[1] F. W. H. Myers.   [2] Cicero, *Ad Quintum Fratrem*, II, 9, 3.

himself the forerunner of the atomic discoveries of today. More-over, Lucretius' belief in mankind brought him the attention and admiration of the Renaissance humanists. The twentieth century, too, has found much to interest it in Lucretius' account of the beginnings of civilisation: Marxists and other materialists have seen in this an anticipation of their own doctrines.

To many, it is true, his originality has seemed of a poetical rather than of a philosophical order. Yet he regarded himself primarily as a philosopher; to him, his artistry was but 'the honey at the edge of the cup'. His main theme was didactic, and it is he above all who justifies the saying of Wordsworth that 'poetry is the impassioned expression which is the countenance of all science'. The *De Rerum Natura* shows that this is not the paradox it seems. And the didactic aim of Lucretius was indeed a serious one. It was his passionate mission to persuade the world of the truth as he saw it. In the same spirit, many centuries later, John Milton—though his God was so different from the gods of Lucretius—was to assert his didactic mission with the prayer:

> That to the height of this great argument
> I may assert eternal Providence,
> And justify the ways of God to men.

3. LOVE LYRIC AND LOVE ELEGY: CATULLUS AND PROPERTIUS

Italian contemporaries of Lucretius were far closer than he was to the Alexandrians. The Roman poets of the first century B.C. who were imbued with the romantic, individualistic, scholarly and experimental ideals of Alexandrianism are described by Cicero as the 'younger school' or 'Neoterics': he employs the Greek word *neoteroi* (=younger men). Cicero also calls them the 'singers of Euphorion', using here the name of a characteristic Greek writer of the Alexandrian movement (third century B.C.) who was one of their models. Another was Callimachus, whose arguments in favour of short poems they strongly supported.

The greatest of the Latin 'Neoterics' was Catullus, who—like many of his contemporaries of this same school—came from North Italy: his home was at Verona. To those who know his poetry it is perhaps surprising that his stock epithet in ancient times was 'learned'. But that virtually means 'Alexandrian', and his works show this Alexandrian influence strongly: for the first time in a Latin writer, one feels the unity of the Eastern and Western Mediterranean. Like the Alexandrians (but unlike earlier Greeks) Catullus writes for recitation and not for singing. Moreover, a long poem in the elegiac metre called *The Lock of Berenice* (no. 66 out of the 116 poems which have survived) is almost a translation from the Greek of Callimachus. Catullus' no. 64 is a poem of 408 hexameters which again shows marked Alexandrian features, and is perhaps the best instance of Neoteric technique that has come down to us. Its subject is Theseus and Ariadne, and it belongs to one of the miniature kinds of poetry which Alexandrian followers of Callimachus loved. It is a 'miniature epic',[1] and one of the finest of its kind. Incidentally, in addition to its Alexandrian affinities, it provides echoes of Catullus's philosophical contemporary, Lucretius. At the same time, it is one of our earliest surviving examples of a poem showing clear rhetorical influences (it may well owe something to discredited but technically influential poems by Cicero). But it is truly Catullan, for example in its appreciation of the beauties of nature:

> As, by the Zephyr wakened, underneath
> The sun's expansive gaze the waves move on
> Slowly and placidly, with gentle plash
> Against each other, and light laugh; but soon,
> The breezes freshening, rough and huge they swell,
> Afar refulgent in the crimson east....[2]

[1] *Epyllion.* [2] W. S. Landor, after Catullus, no. 64, ll. 270 ff.

Poems described as 'miniature epics' may perhaps be defined as short, poetic stories of from 100 to 700 or 800 hexameters, often—as here—containing brilliant word-pictures of a romantic or psychological character. Poems of this length and character in the Latin language include not only Catullus' *Theseus and Ariadne* but a work called the *Ciris* (=a sea-bird), and perhaps the mock-heroic *Culex* (=gnat). These belong—like the gastronomic *Moretum* ('Salad'), and the *Copa* ('Hostess')—to a group of poems called the 'Virgilian Appendix' because they used to be ascribed to Virgil; but the authorship of most of them is now regarded as uncertain.

Two further poems of Catullus, nos. 61 and 62, belong to another relatively small-scale *genre*, the Bridal Song,[1] a Greek 'Kind' with which the Romans blended old traditions of their own. No. 62 consists of some 65 hexameters, including a refrain. No. 61 has 230 short lines of a delicate metre which owed much to the early Greek poetess Sappho—a reminder that, though these kinds of poetry were beloved by the Alexandrians, their inspiration often lies a good way further back. Catullus also twice uses the complete Sapphic metre[2] (later perfected in Latin by Horace). Catullus is one of the very few poets who are worthy to stand beside Sappho for intensity of feeling.

For, despite all such debts, his individuality and freshness are unmistakable. Nor did his debt to the Alexandrians stifle his freshness. On the contrary, it made this articulate by opening his heart to the beauties of style which they had achieved. Those of Catullus's poems which show the strongest Alexandrian influence are mostly collected together between nos. 60 and 70 of his poems. But one of this group is a reminder that the new technical mastery can be used to express profound personal excitement. This is no. 63, a hymn to Attis, the deity whose cult was linked with that of Cybele, the Great Mother, the age-old goddess of

---

[1] The *epithalamium*.   [2] See Appendix 2.

Anatolia. The hymn, like the miniature epic and Bridal Song, was a kind of poetry dear to the Alexandrians. But it was far older. Certain Greek hymns in hexameters are so antique that we know them as 'Homeric'. And there is a direct and visible chain of hymnology from these ancient Homeric hymns throughout Roman literature, from its first known poet Livius Andronicus (who was commissioned to write an expiatory hymn) right down to the end of the Graeco-Roman world—when a nostalgic hymn was written in honour of Venus,[1] and St Ambrose combined traditional forms with new, Christian conceptions, thus initiating the hymns that we know today.

Near the middle of this thousand-year development comes Catullus' strange hymn to the young god Attis. It consists of ninety-three lines written in an unfamiliar, racing, rhythmical metre[2] which was specially associated with this eastern cult. And the hymn is moving and disquieting in an uncontrolled ecstatic fashion—it ends with a prayer that the frenzy may be averted. The whole poem has an emotional intensity which seems modern; the classical spirit would usually have sought to subject it to a more rigorous control. This, like other Latin poems, is quite as 'romantic' as it is 'classical'.

Though Catullus is called the 'learned poet', it is as a poet of emotion that he has won his fame. The religious or orgiastic emotion of the *Hymn to Attis* is exceptional. Catullus is at his greatest as a poet of love. He is not only a sympathetic narrator of the loves of others, like the Greek writers of the Alexandrian movement: Catullus himself was passionately in love—and he tells us of all his ecstasies and miseries. In his poems the subject of his passion is called 'Lesbia', a name which we believe to represent a certain Clodia, a beautiful and unconventional member of a great family. His life was consumed by this passion; and he

[1] The *Pervigilium Veneris*.   [2] The 'Galliambic'.

tells us of it. Roman love-poetry was the product of the brilliant society in which the two of them lived.

We call short love-poems of this kind *lyrical*, because they give 'perfect expression to a mood of the highest imaginative intensity'.[1] In this sense Catullus is one of the greatest lyric poets who have ever lived. Curiously enough, however, the ancients hardly regarded him as a lyric poet at all. That is because Graeco-Roman literary criticism was so largely concerned with classification by *metre*. (Some of the principal metres are summarised in Appendix 2 at the end of this book.) Only five of Catullus' poems were in metres which the critics of antiquity regarded as lyrical—two in Sapphics, two in the shorter lines found in Sapphic metres, and one in a verse known as the Asclepiad (likewise a favourite of Horace). So the educationalist Quintilian completely leaves Catullus out of his survey of Latin lyric poetry. But after neglect during the Middle Ages his fame revived, until in the nineteenth century he was regarded as a much greater lyric poet than Horace, because he was more spontaneous. Landor, Tennyson and Swinburne are among those most greatly moved by his poems—and not only by those in the Sapphic and Asclepiad metres. For Catullus also wrote a good many others which, to modern readers, display his lyric feeling—some are burning love poems, and others show equally authentic feeling about nature. But these poems are in metres which Quintilian would not accept, under the Doctrine of Kinds, as appropriate to lyric poetry.[2]

A large part of Catullus' poetry consists of 'epigrams'; and he must be regarded as a decisive figure in the history of this *genre*. The word *epigramma*, 'inscription', was used in early Greek times

[1] John Drinkwater.

[2] Such are the hendecasyllabic (eleven-syllable) line (the majority of the poems numbered from 1 to 58), the iambic *senarius* (three poems), the 'limping iambic' or scazon (eight poems) and the elegiac couplet (nos. 65–116); see Appendix 2.

to describe metrical inscriptions on gravestones, and also other dedicatory verse in various metres. The great name in the history of the pre-Alexandrian Greek epigram is that of Simonides of Ceos (*c.* 556–468 B.C.). This miniature 'Kind' was well suited to the spirit of Alexandrianism. It gained added popularity when Meleager of Gadara (in Judaea, *c.* 140–70 B.C.) published an anthology, the *Garland*, containing 130 Greek epigrams of his own, decorative, elaborate and varied. In the same spirit Catullus calls one of his books of poems *Trifles*.

Many of Catullus' miniature poems deal with subjects in which wit had no place. That is to say, they are closer to the original, Greek idea of an epigram:

> Time will not be ours for ever,
> He, at length, our good will sever;
> Spend not then his gifts in vain;
> Suns that set may rise again:
> But if once we lose this light,
> 'Tis with us perpetual night.[1]

That is a rendering of a poem of Catullus (in lines of eleven syllables, i.e. 'hendecasyllabic'), itself adapted from a Greek Idyll. Another poem by Catullus in the same metre, a trifle about the death of his lady's pet sparrow—in sentimental Alexandrian vein—was a favourite of the Elizabethans; but some of its unaffected quality is apparent in a modern Scots version:

> Weep, weep, ye Loves and Cupids all,
> And ilka Man o' decent feelin':
> My lassie's lost her wee, wee bird,
> And that's a loss, ye'll ken, past healin'. . . .
> Her bosom was his dear, dear haunt—
> So dear, he cared na lang to leave it;
> He'd nae but gang his ain sma' jaunt,
> And flutter piping back bereavit.

[1] Ben Jonson, after Catullus, 5.

> The wee thing's gane the shadowy road
> That's never travelled back by ony:
> Out on ye, Shades! ye're greedy aye
> To grab at aught that's brave and bonny.[1]

Other short poems are witty, in a variety of metres. Sometimes—and once the dictator Caesar himself was the butt—we find an epigram of just two pungent lines.

> What is an epigram? A dwarfish whole,
> Its body brevity, and wit its soul.[2]

Other poems are of over thirty hendecasyllabic lines—perhaps too long to be regarded as epigrams in the formal sense, but still epigrammatic in character:

> When lounging idle 'mid forensic whirl,
> Friend Varus took me off to see his girl.
> The naughty wench, I very soon was shewn,
> Had got some wit and beauty of her own.
> Arriving, we began a busy chat
> On politics and weather, this and that—
> Then on my province's internal state,
> And 'Had I found the profit adequate?'[3]

Some hendecasyllabic epigrams of Catullus reached a very low level of chivalry:

> All Hail! young lady with a nose by no means too small,
> With a foot unbeautiful, and with eyes that are not black....
> And they call you beautiful in the province,
> And you are even compared to Lesbia.
> O most unfortunate age![4]

[1] Catullus, 3; the translator's name is G. S. Davies. The version is owed to H. W. Garrod.

[2] S. T. Coleridge.

[3] Flecker (1901), after Catullus, 10. Flecker wrote this adaptation when he was seventeen.

[4] Ezra Pound, *To Formianus' Young Lady Friend*, after Catullus, 43, ll. 1–2, 6–8.

Three of Catullus' poems are in the six-foot iambic line which had been used extensively by the Comedians. Eight more are in a metre known as the 'limping iambic'. This differs from the ordinary iambic six-foot line in that the final foot is not an iambus ($\cup$ –) but a spondee (– –) or trochee (– $\cup$). This manner of conclusion, coming after five feet of predominantly iambic metre, produces a curious jerking rhythm capable of vigorous effects (which can hardly be reproduced in translation).

Many of Catullus' limping iambics are scurrilous or abusive.

> Egnatius has fine teeth, and those
> Eternally Egnatius shows....
> 'Tis a disease, I'm very sure,
> And wish 'twere such as you could cure,
> My good Egnatius! For what's half
> So silly as a silly laugh?[1]

It is because of these poems that Quintilian, though he will not admit Catullus as a lyric or elegiac poet, ranks him among those who exemplify the iambic metre. Though this was characteristic of dramatic poetry, short iambic poems had traditionally formed quite another *genre*, devoted to personal attacks and ridicule. This conception is associated with the names of two early Greek poets. One was Archilochus of Paros (eighth or seventh century B.C.); the other was Hipponax of Ephesus (sixth century B.C.), who introduced the 'limping' verse to supplement the true iambic. This type of literature was revived, with varying degrees of abusiveness, by later Greeks of the Hellenistic Alexandrian Age. Next it found a home in Rome, where there was a marked native taste for literary 'vinegar'. If we had today any of the 'Menippean satire' (=mixed verse and prose) of Varro—the scholar of the first century B.C.—we should find in it some examples of iambics used for this purpose (as well as of the less vituperative and more reflective hexameter).

[1] W. S. Landor, after Catullus, 39.

Catullus often uses the limping iambic with a savagery that is partly individual and partly traditional. Yet, if the eight poems in this metre were his only manifestations of this spirit, it is doubtful whether Quintilian would have troubled to rank him among iambic poets—any more than he ranks him among lyrists. But Catullus reveals 'iambic bitterness' in non-iambic metres also, notably the elegiac and the hendecasyllabic; and these two metres tended at times to supersede the traditional iambic as the verse medium of personal abuse (though Horace's early production, the *Epodes*, consists of iambic lines of various length; and, later, Martial's epigrams include many such poems, mostly 'limping').

Other epigrams of Catullus consist of elegiac couplets.[1] Many are less than ten lines long. Sometimes two couplets are enough to make a poem.

> Lesbia for ever on me rails;
> To talk of me she never fails.
> Now, hang me, but for all her art,
> I find that I have gained her heart.
>
> My proof is thus: I plainly see
> The case is just the same with me;
> I curse her every hair sincerely,
> Yet, hang me but I love her dearly.[2]

But Catullus could say the same thing, more grimly, in a single couplet.

I hate and love. Perhaps you ask why I do this. I do not know. But I feel it happening, and I am in torment.[3]

Many of these elegiac poems are about the same disastrous love for Lesbia, which is the driving force for Catullus' whole poetry.

[1] See Appendix 2.   [2] Jonathan Swift, after Catullus, 92.
[3] Catullus, 85.

My love boils up, and like a raging flood
Runs through my veins, and taints my vital blood....
I beg but balsam for my bleeding breast,
Cure for my wounds and from my labours rest.[1]

A few poems in the elegiac metre are of some length: one of them,
The Lock of Berenice (no. 66), is a translation of an elaborate poem
by the Alexandrian master, Callimachus. Catullus' version inspired Alexander Pope's *The Rape of the Lock*.

The characteristic form of the elegy is clear enough; it was
always this couplet. But it is less clear, and harder to state briefly,
what Greeks and Romans regarded as the proper significance and
topics of this branch of poetry. Its origins may well have been
the subject of a misconception on the part of the ancients. Roman
elegists attached to it the epithet 'tearful'. This shows that they
believed its essential character to be that of a lamentation. But it
is held today that the word 'elegy' may rather have been derived
from a non-Greek word meaning 'flute'. In this event the earliest
pre-Alexandrian elegies were presumably sung to the accompaniment of that instrument. By *c.* 700 B.C. there were already Greek
elegists. It is possible to identify, among early Greek productions,
several varieties of elegy in addition to the lamentation—songs
sung at drinking parties, military and political exhortations, stories
of real or imaginary events, dedicatory inscriptions and epitaphs.

The Alexandrian Greeks transferred the elegiac from these
practical purposes to the artifices of a literary form. But at the
same time they put new life into it, according to their own
interests and preoccupations. Callimachus, their foremost exponent of the short poem, also earned the title of the greatest
elegist, the 'prince of elegy' as Quintilian calls him. He gained
this title by his *Causes* (*Aitia*), an elegiac poem of several thousand

---

[1] C. W. Walsh, after Catullus, 76, ll. 21–2, 25–6—reproducing the
sentiments rather than the words.

lines possessing a narrative form. The other sort of elegy which now developed arose from the earlier wine-songs, and dealt with love; a specialised example is Callimachus' *Lock of Berenice*, which Catullus translated. The Alexandrian and Roman elegy was essentially a lover's complaint. Ovid pretends to explain the characteristic pentameter by saying that the foot subtracted from the heroic hexameter was stolen by Cupid. It was fashionable for elegists to offer mock depreciation of their subjective theme by describing it as 'light' or 'trifling' in comparison with the stately and national grandeur of the hexameter.

It was perhaps the Romans, not Callimachus, who first produced elegiac poems that were concerned not only with stories of love, but with the poet's own love—like the couplets of Catullus. Elegy became the most subjective of all forms of poetry. Much is hidden from us of its origins among the Romans; but Catullus may have been the first to take this momentous step, with its great effects on subsequent Roman elegy and so on the literature of the world. However, a poet did not usually take such a step without suggestions having reached him from earlier poetry; and 'Alexandrian' Greek elegists had hinted at this more intimate treatment. Yet they had only hinted at it, and the chain of influences is more complex. Latin elegiac poetry draws on many sources: lyric, epigram, pastoral and the Athenian New Comedy. It draws much subject-matter from Greek mythology. Later, the effect of rhetorical schools becomes strong. The resultant blend is highly individual, and well may Quintilian say 'in elegy we challenge the Greeks'.

Love became the principal theme of elegy—and indeed, in the end, it was to become the chief theme of poetry. But it was the elegists who used their medium most skilfully and tenderly to work upon the emotions. 'From the Latin elegiac, as well as from the Roman oratory, we derive great part of such power as we have over pointed and balanced expressions. It has touched our insular slovenliness and inconsequence with something of the Latin gift of clear thinking and the classical sense of form.'[1]

Some stress has here been laid on the part played by Catullus in the development of the Latin elegy. But the ancients would not have agreed. For Quintilian, while omitting him (as has been noted) from the lyric poets, likewise does not mention him among the elegists. This is probably because the output of Catullus in this field did not seem to the critic to be substantial enough to warrant his description by this title. It may also be that Quintilian had in mind a metrical consideration. The elegiac couplet of Catullus and other 'Neoteric' poets, though on occasion it could have both tenderness and force, was lacking in the refinement which it later acquired.

Of uncertain authorship, at the end of the Republic or beginning of the Principate, is a charming elegy of nineteen couplets called the *Copa* ('Hostess'). The landlady of an inn sings (and dances) an invitation to passers-by to come into her garden. This poem used to be attributed to Virgil. But it is too gay for him; even if he was an Epicurean in his early days, as some believe, he was never this sort of an 'extrovert'.

> It's very hot.
> Cicadae out in the trees are shrilling, ear-splitting,
> The very lizard is hiding for coolness under his hedge.
> If you have sense you'll lie still and drench yourself from your
>   wine cup,
> Or maybe you prefer the look of your wine in crystal?...
> Set down the wine and the dice, and perish who thinks of
>   to-morrow!—
> Here's Death twitching my ear, 'Live,' says he, 'for I'm coming.'[2]

The four Latin elegiac poets included in Quintilian's patriotic claim to 'challenge the Greeks' are Gallus, Propertius, Tibullus

[1] J. W. Mackail.   [2] Helen Waddell, after *Copa*, ll. 27–38.

and Ovid. Catullus had died in *c.* 54 B.C. Gallus, who came from southern Gaul and was a younger member of the 'Neoteric' Alexandrian circle, was writing a decade and more later—at the time when Virgil was composing his *Eclogues*, of which the last is dedicated to Gallus and is in some sort a commentary on his poetry. Gallus rose to a brilliant position in the society and politics of his day. After Actium, while serving as the first Roman governor of Egypt, he lost the favour of Augustus, and with it his life. But, long before that, he had written his four books of *Loves* (*Amores*). These entitle him to be called, if not the founder of Roman elegy, at least the first to write it on an extensive scale. We cannot judge his poetry, for it has not survived; according to Quintilian it had not yet achieved the metrical delicacy which the elegiac was later to possess.

Gallus, as has been said, was already prominent when Virgil was writing the *Eclogues*. But the Latin love-elegy reached its climax in the years when Virgil was concluding, or had just concluded, his *Georgics*. The *Georgics* were written in *c.* 36–29 B.C. The first book of the elegies of Propertius cannot be dated exactly, but it is likely to belong to the years *c.* 33–28 B.C. Propertius, the son of a gentleman from Assisi in Umbria who had lost his estate in the civil war, was at this time in his late teens and early twenties. His genius developed at a much younger age than Virgil's; and this first book contains love-poetry of unparalleled quality. It was called by the Romans *Cynthia Monobiblos*, for it deals almost entirely with the poet's stormy and passionate love-affair with 'Cynthia', a beautiful girl of no reputation.

> Yet you ask on what account I write so many love-lyrics....
> Neither Calliope nor Apollo sung these things into my ear,
>   My genius is no more than a girl.[1]

[1] Ezra Pound, *Homage to Sextus Propertius*, v, after Propertius, II, i, 1–4.

Propertius was pale, slight, excitable, veering rapidly at Cynthia's nod from ecstasy to wild abasement and depression. His self-pity owes something to Alexandrian convention, but much also to himself; he has been described (despite protests) as the first young neurotic of European poetry. His surrender to his own emotions makes him seem nearer to the subjectivity of modern poetry than to customary classicism. 'There is a romance in Propertius, the Roman Rossetti, whose cloudy colours are so far, already, from the sharp flame-tongues of Sappho.'[1] He exhibits a morbid, melancholy quality known to the Romans as *mollitia*, 'susceptibility in harmony with a luxurious and voluptuous sentiment'. He evokes nature by a sensuous choice of Hellenic names:

> There's a clear well beneath Arganthos' screes
> Wherein Bithynian Naiads take their ease,
> > By leafage overarched, where apples hide
> Whilst the dew kisses them on the unknown trees.[2]

But love is the motive power of his poetry. Inspired by it, his imagination is compelling. It finds expression by means of a new mastery of the elegiac metre. In his hands the pentameter, which easily becomes trivial in lesser poetry, has strength and emotion. Propertius knew his own merits. He called himself the Roman Callimachus; for he claims to be the first Roman to reproduce Alexandrian artistry. This was hardly just to the 'Neoterics' of the 50's and 40's. But Propertius moved on far beyond them.

He did so while he was still very young. The inspiration of his *Cynthia Monobiblos* is uneven; classical self-control is not always there; the language is often obscure and confused, and there are abrupt transitions (which increase in the unhappy second book). But the passion of love sounds through this poetry, and there is a complete integration of feeling and metre, of subject and form.

[1] F. L. Lucas.   [2] Flecker (1904), after Propertius, I, xx, 33–6.

But Propertius, in this and later books, seems also to show an occasional irony, a deliberate variation of Horace's disavowals of grandiose epic—duly complimentary to Augustus, but mock-modest and independent: to the pathos of Greek elegy he adds the cleverness of epigram.

Oh august Pierides! Now for a large-mouthed product.
Thus:
'The Euphrates denies its protection to the Parthian and apologizes
    for Crassus,'
And 'It is, I think, India which now gives necks to your triumph,'
And so forth, Augustus. 'Virgin Arabia shakes in her inmost dwelling.'
If any land shrink into a distant seacoast, it is a mere postponement of
    your domination.
And I shall follow the camp, I shall be duly celebrated for singing the
    affairs of your cavalry....[1]

Another such reference to patriotic poetry leads to an assertion, as convinced and self-conscious as that of Horace (though with a different sort of sophistication), of Propertius' future renown:

Upon the Actian marshes Virgil is Phoebus' chief of police,
        He can tabulate Caesar's great ships.
He thrills to Ilian arms,
        He shakes the Trojan weapons of Aeneas,
And casts stores on Lavinian beaches.

Make way, ye Roman authors,
        clear the street, O ye Greeks,
For a much larger Iliad is in the course of construction....[2]

Propertius is concerned with his posthumous glory, because he is continually preoccupied with death. In this spirit he prays to the powers of the underworld for his beloved's life—with

[1] Ezra Pound, *op. cit.* v, after Propertius, II, i, 11–20.
[2] Ezra Pound, *op. cit.* XII, after Propertius, II, xxxiv, 66–70.

mythological allusions that are not merely superficial but lie at the heart of his feeling.

> Here let thy clemency, Persephone, hold firm,
> Do thou, Pluto, bring here no greater harshness.
> So many thousand beauties are gone down to Avernus,
> Ye might let one remain above with us.[1]

Cynthia died before Propertius, but long before she was dead his love for her, after great unhappiness, had faded. His later books contain many love-poems—sometimes tortured and torturing—which achieve great beauty. But it was impossible to improve on *Cynthia Monobiblos*. It is the culmination of the elegy.

It also marks the end of a historical epoch.[2] It was published soon after the battle of Actium, and is one of the last surviving works to retain a personal and individual character, outside the orbit of the emperor. Its absorption in violent personal emotion might well have been displeasing to Augustus, who was shortly to press ahead with moral legislation. But these poems were so good that the more flamboyant character of Augustus' minister Maecenas was attracted by them. This patronage, and the collapse of his love for Cynthia, led Propertius gradually into the writing of a different sort of poetry, of which something will be said on a later page—a new, archaeological variant of the patriotic verse which he had at first disowned.

It is not surprising that the ancients were inclined to withhold admiration from a poet who was a spiritual 'deviationist' from classical austerity. There was a tendency to prefer a contemporary, Tibullus, whom Quintilian aptly sums up as 'smooth and grace-ful'. Tibullus' elegies on his love for 'Delia' lack the faults of Propertius but also lack his greatness. Ovid, writing of Tibullus in tender terms, speaks of him as prior to Propertius, but it seems

[1] Ezra Pound, *Prayer for his Lady's Life*, after Propertius, III, xxvi.
[2] As O. L. Richmond has noted.

likely that the latter's first elegies were published at least a year or two earlier than those of Tibullus.

Tibullus reminds us that Maecenas was not the only literary patron of the day. For this poet belongs to another circle, that of the soldier, orator and statesman Messalla Corvinus. (One member of this circle, Messalla's ward Sulpicia, wrote passionate, direct love-elegies, which illustrate the freedom and culture of upper-class Roman women.) Tibullus sings Messalla's praises, and, by occasional allusions to national affairs, reminds us that his patron, though he had been a fearless Republican, accepted the Augustan order and took high office under it. What impressed Tibullus about the new regime was that it brought peace. That is why other Augustan poets, too, welcomed the Principate. But Tibullus more than any of them is the poet of peace—and of the countryside which he associates with this blessing, herein strongly influenced by the *Eclogues* and *Georgics*, written by a poet as fastidious as himself; and Tibullus 'walks in a dream', with his delicate sadness, like the writer of the *Eclogues*.

Tibullus is called by Ovid *cultus*—civilised. His elegies like his sentiments show a new refinement. His happiness and un-happiness are real, but not passionate. The 'liquid smoothness' of his versification brought the elegiac metre to a new perfection: and thereby he contributed much to the Roman elegy—though not to the elegy as a real love-poem; it had a future of another kind. Tibullus died in the same year as Virgil, 19 B.C. Propertius may have lived on; they were both outlived by their friend Ovid. But Ovid's elegies were to raise still further the artistry of the *genre* at the expense of its passion; and it has seemed preferable to mention Propertius and Tibullus here, as leading and final exponents of the love-elegy—whose most distinctive work was done at the very outset of the Augustan era—rather than to group them as 'Augustan elegists' with Ovid, whose conception of the elegy was for the most part so different.

CHAPTER IV

VIRGIL

1. PASTORAL POETRY: THE 'ECLOGUES'

A COLLECTION called the *Catalepton* ('Trifles') includes some small poems which may represent Virgil's youthful work, but his first important writings were the *Eclogues*, written in *c.* 42–37 B.C., at about the same time that his friend Gallus was developing the love-elegy. The *Eclogues* of Virgil are the earliest and by far the best known examples in Latin of the kind of poetry known as 'pastoral' or 'bucolic' Idylls ('miniature pictures').

As the two epithets suggest, these are poems of country people. Early in Greek history, herdsmen had no doubt sung simple songs, accompanied by the pipes as they still are in some parts of the Mediterranean today. It seems that the Greek land to which these songs can first be traced is Sicily. But a great portion of Greek literature had already been written before it produced a literary master of the pastoral poem. That master is Theocritus (early third century B.C.). It is not to be supposed that Theocritus had no predecessors, that no influences contributed to his achievement. For instance, a 'pastoral' choral Ode was written by the lyric poet Stesichorus (*c.* 600 B.C.). But, otherwise, who and what those predecessors and influences were is a matter of conjecture.

Theocritus was a Greek born at Syracuse. But in Sicily he failed to attract enough support or subsidy. So he emigrated— first perhaps to the island of Cos (off the S.W. coast of Anatolia), and then to the centre of Hellenistic learning, Alexandria. It was probably there, in the 270's and 260's B.C., that he wrote, in hexameters, his 'bucolic' poems. They do not, it is true, all deal with bucolic subjects (there is also miniature epic, and poems with a humorous element akin to 'mime', parody and burlesque). They also include a number of topical references. But Theocritus is the classic exponent of the bucolic in Greek literature. He deserves to be called classic, although he lived when the classical epoch of Greek literature, according to usual definitions, was at an end, and the Hellenistic epoch had begun. Though a true 'Alexandrian'—and, in particular, a supporter of Callimachus' crusade in favour of short poems—Theocritus did 'for the last time what the Greek genius had so often done in its great days; he created, and brought to perfection, a new kind of poetry, which alike in form and substance presented a new pattern of life'.[1]

The 'new pattern of life' presented by Theocritus, in so far as it relates to rustic matters, deals with such topics as shepherds' singing contests and mutual bantering, laments for rustic lovers, and the like. And these topics are written of in poetry of an artfully elegant simplicity, in a language of 'rustic' artificiality which had never been spoken. This is the pastoral poetry of an urban civilisation, written for the townsman, with a subtle humour which combines bucolic simplicity and realism with some of the traditional trappings of refined poetry.

Theocritus, if he did not 'invent' this bucolic *genre*, developed it into a branch of Greek literature. But he has not influenced the world so much as Virgil, who adapted the bucolic theme to Latin. There are beautiful pastoral poems in our own language, and it is to the *Eclogues* of Virgil that they go back. The *Eclogues* are ten short poems written by Virgil when he was between twenty-eight and thirty-two (or thirty-three) years old. They contain a good many echoes of Theocritus, whose Romaniser Virgil claims to be. There are also signs of the influence of more recent writers. One of these is Meleager (first century B.C.), whose *Garland* of Greek epigrams was very popular at Rome in Virgil's youth. There are

[1] Gilbert Murray.

implied allusions in the *Eclogues* to Catullus, too, and to the contemporary love-elegies of Gallus.

But the *Eclogues* have a peculiar fascination that is all their own. Horace later tried to define their intangible quality. But his words seem to us cryptic, and their meaning has hardly survived. What he appears to say is this: 'The Muses, who love country life, have granted to Virgil delicacy and graceful charm.' It is possible that this is a piece of semi-technical literary criticism, intending to ascribe to Virgil's rural poetry those qualities which are the *opposite* of heroic or pretentious. Horace seems to be stressing the susceptibility and sympathy apparent in the *Eclogues*—sympathy with man, and no less sympathy with nature.

Virgil is one of the great poets of nature, the model of the nature poetry which plays so great a part in European literatures. When he was writing the *Georgics*, if not earlier, he was living in a villa near Naples, where he spent most of the rest of his life in retirement. But when he had left his family's farm near Mantua, he had been old enough to remember the spirit of the country-side—yet young enough for his memories in later years to require, for their expression, conscious art rather than a mere recording of remembered observation. Herein lies part of the fascination of the *Eclogues*. They display a satisfying and piquant balance, a harmonious contrast, between the simplicity of their subject and the artistry with which it is treated. 'The Eclogues look at us with dark enigmatic eyes, from the fascination of which it is not easy to escape.'[1] One feature of the enigma is this contrast.

Another is the apparent weakness of unity between one poem and another. This absence of unity is, perhaps fortuitously, reflected in the very name 'eclogue' (Greek *ekloge*=selection). This was not Virgil's own name for these poems; it was probably invented in the later Empire. Perhaps it was first used of the copying, by someone (and for some purpose) unknown, of

[1] F. Skutsch.

a single one of these bucolic poems—i.e. it was a 'selection' from the *group* of poems. But 'selection' is not a bad title for the whole set, since it prepares us for a lack of rational completeness or continuity.

These poems nevertheless have one sort of unity, one with another; and each one has an elaborate and well-rounded unity within itself. This, however, is the unity not of reason but of art, without the intervention of any of Theocritus' realism. Here, the links that make the unity are links of emotional association. The connection of ideas in the *Eclogues* is akin not to our real lives but to our idle day-dreams or the dreams of our sleep. A comparably unreal beauty is seen in the landscape-paintings of J. M. W. Turner in the nineteenth century. When someone remarked to him, of one of his pictures, that he had 'never seen such a sunset', Turner's answer was, 'No, but don't you wish you had?' The same comment, it has been suggested, would be appropriate to the atmosphere of the *Eclogues*. This characteristic has caused them to be described by phrases like 'enchanted light', 'a medium of strange gold', and 'unearthly day'.[1]

Thus, in spite of the reconstructive efforts of scholars, the scenery of the *Eclogues* is not usually to be identified at any one place; it is composite and imaginative. The shepherds are from Arcadia, a rustic land in the Peloponnese where the countrymen were believed to have competed of old in singing contests; but references to this Greek countryside are blended with Sicilian and north Italian allusions. The scene of the *Eclogues* is not anywhere in the real world. The second and seventh poems are true pastoral idylls, containing evocative, sensuous descriptions of this poetically conceived nature and her beauties.

Can you not see the Nymphs, laden with baskets of lilies, all for you? See the white Naiad, plucking, for you, pale irises and poppy-heads, binding narcissus to the fragrant anise-flower, with cassia and

[1] J. W. Mackail.

other scented herbs twined in and flaming marigolds to make the
modest blueberries look their best. Myself I'll pick you quinces with
their white and tender bloom, and the chestnuts Amaryllis loved
when she was mine. And waxen plums....[1]

Such evocations and enumerations have fascinated many English
poets of many (including the most romantic) epochs. Among
them was Tennyson, who explicitly asserts his debt to the Virgilian
'shepherd pipe' in 'a small Sweet Idyll':

> So waste not thou; but come; for all the vales
> Await thee; azure pillars of the hearth
> Arise to thee; the children call, and I
> Thy shepherd pipe, and sweet is every sound,
> Sweeter thy voice, but every sound is sweet;
> Myriads of rivulets hurrying thro' the lawn,
> The moan of doves in immemorial elms,
> And murmuring of innumerable bees.

Virgil had written: 'the roof-tops of the farms are already putting
up their evening smoke' and 'the turtle-dove high in the elm
will never bring her cooing to an end'.[2]

But, like the Bucolics of Theocritus, these Idylls of Virgil are
not all of the countryside. The poem which Tennyson is adapting
(I), as well as another (IX), hints in unmistakable though indirect
terms at a disaster which, during Virgil's youth, overtook his
fellow townsmen of Mantua. In c. 41 B.C. it lost a great part of its
lands to settlements for demobilised veterans—settlements such
as were continually and sweepingly allotted during the civil wars.
Sufferers from the confiscations of this grim epoch include Horace,
Propertius and Tibullus; whether Virgil himself lost his patrimony
in the plundering of Mantua is uncertain, though there is a persistent tradition that he did.

[1] *Eclogues*, II, 45–53.
[2] *Eclogues*, I, 82, 58. Tennyson's poem is *The Princess: a Medley*. The
prose-translation used here and in other passages is that of E. V. Rieu.

The last poem of the collection (x) is again by no means limited to purely pastoral themes. It honours in haunting verses a poetic contemporary, the Roman elegist Gallus, and goes half way towards the love-themes which he had developed. In this poem, Virgil makes his farewell to pastoral poetry. This farewell inspired an acknowledgement by John Milton of his great debt to Virgil. Milton's poem is *Lycidas*; it is a poem bewailing the death of a friend, and Virgil's poem too, in cryptic and not wholly comprehensible terms, speaks of Gallus as dead and mourned:

> The laurels and the myrtle-copses dim,
>   The pine-encircled mountain, Maenalus,
> The cold crags of Lycaeus, weep for him;
>   And Sylvan, crowned with rustic coronals,
> Came shaking in his speed the budding wands
>   And heavy lilies which he bore: we knew
> Pan the Arcadian.[1]

The last lines of Milton's *Lycidas* echo a revealing hint with which Virgil concludes this poem.

> And now the sun has stretched out all the hills,
> And now was dropt into the western bay.
> At last he rose, and twitched his mantle blue;
> Tomorrow to fresh woods and pastures new.

'Pierian goddesses,' Virgil had written, 'let these lines suffice for your poet to have sung.... Now let us go. The shade is bad for singers....'[2] Virgil is on the way to fresh woods, to different sorts of poetry. Yet even these Idylls, as has been said, had not stayed within the comparatively narrow scope of simple bucolic subjects. The first, ninth and tenth *Eclogues* have wider themes. But what has earned the poet special fame throughout the ages is the fourth *Eclogue*.

[1] Shelley, from *Virgil's Tenth Eclogue* (after Virgil, *Eclogues*, x, 6–15, 24–7). His *Adonis* also owes much to this poem.

[2] *Eclogues*, x, 70, 75.

This is one of three poems (III, IV, VIII) which honour a great orator and public man of the epoch, Pollio. It appears that Virgil may have intended to dedicate the whole collection to him, but that he finally changed his mind and prefaced it instead by an honorific mention of the young Octavian (the future Augustus). However, the fourth *Eclogue* confers signal honour on Pollio.

With reference to the date of Pollio's consulship (40 B.C.), it prophesies the birth of a boy who will inaugurate the Golden Age—the birth of a Messiah.

Time has conceived and the great Sequence of the Ages starts afresh. Justice, the Virgin, comes back to dwell with us, and the rule of Saturn is restored. The Firstborn of the New Age is already on his way from high heaven down to earth.[1]

> The world's great age begins anew,
> The golden years return,
> The earth doth like a snake renew
> Her winter weeds outworn.[2]

It has been endlessly argued what, and in particular whom, Virgil meant. His poem was written when the wives of the two rulers of the Roman world, Antony and Octavian, were both expecting children. It has been supposed that he was alluding to one or the other of the awaited births. But scholars still do not agree on their choice between the two; and it has been suggested that, whatever Virgil wrote originally, the text as we have it may be that of a revision twenty years later.

But this fourth *Eclogue* owes its overwhelmingly great reputation to special circumstances. In the fourth century A.D., when Christianity became Rome's state religion, many Christians believed that Virgil was here prophesying the birth of Christ. This

---

[1] Virgil, *Eclogues*, IV, 5-7.
[2] Shelley, *Hellas*, after Virgil, *Eclogue* IV.

view obtained the support of Constantine the Great and St Jerome. It led, in the Middle Ages, to the actual comparison of Virgil to the Biblical prophets. This strange development is illustrated by medieval prayers, at Rheims Cathedral, for Virgil as 'prophet of the Gentiles'; by his appearance, in the eleventh century, in Nativity Plays at Limoges; and in fourteenth-century Spain, by his inclusion among the prophets of the Old Testament.

In modern times the question has been put rather differently. Had Virgil, it has been asked, read the Messianic prophecies of the Book of Isaiah? Even if we decide that such a conclusion is unproved, it remains true that Virgil, like the earlier prophet, was reflecting a feeling, widespread in the Mediterranean and Middle Eastern area, that a Saviour was about to come and rid the world of the miseries into which it had fallen. At all events, whatever the precise explanation may be, Virgil's echo of the principal theme of Christianity had an incalculable influence on many successive generations.

The other *Eclogues*, too, have had their fame. In antiquity, it is true, few poets attempted to rival or imitate them; there were two graceful attempts under Nero, but in general the originals were felt to be too good. In the Middle Ages the 'Messianic' *Eclogue* often almost monopolised attention. But in the Renaissance the whole collection came into its own again. Pastoral writers in France and Italy sought to adapt the *Eclogues* to their own languages. Edmund Spenser, imbued with the classics more than any other English poet, wrote his *Shepherd's Calendar* (1579) in the form of twelve *Eclogues*, one for each month. And then in the poems of John Milton—not only in *Lycidas*, but in *L'Allegro*, *Il Penseroso* and *Comus*—the true spirit of Theocritus and of Virgil's *Eclogues* is at work.

It remained active in the eighteenth century, which was an epoch of bucolic poems beyond all count. The most beloved lines of Gray's *Elegy* are pastoral:

There at the foot of yonder nodding beech
    That wreathes its old fantastic roots so high,
His listless length at noontide would he stretch,
    And pore upon the brook that babbles by.

And the French court at Versailles cherished the pastoral spirit. 'The ideals of Arcadia were perfectly real and active for several hundred years. Dresden-china shepherdesses and Marie Antoinette's toy farm in the Petit Trianon look childishly artificial to us now; but they were closer to reality than the enormous operas about Xerxes and the enormous mural paintings representing His Serene Highness as Augustus or Hercules.'[1]

The metre of the *Eclogues*, *Georgics* and *Aeneid* is the hexameter. It had also been employed by Theocritus. It was the oldest and most venerated of classical metres, employed in Homeric Greek before any prose-writing had been seen. Virgil's total achievement is inseparably linked with his brilliant development of this metre. With a thousand devices he achieves previously unimaginable beauties and subtleties. This is already true of the *Eclogues*; and his metrical achievement grew ever greater, more complex and more profound, as he passed from them to the *Georgics*, and from the *Georgics* to the *Aeneid*.

The commonest sense-unit in the hexameters of his predecessors had been the single line. Virgil soon experiments with units of two lines. In his later poems, the *Georgics* and the *Aeneid*, he handled, on occasion, units of ten or twelve lines. In these, the pauses were delicately interspersed with an infinite variety of weight, sound and significance. Every resource of an incomparably sensitive imagination was developed until the lines seem to possess an almost magic quality. So he came to forge the superb instrument of his hexameter.

[1] Gilbert Highet.

2. DESCRIPTIVE POETRY: THE 'GEORGICS'

The *Eclogues* were published in *c.* 37 B.C. Soon afterwards, Virgil began his second great poem, the *Georgics*. This took seven years to complete, and was published in *c.* 29 B.C., at about the same time as the elegiac *Cynthia* of Propertius—soon after the battle of Actium, at which Octavian, the future Augustus, by his defeat of Antony and Cleopatra obtained the mastery of the Roman world. The *Georgics*, like the *Eclogues*, are written in hexameters; and like the *Eclogues*, they evoke wonderfully the Italian countryside. But, for all that, the two works are very different.

The subject of the *Georgics* is farming, as the meaning of the title in Greek indicates. The choice of this subject illustrates the complexity of a great Roman poet's literary debt to his Greek and Roman predecessors. The general idea of hexameter poetry on such a topic goes right back to the dim Greek past of Hesiod; and just as Horace later wished to be regarded as the 'Roman Alcaeus', so Virgil, in the *Georgics*, claims to be the 'Roman Hesiod'. It was a patriotic task to bring the spirit of Hesiod to the Latin language and to Roman audiences. But the patriotism goes far deeper than that; this is patriotic poetry of an unequalled splendour. The whole four books of the poem are paeans to the Roman homeland and the countryside of Italy. Italy is now a word of deep emotional associations. But the unity of Italy was something new; well within living memory it had been split by the savage Social (Marsian) War. Here a dominant, emphatic theme is peace.

> The wicked War-god runs amok through all the world.
> So, when racing chariots have rushed from the
>   starting-gate,
> They gather speed on the course, and the driver tugs at
>   the curb-rein—
> His horses runaway, car out of control, quite helpless. . . .

Surely the time will come when a farmer on those frontiers
Forcing through earth his curved plough
Shall find old spears eaten away with flaky rust,
Or hit upon helmets as he wields the weight of his mattock
And marvel at the heroic bones he has disinterred.
O Gods of our fathers, native Gods, Romulus, Vesta
Who mothers our Tuscan Tiber and the Roman Palatine,
At least allow our young prince to rescue this shipwrecked era![1]

'Our young prince' is Augustus. For the peace stressed here was
given to the world by him; and the poem is dedicated to Augustus'
associate, Virgil's friend and patron, Maecenas. Indeed, Virgil
attributed to Maecenas the inspiration of the poem; whether he
was speaking literally, or referring in general terms to the encouragement Maecenas had given him, it is hard to say.

Another difficult question is this: had Virgil some contemporary, topical purpose in mind? At least a decade or two later,
Augustus, to meet a long-standing and increasingly urgent agricultural problem, was urging people 'back to the land'. Was he
doing so already? And, if so, were the *Georgics* an attempt to
encourage this movement? Perhaps not; but at least Virgil was,
in his poetic fashion, in harmony with Augustus' movement; he
was what Horace called 'useful to Rome'.

In harmony with this aim, too, was the moral of the *Georgics*,
the necessity of hard work and the dignity of labour—a creed
which is expressed in the spirit of Virgil's greatest forerunner,
Lucretius.
                        For the Father of agriculture
Gave us a hard calling: he first decreed it an art
To work the fields, sent worries to sharpen our mortal wits
And would not allow his realm to grow listless from lethargy.
Before Jove's time no settlers brought the land under subjection;
Not lawful even to divide the plain with landmarks and boundaries:

[1] Virgil, *Georgics*, I, 511–14, 493–501. The translations from the
Georgics reproduced here are those of C. Day Lewis.

All produce went to a common pool, and earth unprompted
Was free with all her fruits.
Jove put the wicked poison in the black serpent's tooth,
Jove told the wolf to ravin, the sea to be restive always,
He shook from the leaves their honey, he had all fire removed,
And stopped the wine that ran in rivers everywhere,
So thought and experiment might forge man's various crafts
Little by little, asking the furrow to yield the corn-blade,
Striking the hidden fire that lies in the veins of flint.[1]

This emphasis on the laborious tasks of mankind deliberately
recalls Hesiod. But any attempt to compare Virgil with Hesiod too
closely would be misleading. There was an enormous gulf of time
and civilisation between the two poets. In this intervening epoch
came not only classical Greece, but the Alexandrian movement.
Though Virgil himself was not one of the Roman 'Alexandrians',
they were fashionable when he was a young man; and the debt of
the *Georgics* to the movement is considerable. The Alexandrians
had loved to write of nature; they wrote as 'townsmen playing at
being countrymen', and Virgil, who had long ago left his farm,
reflects some of this spirit. The very title of his work echoes that
of a Greek poem of the Alexandrian epoch and school, the
Georgica of Nicander (? second century B.C.). The contents, too,
of Virgil's poem owe material to another 'Alexandrian' Greek,
Aratus of Soli in Cilicia (*c.* 315–240 B.C.), whose poem the *Phaeno-
mena*, though its subject was astronomy, was fashionable enough
at Rome to be translated by Cicero and an imperial prince,
Germanicus.

Virgil also owes to the Alexandrians certain of the technical
achievements which now enabled him to attain a new brilliance
and refinement of language. The hexameter of the *Georgics* is
a more powerful and varied instrument than that of the *Eclogues*,
more polished than that of Lucretius. Its rhythmical perfection

[1] Virgil, *Georgics*, I, 121–35.

was due to extreme subtlety of poetic expression. It was also the outcome of a deep sensibility—a sensibility that was truly romantic, pointing to the falsity of the opinion that there is nothing romantic in the classics. In the *Georgics*, in even more refined form, is that duality of nature and artistry—merged in piquant varieties of proportion—which is also one of the chief charms of the *Eclogues*. The masterpiece was brought about by Alexandrian means, but the result was something new. This was partly because nothing in Latin could be quite like anything in the different Greek language. But the result was chiefly original because Virgil was a greater poet than his forerunners.

It was a sign of genius to bring into brilliant life a subject so apparently unpromising for poetry as farming. For the main part of the subject-matter remained directly connected with this topic. Book I deals with crops; Book II with fruit-trees, especially the vine and olive; Book III with the animals of the farm; and Book IV with bee-keeping (then a more important activity than it is now, since there was no sugar). Much of the agricultural material described in these accounts must have been derived, not only from Greek didactic poetry, but from prose text-books on agriculture. Such books were a feature of Hellenistic Egypt, and there were already at least two Latin works on such subjects. The first was the book 'On Agriculture' (*De Agri Cultura*) by Cato the Elder (*c.* 160 B.C.). But more important for our present purpose was the second, the work of a man who was still alive when the *Georgics* were published. This was the scholar Varro. His three-book treatise was on 'Country Life' (*Res Rusticae*).

This influential and detailed study by Varro was published only about a year before the *Georgics* were begun. The latter work does not imitate the former in obvious ways, but owes a good deal to its existence and to the interest which produced it and was produced by it. The just previous publication of Varro's treatise gives us a hint regarding Virgil's purpose. It has sometimes been said that he intended the *Georgics* as an agricultural treatise. But that is not the case. As a text-book on farming it is far slighter than the very recent and exhaustive study of Varro. Many important topics, such as slave-labour, are not mentioned at all. Virgil has no need to be thorough; his aim is not that of prose essayist or instructor. So this is not truly 'didactic' poetry. Its aim is not wholly informative, for all the necessary information had recently been given, in prose, by Varro. It is true that the title and subject are taken from Alexandrian poems of a more thoroughgoing didactic character. It is also true that their metre, the hexameter, is employed; and that Virgil, in these *Georgics*, echoes (in his praise of labour and in many turns of phrase and verse), and may deliberately compliment—despite antipathy to his austere materialism—the great Roman writer of didactic hexameter poetry, Lucretius. The *Georgics* do seek to be 'improving'—but in a moral rather than an informative way. They are not chiefly concerned to tell us about the technicalities of farming. They are concerned with the glories of the countryside, Virgil's Italian countryside, and with the life of the men who lived there and worked there. They are descriptive rather than didactic.

The *Georgics* are also beautiful poetry. So too had been Lucretius' poem. But he had used its beauty to make his instruction the more palatable, as 'the honey at the edge of the cup'. The poetry of the *Georgics* does not seem so clearly subordinated to their moral purpose. Seneca, who greatly admired them, wrote of 'our beloved Virgil, who considered not the most accurate way of writing, but the fittest way of writing; he did not seek to instruct farmers, but to delight his readers'.[1]

So the *Georgics* contain many passages which rise far above the rustic theme. In the second book there are famous praises of country life (and of Lucretius?). In Book III there is a eulogy of

[1] Seneca, *Ep.* LXXXVI, 15.

the young Augustus. The last book tells of Orpheus' visit to Hades in search of Eurydice—a theme which fascinates French dramatists today. This story, of 106 lines, forms the concluding part of a separate episode, the tale of one Aristaeus. This is, in its own right, a self-contained hexameter poem, of 245 lines—almost a miniature epic in itself.

Other episodes are shorter, and have the perfection of a small landscape painting. Of such a character is the story of the pirate from Corycus in Asia Minor, who retires and settles in the rich Italian lands of Tarentum:

> Indeed, were it not that already my work has made its landfall
> And I shorten sail and eagerly steer for the harbour mouth,
> I'd sing perhaps of rich gardens, their planning and cultivation.
> The rose beds of Paestum that blossom twice in a year,
> The way endive rejoices to drink from a rivulet,
> The bank all green with celery, the cucumber snaking
> Amid the grass and swelling to greatness: I'd not forget
> Late-flowering narcissus or gum-arabic's ringlet shoots,
> Pale ivy, shore-loving myrtle.
> I remember once beneath the battlements of Oebalia,
> Where dark Galaesus waters the golden fields of corn,
> I saw an old man, a Corycian, who owned a few poor acres
> Of land once derelict, useless for arable,
> No good for grazing, unfit for the cultivation of vines.
> But he laid out a kitchen garden in rows amid the brushwood,
> Bordering it with white lilies, verbena, small-seeded poppy.
> He was happy there as a king. He could go indoors at night
> To a table heaped with dainties he never had to buy.
> His the first rose of spring, the earliest apples in autumn:
> And when grim winter still was splitting the rocks with cold
> And holding the watercourses with curb of ice, already
> That man would be cutting his soft-haired hyacinths, complaining
> Of summer's backwardness and the west winds slow to come.
> His bees were the first to breed,

Enriching him with huge swarms: he squeezed the frothy honey
Before anyone else from the combs: he had limes and a wealth of
    pine trees:
And all the early blossom, that clothed his trees with promise
Of an apple crop, by autumn had come to maturity.
He had a gift, too, for transplanting in rows the far-grown elm,
The hardwood pear, the blackthorn bearing its weight of sloes,
And the plane that already offered a pleasant shade for drinking.[1]

The *Georgics* have not failed to exert their fascination on later
ages.[2] Parts of Milton's *Paradise Lost* are so imbued with the
spirit of the *Georgics* that, though they lack its fluency, they might
be translated from it. John Dryden called the *Georgics* 'the best
poem of the best poet'. In the years preceding 1800, their direct
or—more often—indirect influence was ubiquitous. There was
an immense crop of eighteenth-century *Georgics*, among which
James Thomson's *Seasons* are conspicuous. Virgil even had his
effect on the new, romantic, yet often didactic, nature poetry
written by Wordsworth: To me

> The meanest flower that blows can give
> Thoughts that do often lie too deep for tears.

To many today Virgil remains the poet who, for all his later
achievement, is—in the words of Cecil Day Lewis—

> chiefly dear for his gift to understand
> Earth's intricate, ordered heart.

3. ROMANTIC EPIC: THE 'AENEID'

Epic is the third and greatest of the types of poetry of which Virgil
was the master. An epic poem must be 'a narrative of some length,
and deals with events which have a certain grandeur and importance and come from a life of action...it gives a special

[1] Virgil, *Georgics*, IV, 116–48.
[2] In the sixteenth century they were Montaigne's favourite reading.

pleasure because its events and persons enhance our belief in the worth of human achievement and in the dignity and nobility of man'.[1] Epic poetry, with its heroic themes, enjoyed a special, exalted reputation among the 'Kinds' of ancient poetry; lyric and elegiac poets professed themselves in awe of it.

Aristotle said that the epic had a good deal in common with tragedy—including a plot leading to an *outcome* such as history, for example, cannot possess. But epic and tragic poems, he continued, differ in length and in metre; and what he said was reflected in the Doctrine of Kinds. A tragedy is shorter than an epic poem. And, although both possess six-foot lines, most lines of the former are iambic ($\cup$ –), whereas the epic foot is the dactyl (– $\cup$ $\cup$) or spondee (– –). Tradition had made the dactylic hexameter the inevitable instrument of epic poetry.

The model for epic poets was Homer. In Greece the earliest known poetry—the earliest known literature—had been epic. The unequalled, unapproachable Homeric epics, the *Iliad* and the *Odyssey*, were 'lays' sung by bards; they were *oral*. Yet it is a mistake to regard them as possessing a natural, artless, spontaneous character which ought to be contrasted with the literary character of Virgil's epic. The poems of Homer are far from spontaneous or artless. On the contrary, they are highly artificial. They only seemed to be otherwise because the civilisation that they record is a past, lost one which has disappeared without leaving us any other literary trace—without disclosing to us any part of the long, elaborate development which must have preceded the Homeric poems.

The *Iliad* and *Odyssey* fixed the hexameter for ever as the proper medium for epic poetry. But in other respects this poetic realm changed greatly before the Greeks completed their sojourn in it. The Homeric poems possess the extrovert, external character of a ballad. Centuries later, the Alexandrians infused the Greek

[1] Sir M. Bowra.

epic with their three characteristic qualities—romantic personal feeling, scholarly elaborateness and experiments of phrase and subject. The result was a new sort of poem, the Romantic Epic.

It only came into existence in the face of powerful opposition. The Alexandrian rebel, Callimachus (*c.* 305–*c.* 240 B.C.), held that the day of the epic was done. 'A big book is a big nuisance', he observed. In his opinion, the proper development of this kind of poetry was towards its miniature version, the *epyllion*, a hexameter poem which had fewer hundreds of lines than the old epic had thousands. This attitude was later revived by fashionable young Romans.

Yet, in the evolution of epic poetry, the miniature epic remained unusual, almost a freak. Long Hellenistic epics continued to be written. In particular, one pupil of Callimachus stood out against his attitude. This was another member of the 'Alexandrian school', Apollonius of Rhodes. He became Chief Librarian at Alexandria, and his former teacher Callimachus may have worked under him there. Apollonius wrote a Greek epic of traditional length and structure, the *Argonautica*. Callimachus sneered at him, saying that in this sort of field there were no more laurels to be won— 'another has them'. But this was not quite true. For Apollonius gave the world a virtually new kind of Greek poetry, combining the traditional epic with the new romantic spirit. The characters of his Medea and Jason have a psychological subtlety infinitely removed from the extrovert heroes of Homer. This characterisation owes much to the classic Athenian tragedy of the fifth century B.C.—Aeschylus, Sophocles and particularly Euripides. Apollonius imports their tragic conflicts into epic, with the additional infusion of Alexandrian romantic individualism.

Yet Apollonius, it has been said, opened a new door to poetry, but did not quite pass through it. He spent most of his life revising his *Argonautica*. But in spite of this—or because of it—the poem never quite comes to life. The scope is too great for the poet's talent. His romantic sympathy is suffocated by the traditional trappings. However, even if the *Argonautica* was not in itself a complete success, it enjoys a special fame. For it handed on to a poet in another language, Virgil, a new literary *genre*, marrying epic and romance. The association of these two 'Kinds' by Apollonius inspired the story of Dido and Aeneas, which to many is the supreme achievement of the *Aeneid*. Virgil grafted their passionate tale on to the old heroic epic which descended from Homer. It is true that the first half of the *Aeneid* is an *Odyssey* of travel, and the second half an *Iliad* of war. But Virgil writes and thinks differently from Homer, partly because they are separated by great gulfs of time and civilisation. Between them comes Apollonius, and all that Apollonius represented.

But there was another strand in the tradition inherited by the *Aeneid*. This was the earlier epic in the Latin language itself. This began—as far as we know—with Livius Andronicus' translation of the *Odyssey* (a successful school-book). But Latin epic became a *national* epic—'epic embodying the nation's conception of its past history'—an idea natural to the Romans, who tended to think of the prime function of literature as patriotic. The great names of the early Roman epic were Naevius (*c.* 264–194 B.C.) and Ennius (born 239 B.C.). Both were Italians, not Romans— Naevius from Campania (S.E. of Rome) and Ennius from Calabria in S. Italy. Naevius boldly chose a contemporary subject, the Second Punic War (*Bellum Poenicum*). He chose also a native metre, not the hexameter but the cruder (though to us still obscure) medium of the 'Saturnian' which was apparently not based on quantity. Though his main subject was of his own day, he prefaced it by a mythological account of the origins and pasts of Rome and Carthage, thus satisfying the Roman love of chronicling stories from the beginning.

The epic poem of Ennius, too, went back to the dim past. His great work was the *Annals*, in eighteen books. This made metrical history; for its metre was the heroic, dactylic hexameter imported from Greece. And Ennius, completing a process begun by the comic poet Plautus, also imported the Greek poetic custom of scanning, not according to the natural stress-accent of words—like Naevius (and our own poetry)—but according to formally, quantitatively long and short syllables.

The poem of Ennius is in some respects hardly an epic at all; as its title the *Annals* suggests, it is rather a chronicle in verse. Yet his position is secure: he is the father of Roman epic and Roman poetry. As 550 surviving lines show us, the *Annals* contained many passages of rugged, if crude, splendour. Cicero revered his memory. Lucretius too, offered him high tribute: Ennius 'was the first to bring from pleasant Helicon (the home of the Muses) a garland of leaves that fade not'.[1] Quintilian sums up the unassailable position of Ennius in Latin letters. 'Let us venerate Ennius as we venerate groves sanctified by antiquity, in which there are ancient mighty oaks which are now not so much admired for their beauty as revered.'[2]

Virgil offers many conscious echoes of Ennius, his forerunner in the writing of the national epic. Homer, Lucretius, Apollonius, Naevius and Ennius—these were only a few of the many influences interwoven in the fabric of the *Aeneid*. The extent and variety of its borrowings is startling. Yet it is equally outstanding in its originality. In the nineteenth century, Virgil's achievement was thought to be derivative; he was considered an imitator of Homer. But this was due to a serious misconception. It had begun with the ancient Roman critics, who had insisted on comparing Latin writers with Greek ones. So they compared their own greatest epic poet, Virgil, with Homer. Many nineteenth-century scholars did the same. So many of them, starting with the belief that Homer was 'natural', found Virgil artificial by comparison. Homer, as we have seen, was not 'natural'. But in any case such comparisons

[1] *De Rerum Natura*, I, 119.   [2] *Inst. Or.* x, i, 88.

are valueless. Society had changed as much between the times of Homer and Virgil as it has changed between the age of Virgil and the present day. The two poets reflect totally different beliefs, aspirations, societies.

Two of the chief literary developments of the intervening centuries, the romantic epic of Apollonius and the national epic of Naevius and Ennius, are both decisively represented in the *Aeneid*. The story is that of Aeneas, who escapes from the ruins of Troy— captured by the Greeks and in flames. After many wanderings and adventures, he and his band of followers reach the shores of Italy. After violent resistance by the Latins, peace is made, Aeneas marries a Latin bride—and their descendants will be the founders of Rome.

The plan of the *Aeneid* is as follows: Book I. Aeneas and the Trojans land in North Africa. II. He tells Dido the story of the fall of Troy. III. He tells her of his subsequent wanderings. IV. He leaves her, and she dies. V. In Sicily the Trojans celebrate funeral games on the anniversary of the death of Aeneas' father, Anchises. VI. The Sibyl conducts Aeneas to the Underworld. VII. He arrives in Latium, and Latinus its king reluctantly arms against him at the bidding of Turnus. VIII. Aeneas visits king Evander on the site of the future city of Rome. IX. Turnus nearly captures the Trojan camp. X. Turnus kills Evander's son Pallas, Aeneas kills the Etruscan Mezentius and his son. XI. The Trojans win another battle, despite the heroism of the Amazonian Camilla. XII. Aeneas kills Turnus and the war is over.

In the course of his wanderings on the seas, Aeneas lands in North Africa, where the Queen of Carthage, Dido, falls in love with him, and her love is returned. But Destiny is calling him on to Italy (and Italy is doomed to be Carthage's enemy); he has to leave her. She kills herself. Book IV of the *Aeneid*, where this story is told, is the climax of romantic epic and (despite debts to Apollonius Rhodius) of Virgil's own unique sensibility. It includes passages of harrowing poignancy. And when Aeneas has arrived in Italy, there is pathos in the Latin warrior Turnus. He resists the invader, but is fated by the remorseless intervention of heaven to lose his promised bride Lavinia to Aeneas, and to die at his hand. The picture of their changed fortunes struck Turnus dumb, bewildered him.

Speechless and staring, he stood there, his heart in a violent conflict,
Torn by humiliation, by grief shot through with madness,
By love's tormenting jealousy and a sense of his own true courage...
'The fates are too strong for me, sister—I see it now. Don't hold
           me back;
Let me go where God and my own unmerciful fortune call me.
      ...You shall not see me disgraced
Any longer. Just let me indulge this madness of mine ere I die.'[1]

Both Dido and Turnus symbolise conflicts. Fate overrides strong love and strong manhood. The situations are tragic; and their inspiration, though it is due to Virgil's own genius, is not unconnected with Apollonius—and the conflicts of Athenian tragedy before him. The *Aeneid* gains added fascination from these conflicts. If there had been no such dilemmas, it would not hold the attention in the same way.

Indeed, many modern critics have felt that Virgil's sympathy for losing sides is so great that it obscures the main issue. So nobly, it is said, are Dido and Turnus portrayed, that the character of Aeneas is insipid in comparison: Dido and Turnus are human, but Aeneas is only the servant of Fate. This is a modern point of view, and it ignores a very different attitude in Virgil's own day. Aeneas represents the Stoic ideal—much admired by the poet and many of his contemporaries—of the man who presses on regard-

---

[1] Virgil, *Aeneid*, XII, 665–8, 676–80. Unless otherwise stated, the translations of the *Aeneid* given here are those of C. Day Lewis.

less of the buffets and obstacles of life. And there is a dramatic development of his character. He does not at once become the complete Stoic Wise Man. He has his weaknesses, and only gradually overcomes them.

The turning-point comes in Book VI, when Aeneas, after landing in Italy, is granted initiation into his new world. He is guided to the Golden Bough, and allowed, in the company of the Sibyl, to penetrate to the Underworld—a conscious echo of Odysseus' communion with the Shades in the eleventh book of the *Odyssey*—braving all the horrors and dangers that encompass the route:

> Hence leads a road to Acheron, vast flood
> Of thick and restless slime: all that foul ooze
> It belches in Cocytus. Here keeps watch
> That wild and filthy pilot of the marsh
> Charon, from whose rugged old chin trails down
> The hoary beard of centuries: his eyes
> Are fixed, but flame....[1]

When Aeneas has overcome these obstacles, he is vouchsafed, under the guidance of his father Anchises, a prophetic vision of the glories of Rome which his line are to found. But the task is still a desperately hard one. For Turnus and the Italians arm against him. His harrowing anxieties are described by a simile borrowed from a wholly different context in Apollonius:

> So things went in Latium. Aeneas, seed of Laomedon,
> Seeing them so, was much agitated by surging worries,
> His mind in feverish conflict, tossed from one side to the other,
> Twisting and turning all ways to find a way past his dilemma;
> As when, in a bronze basin, the quivering water reflects
> A sunbeam or the round of the radiant moon, a light
> Goes glancing hither and thither, now shooting up from the water

[1] Virgil, *Aeneid*, VI, 295–300, tr. Flecker.

And jigging upon the fretted ceiling over your head.
It was night, and throughout the earth deep slumber lay upon
All weary creatures, lay on bird and beast alike....[1]

But in the end Aeneas prevails over all his troubles, with the aid of Providence. He is the poetic creation of the Stoic conception of man, the finest conception before Christianity—and his Stoicism is harnessed to Roman nationalism.

The personal tragedies of Dido and Turnus are incidental to this ideal. The main theme is the preparation for the foundation of Rome by Aeneas' descendants. For this is not only a romantic epic with a debt to Apollonius; it is a national epic, in the tradition of Naevius and Ennius. The choice of subject is significant. Not only was Carthage Rome's traditional enemy, but the claim to follow and equal Greek literature required a theme from the Greek epic cycle—while Rome's tradition of wars against Greeks (including, finally, Cleopatra, regarded as the epitome of un-Romanness) required that the Greeks should be foes. 'You must never feel safe with the wooden horse, Trojans. Whatever it is, I distrust the Greeks, even when they are generous.'[2]

The national character of the epic is another reason why we today are affected by misgivings and misconceptions when we think of Aeneas. For today, patriotic poetry is not fashionable. Kipling, though a fine stylist, brings a blush to many cheeks, and it has been doubted whether Tennyson's national poems should be regarded as an essential product of his genius. But such feelings should not be applied to the *Aeneid*. It is a patriotic poem. In the most sincere and moving terms, it glorifies Rome and Italy. It glorifies this land as the enlightened ruler of the world—just as the *Georgics* had glorified the land itself.

At the end of his life, in 19 B.C., Virgil had left Italy, proposing to spend three years in Greece and Asia Minor, and there to finish the *Aeneid*. But in Greece he fell ill, and was brought back to

[1] Virgil, *Aeneid*, VIII, 18–25.   [2] *Aeneid*, II, 48–9.

Italy, where on landing at Brundusium (Brindisi) he died. On his death-bed he sought to have the poem destroyed, since it was not complete—though what changes he would have made, apart from the removal of minor inconsistencies, we cannot tell. The *Aeneid* was saved, and its publication by the poet's literary executors (Varius and Tucca) ensured, by Augustus. And this act of admiration was warranted by the admiration which Virgil had felt for his patron. The *Aeneid* does not only glorify Italy; it also honours Augustus. Aeneas is not, indeed, his replica—but very clearly his forerunner. Here, too, is a difficulty for modern taste. If patriotic poetry is unfashionable, poetry praising our rulers is likewise not in vogue. But Augustus had performed what seemed to be a miracle. Fulfilling the hopes which Virgil had voiced in the *Eclogues*, he had after almost superhuman exertions terminated a long, terrible phase of civil war and misery. The horrors of those years, and their leading perpetrators Pompey and Caesar, are prophetically revealed to Aeneas in the Underworld by his father Anchises, in terms which seem to imply a rebuke to Caesar (whose dictatorial acts Augustus—though Caesar was his adoptive father and a god of the Roman state—omitted to stress).

See those twin souls, resplendent in duplicate armour: now
They're of one mind, and shall be as long as the Underworld
   holds them;
But oh, if ever they reach the world above, what warfare,
What battles and what carnage will they create between them....
Lads, do not harden yourselves to face such terrible wars!
Turn not your country's hand against your country's heart!
You, be the first to renounce it, my son of heavenly lineage,
You be the first to bury the hatchet!...[1]

The waste and tragedy had been ended by Augustus when he defeated Antony and Cleopatra at Actium. But Victory is not a triumphant, Homeric affair. We today are able to see in the

[1] Virgil, *Aeneid*, VI, 826–35.

regime of Augustus certain unsympathetic, even grim, features of which a man of Virgil's gentle and sensitive nature could hardly have approved. Yet he was an enthusiastic Augustan. This must be because to him, as to multitudes of his contemporaries, the gift of peace far outweighed everything else.

Yet there is much about war in the *Aeneid*. Its first part is a tale of travel, but its second half is a tale of war. However, in telling of war Virgil is the spokesman of his war-weary age. There is none of Homer's simple satisfaction in warlike exploits. Even victory over the Tuscan arch-tyrant Mezentius, cruellest of rulers, brings little but pathos.

> The Tuscan, recovering consciousness,
> Gazing up at the sky, gulping the air, answered:
> '...I know I'm beset by my people's
> Bitter hatred. I ask you, protect my remains from their fury,
> And let me rest in the same sepulchre as my son.'[1]

This damps any sense of triumph. Virgil sees the weariness and frustration of war. He is hundreds of years away from Homer, and his standards are proportionately remote. We come away from the *Aeneid* with the impression that its poet saw real merit not so much in military conquest as in a man's conquest of himself. This was an idea which owed much to the philosophers.

But Virgil was not only a blend of patriot and philosopher. He was also deeply religious. The main intention of the *Aeneid* is religious. Virgil uses a word *pietas* to mean something very like 'religion', and it provides the stock epithet of Aeneas, *pius*. In Latin this refers to family feelings, to patriotism, and to harmony with the will of Providence. Virgil was lovingly attentive to the traditional tales of the gods and especially to the old stories of native Italian cult. But he was at heart a monotheist who believed—

[1] Virgil, *Aeneid*, x, 898–9, 904–6.

as the Stoics did—in the rule of the world by an omnipotent deity who was also Fate; and, if he had lived, he would have turned to philosophy. The most profoundly religious part of the poem is its sixth book. For when Aeneas descends to the lower world, guided by the Sibyl of Cumae, there he is told by his father Anchises, not only the future of Rome, but the mysteries of the universe. This is his initiation: he is on Italian soil, and though his troubles are not yet at an end, his wanderings are.

The spiritual aspects of Virgil's religious feeling are constantly apparent. But, without any feeling of contradiction, he also uses the traditional epic machinery of the Olympian deities. Venus is the mother and patroness of Aeneas; Juno supports the Latins. They intervene as much as they can, and the 'wrath of Juno' against Troy is in the tradition of divine wraths in Homer. But their interventions, and arguments with Jupiter, are not relevant to religion at all. They are part of the dramatic machinery, further opportunities for dramatic conflict and tension, and for the display of Virgil's rhetorical gifts.

For a large part of the fascination of the *Aeneid* lies in its mastery of words. Here we are far from the rapid language of the *Iliad* and *Odyssey*. Here are subtleties infinitely removed from the ballad-style of Homer. Homer's poems had been sung— were oral; Virgil's were written down. He recited parts of them, it is true, and such recitations need to be remembered as an essential feature of Roman poetry in general, and not least of the *Aeneid*. But this was a different matter from the Homeric 'lay'. Augustan society was too sophisticated to be satisfied by a racy, straightforward Homeric style. A good strong story was not enough. Virgil's poem has good stories. But his theme contains infinite profundities—'an unparalleled variety of appeal....It has helped many generations of men to formulate their views on the chief problems of existence.'[1] And this is due not only to what

[1] Sir M. Bowra.

Virgil says, but to the fact that he says it with the supreme beauty and refinement of which the Latin language was capable.

The *Aeneid* shows him as an innovator in the manipulation of words, though not in the actual vocabulary which he used. He made the most of the elaborate inflections of the Latin tongue and of the varied potentialities of its word-order. Also, he possessed unique insight into the close relation which should exist between style and metre; harmonising them perfectly, he entered new and hitherto unimaginable worlds. One of his most fruitful experiments was in the *groupings* of his lines. Lucretius had usually treated each hexameter as a unit. Virgil increasingly thought in terms of a larger grouping of several hexameters.

The implications and effects of this wider scope can best be appreciated by reference to poets in our own language who have deliberately and successfully imitated the same complex structure. Tennyson is one of them. But first and foremost was John Milton, whose debt to Virgil goes far beyond the usual practice of literary debts. Milton, who attained international renown as a Latin poet, remade English poetry in a Latin mould so as to reproduce the rhythmical and periodic structure of Virgil. *Lycidas* was inspired by an *Eclogue*; there are also important echoes of the *Georgics*. But *Paradise Lost* is divided into twelve books like the *Aeneid*, and its opening proclaims in all its complex fabric that the *Aeneid* is its model:

> Of man's first disobedience, and the fruit
> Of that forbidden tree, whose mortal taste
> Brought death into the world, and all our woe,
> With loss of Eden, till one greater Man
> Restore us, and regain the blissful seat,
> Sing, Heav'nly Muse.

It was Virgil who had created these stately periods, and brought a new symphonic grandeur into poetry. This intricate composition is the very antithesis to the unclassical idea that the poet has nothing to do but to wait upon inspiration. Virgil's inspiration was extraordinarily rich, but he translated it into poetry by a technique of almost incredible subtlety. Within lines or groups of lines, words and phrases and rhythms are interlaced with an elaboration which is carried to the furthest possible extent.

His main principle is compression into density of meaning. Virgil's Latin is the art 'of making two or three words, chosen to go together, have quite definitely a meaning far more than the total of the meanings of each word, added together'.[1] It is hard for us to understand this process fully. Yet the *Aeneid* is put before children whose knowledge of the language is far from profound. This is partly because Virgil does not use very difficult words: so it is not too hard to extract some sort of a translation from what he writes. But to extort, from any passage of the *Aeneid*, anything like its full meaning is one of the hardest tasks in the whole field of literary study—and one of the most rewarding. Many phrases cannot be rendered in a phrase of even approximately similar length in English: they often mean several things at the same time—on different planes of thought.

Let us consider for a moment that pathetic outcry *sunt lacrimae rerum*:[2] literally, 'there are tears of things'—

> the Virgilian cry,
> The sense of tears in mortal things.

'Aeneas, arriving at Carthage, sees pictures of Trojans fighting painted on the walls; emotion overcomes him, and he says:

> sunt hic etiam sua praemia laudi,
> sunt lacrimae rerum et mentem mortalia tangunt:

which seems to mean, in prose, not much less than: "There is no denying that even in this far land honour gets its due, and they can weep at human tragedy; the world has tears as a constituent part of it, and so have our lives, hopeless and weary; and the

---

[1] W. F. Jackson Knight.   [2] Virgil, *Aeneid*, I, 462.

thought how things have always their own death in them breaks our hearts and wills and clouds our vision.... The first of the two lines might seem to limit the statement to the particular plight of the Trojans. But almost the whole point is that in the second the meaning expands to all the world."' [1]

This complex profundity of Virgil's meaning is served by a far greater flexibility of word-order than we have in our own poetry. Use is also made—to a degree beyond our own experience or easy understanding—of all possible devices of sound and rhythm. These include alliteration 'assonance' in the beginnings (and also the middles and ends) of words; and there are the most vivid and varied groupings and contrasts of vowels and consonants alike. All these stylistic resources made it possible to dispense with grandiloquence of vocabulary. Here was a new sort of poetic diction. It immediately attained overwhelming fame. One of the few who hung back suspiciously was Augustus' admiral Agrippa, who unappreciatively described the poet as 'the inventor of a new sort of affectation, neither florid nor plain, but made out of ordinary words and thus concealed'. But throughout the ages others have rather felt that Virgil's poetry has achieved the most significant music of which words are capable.

[1] W. F. Jackson Knight.

CHAPTER V

HORACE, OVID AND AFTER

I. LITERARY LYRIC AND SATIRE: HORACE

HORACE'S mind differed profoundly from the mind of his older contemporary Virgil. Yet Horace's poetry is the second great achievement of the Augustan Age. His *Odes* are lyric poetry. Yet they are far removed from the personal, spontaneous lyric of Catullus. For Horace's *Odes* are literary lyric. Inspiration and emotion cannot have been lacking in their composition—at their best these *Odes* are much too good for that—but these qualities are modified and transformed by a calm, meticulous intellectual process. These *Odes* were begun under the influence of poetic inspiration, and then, as in the poems of Donne and Baudelaire, 'the first wild onslaught yields to something more meditated and more complex'.[1] Public opinion today is inclined to see in this something different from lyricism—of which the second dictionary definition is 'high-flown sentiments'. The sentiments of Horace seem to many moderns to have been too much chastened by technique to be truly lyric. But the ancients, who attached vast importance to technique, held the opposite view. Quintilian says that Horace—not Catullus—is practically the only Roman lyric poet worth reading.

The four books of *Odes* are work of Horace's maturity. Books I–III were published in *c.* 23 B.C., some four years before the *Aeneid*; Book IV in *c.* 13 B.C. These poems deal with many matters in many moods. They sing of love, and wine, and nature, and the transience of life; of the gods and of Augustus and Horace's

[1] Sir M. Bowra.

patron Maecenas; of Roman virtues and the foolishness of exaggeration. This variety is one of the most conspicuous of Horace's gifts; and it was far greater than even the manifold pleasures of the *Odes* suffice to show, for Horace was also the poet of the *Epistles*.

The *Odes* make rapid transitions from grave to gay, from solemnity to laughter. Such *volte-faces*, even within a single poem—and equally rapid returns to seriousness—have caused shock and misunderstanding among moderns, who feel that Horace is, in spirit, flouting the ancient Doctrine of Kinds. Yet he manages the transitions with so consummate skill that such criticism, whether based on ancient or modern ideas about Kinds, is very rarely valid. On the contrary, he deliberately gives us surprises, dramatic turns and changes. His sense of drama is superlative.

And sometimes the surprise takes the form of a deliberate anticlimax. Horace laughs gently at us, and also at himself. He sometimes pictures himself with the ponderous trappings of heroic poetry; but he does not really mean it, and shows that they do not fit him. Mock-solemnity is his favourite form of irony. To some extent he means what he says when he contrasts the grandeur of epic with his own 'frivolous lyre'.

> No history, please! Work out some other time
> The pedigree of Aeacus,
> Settle the dates of Inachus
> And Codrus, in his death sublime.
> Even your outline of the Trojan War,
> Just now, would be a bore.
> For sooner would we have you say
> What price a cask of Chian is today,
> Or where, and what o'clock, we dine.[1]

[1] *Odes*, III, xix, 1–8. This and the two next adaptations are by the late Sir Edward Marsh (1941).

Tibullus, pull yourself together!
You mustn't make such heavy weather
    When women throw you over.
All day you melt in songs of woe,
Merely because a younger beau
    Is now Neaera's lover.[1]

It would seem a girl is doomed to be a saint:
They tell us what we may and what we mayn't:
    We mustn't have affairs,
    We mustn't drown our cares,
Or we're lectured by an uncle till we faint.[2]

Yet an assessment of Horace on the basis of such poems would be very misleading without extensive qualification. It is true that, in matters of love, he is generally flippant and 'hearty'. He has a double standard of feminine values, one for true-born Roman women, and one for others. Augustus himself approved this attitude, as calculated to protect the virtue of Roman womanhood. But, as a result, Horace has been called the least serious of all love-poets. Yet, even when he writes of love, Horace is not always frivolous: occasionally he touches a deeper chord.

Were he more lovely than the evening star,
    Thou lighter than a cork and more awry
Than billows of the Adriatic are,
    With thee I'd love to live and gladly die.[3]

But Horace also makes a loftier claim. He asserts his right to be the Roman Alcaeus. Greek lyric poetry had come to a wonderful climax as early as the sixth century B.C., in the Aeolian island Lesbos—the home of the poet Alcaeus and poetess Sappho. Horace believed it to be his patriotic task and achievement, which posterity would recognise (and it has), to give Rome the glories

[1] *Odes*, I, xxxiii, 1–4.   [2] *Odes*, III, xii, 1–3.
[3] Lord Dunsany (1947), after Horace, *Odes*, III, ix, 21–4.

which Alcaeus and Sappho gave to Greece. And he claimed that he was the first to do so—that this was his originality. Catullus had written a few Sapphic poems, but they were not regarded as substantial enough to qualify Horace's statement. And indeed Horace displays his debts to the Greeks in a highly original manner. He is infinitely far removed from being a mere translator. His poems have the ring of his own day and people, and of his own genius.

His particular pride was to have adapted to the very different Roman tongue the delicate metres of the Aeolian poet and poetess. This extraordinarily difficult feat is one of the greatest of Horace's achievements. Two metres which he employs constantly are those which take their names from his Greek forerunners, the 'Alcaic' and 'Sapphic'.[1] Horace revises these metres in certain respects for adaptation to Latin—with its heavier rhythms and more frequent long syllables—and he fixes a few points of usage which had been fluid before. The patterns which emerge are brilliant and intricate.

But Horace's claim to be the Roman Alcaeus requires one fundamental qualification. The poems of Alcaeus had been written to be sung. Those of Horace—with exceptions such as the *Secular Hymn* (*Carmen Saeculare*), composed for singing on a religious occasion in 17 B.C.—were written to be recited or read. This change had occurred during the intervening centuries. It had been introduced by the Greek writers of the Hellenistic Age, the movement centred on Alexandria. Horace does not emphasise his debt to Alexandria, for he wished himself to be thought the direct heir of Alcaeus and Sappho. But his metrical brilliance and experiment are in the Alexandrian tradition, and would have been unthinkable without it. His sensitive love of nature also owes something to Alexandria. So does his love-poetry. It is true that he has nothing in common with the sentimentality of Alexandrian

[1] See Appendix 2.

Greeks. Yet his more flippant light touch, in regard to affairs of the heart, is far from the passion of the Aeolians; and it is not fortuitous that his love-poems are often cast into Alexandrian forms.

Indeed, it is also Alexandria which, by the characteristic Graeco-Roman paradox, inspires one of the glories of Horace's *Odes*—their brilliant use of language; and the paradox is increased by the fact that very little Alexandrian lyric is known. There is an exquisite compactness in Horace's poetry, an 'inevitability' according to which each word is unchangeably fixed in its right place, and in its right order, and with the right word next to it. This is Horace's most famous talent, his demonstration that great poetry, in the classical sense, needs not only inspiration but perfect arrangement, effected by means of unremitting care. Horace possessed 'a capacity for taking pains pushed to the point of genius'. The ancient critic and novelist Petronius spoke of his 'careful felicity'—the quality of success achieved by a mixture of luck and skill, the achievement of the man who hits the mark because of the care which he has taken.

The Alexandrians had taught themselves a sensitive and intricate feeling for the possibilities of language. But Horace outdoes the Alexandrians in a number of ways. Like Virgil, he avoids the use of high-flown or queer words. He does not need the 'purple patch'—the phrase is his own—to achieve his effects. He achieves them instead by ordinary words, placed and ordered perfectly. It was Horace himself who said 'there is much power in word-order and word-connection'. Clever groupings could achieve more than unusual words, and it is of the former that Quintilian is thinking when he describes Horace as 'most happily bold in his words'.[1] And one of Horace's felicities is his almost startling economy of language, displayed by every possible device of compactness. His phrases and periods are so compactly

[1] *Inst. Or.* x, i, 96.

welded together that they mean much more than the sum total of their component words.

There is another way also in which Horace, like Virgil, far exceeds his Alexandrian forerunners. That is in his use of sound-effects. They are employed in a hundred different fashions. This phenomenon does not come easily to the understanding of the modern reader, who is unaccustomed, in his own language, to this practice being carried to such lengths. The sound of every word is given by Horace its fullest weight, and deliberately woven into the total sound-complex which constitutes each stanza and each Ode. There are skilful repetitions; there are alliterations; the same meticulous and harmonious attention is devoted to every syllable, every consonant and every vowel. There is not a word and not a letter which does not contribute to the total feeling and mood of its poem. Every smallest part of it is an integral part of its meaning. The mosaic is only seen in its full brightness when every piece has been fitted into place.

The Alexandrians had not integrated meaning with sound nearly so fully as this. In any case, their problem had been different, for their language was different. The sound-effects which Horace reveals are not those of Greek but of his own monumental and sonorous tongue. In his more serious poems he raises the lyric Ode to a dignity and solemnity which it had not known before in either language.

Horace may not have been religious in any modern sense of the word. But when he speaks of the religious traditions and rituals of the Roman State he rises to notable heights. He was a Roman patriot, and a sincere admirer of Rome's living leader, Augustus. Though he differed so greatly from Virgil in many respects, his attitude to Augustus was, in its essentials, like Virgil's. Both men owed to him many practical benefits. Both so deeply admired him for ending a nightmare period of war that they were prepared to overlook any crudities which the imperial regime still possessed.

Horace, as a young man, had fought at Philippi (42 B.C.) with Brutus against the youthful triumvir who was to become Augustus. The poet had returned to Rome penniless and without prospects, and had taken a minor job. Then Maecenas had 'discovered' and encouraged him—as he also discovered and encouraged Virgil. A spacious farm on the slope of the Sabine Hills was a present from Maecenas to Horace, who found it a constant source of joy and refreshment.

The progress of Horace's political views is shown in two of his early iambic poems, the *Epodes*. In the earlier of the two (the ninth), he urges escape to the far-off, legendary Blest Isles, since he despairs of Rome. But in the sixteenth Epode he celebrates the victory of Actium (31 B.C.). Maecenas had introduced him to Augustus, who later entered into a more direct relationship with the poet and, in 17 B.C. (two years after the death of the previous 'poet laureate' Virgil), commissioned him to write the *Secular Hymn*. This was the product of Horace's wholehearted support of Augustus. So was the fourth and latest book of the *Odes* (published ten years after the other three books), in which imperial personages are celebrated in a similar spirit.

But Horace, like Virgil, retained his essential independence. Augustus tried to secure his services as secretary, but there is no evidence or likelihood that Horace accepted the offer. His poems show several references, all as tactful as only Horace could have made them, to his escapes from excessive dependence. With typical mock-modesty, he declines the epic task of celebrating the victories of Augustus' admiral Agrippa; and he refers openly to his own service under the high-principled Brutus at Philippi.

With characteristic self-depreciation he says that what he himself did at Philippi was to run away—and to throw down his shield. But when we compare this statement with poetry of earlier periods, it becomes apparent that more than one Greek poet had said the same about his own martial efforts. It does not mean what it says; it is a traditional expression of the unsuitability of poets for war. Horace's *Odes* are full of these well-worn sayings, echoing down the centuries. They were known as 'commonplaces'; and they played a part in ancient literature and especially ancient poetry which it is hard nowadays to appreciate. They must not be dismissed as mere platitudes, for they were not so regarded in ancient times; they were considered to be the legitimate property of all literature, and originality consisted in expressing them in new terms and in the best possible way. This is a fundamental feature of Horace's talent. What he says is not new, but he says it more successfully than anyone else before or since.

The effect is all the better because Horace has the 'personal touch'. He lightly reveals his own personality. We see a man who is kindly, affectionate and sensible. He is also tolerant. One aspect of his tolerance is his broad, receptive attitude to philosophical beliefs. He has, in many matters, the Roman moral sense. But he is the model of the contemporary 'eclectic' who took what he thought best from every philosophy.

> But ask not, to what Doctors I apply:
> Sworn to no Master, of no Sect am I.[1]

Like most educated Romans of the day, Horace owes his moral principles to the Stoics:

> The man of life upright,
>   Whose guiltless heart is free
> From all dishonest deeds
>   Or thought of vanity....
>
> He only can behold
>   With unaffrighted eyes
> The horrors of the deep
>   And terrors of the skies.[2]

[1] Alexander Pope (1688–1744), after Horace, *Epistles*, I, i, 13–15.
[2] Thomas Campion (*c.* 1567–1619), after Horace, *Odes*, III, iii, 1–8.

This is the independent, imperturbable Stoic sage. But in another way Horace is the follower of Aristotle's school, the Peripatetics. For their philosophical principle was the 'Mean', and Horace is a devoted adherent of the Golden Middle Path. He constantly warns against excess—in any of life's activities, and in any direction.

> More justly will you live, Licinius,
>   Not always pushing out into the deep,
>   Nor, while you wisely fear the tempest's sweep,
> Hugging too close the shore so hazardous....
>
> More often by the gales the mighty pine
>   Is shaken, and more heavy is the fall
>   Of lofty towers, and the lightnings all
> Strike where the pinnacles of mountains shine.[1]

Horace is often negative—refusing, deprecating, dissuading. He deplores excess and urges frugality. But his frugality, like all his other characteristics, is far from fanatical. Indeed, nobody is fonder than he is of simple pleasures such as the enjoyment of Sabine wine; and here Horace is Epicurean. 'Gather ye rosebuds while ye may' is an important part of his beliefs.

> Enjoy the present smiling hour,
> And put it out of Fortune's power....
> Happy the man—and happy he alone—
>   He who can call today his own,
>   He who, secure within, can say
> 'Tomorrow, do thy worst, for I have lived today:
>   Be fair or foul or rain or shine,
> The joys I have possessed in spite of Fate are mine,
>   Not Heaven itself upon the Past has power,
> But what has been, has been, and I have had my hour.'[2]

---

[1] Lord Dunsany, after Horace, *Odes*, II, x, 1–12.
[2] John Dryden (1631–1700), after Horace, *Odes*, III, xxix. Dryden writes of this that he tried 'to make it his masterpiece in English'.

Here is the unshakeable Stoic sage, pursuing the Mean in Peripatetic fashion, but making the most of its simple pleasures like a good Epicurean.

The reason why we must enjoy our modest pleasures, feels Horace, is that death is coming to us anyway; and there are those who have felt that he is at his greatest when he writes of life and death.

> Thaw follows frost; hard on the heel of spring
>   Treads summer sure to die, for hard on hers
> Comes Autumn, with his apples scattering;
>   Then back to wintertide, when nothing stirs.
> But oh, whate'er the sky-led seasons mar,
>   Moon after moon rebuilds it with her beams;
> Come we where Tullus and where Ancus are
>   And good Aeneas, we are dust and dreams.[1]

So the moral is to enjoy life while we can; 'the joys I have possessed in spite of Fate are mine'. And one of them, which death cannot reverse or cancel, a joy in which there is impregnable permanency, is human friendship. Horace was again an Epicurean in the high value which he placed upon personal friends. Many of his *Odes* are dedicated to friends—one of them to a 'Vergilius' who may well be Virgil. Horace also liked feminine society; but his friends are men. Perhaps his feeling towards these friends is, in the end, the most persistent feature of his many-sided character. And he makes it clear that he felt able to confer immortality on them by the dedication of his poems. 'Many heroes lived before Agamemnon; but all of them are pressed down by endless night...because they have no poet.'

> Vain was the chief's, the sage's pride.
> They had no poet, and they died.
> In vain they schemed, in vain they bled.
> They had no poet, and are dead.[2]

[1] A. E. Housman (1859–1936), from Horace, *Odes*, IV, vii, 9–16.
[2] Alexander Pope, after Horace, *Odes*, IV, ix, 25–8.

Horace's claim to bestow this immortality has been justified by his fame throughout the centuries. He has had gifts to give to most generations and to innumerable readers. When he died in 8 B.C., in the same year as his friend Maecenas—fifteen years after the publication of the first three Books of the *Odes*—he had already attained the fate, which he humorously deprecated, of becoming a school-book.

Horace was so good that he had scarcely any imitators. Subsequent Latin lyrics are scarce. The emperor Hadrian (A.D. 117–38), with a quite different lyricism, wrote a pathetic invocation to his own departing soul. There was a brief flash of lyric genius two (?) hundred years later when an unknown poet wrote a poignant hymn to the fading vision of Venus. St Ambrose's Christian hymns are lyrics of great purity and sincerity; and the greatest of the Christian Latin poets, Prudentius, wrote two books of original, arresting lyrics in varied metres.

The *Odes* of Horace did not enjoy their greatest repute in the Middle Ages. Medieval piety found them too little dependent on Providence, too much devoted to pleasure, and too infrequently concerned with moral matters. So they were felt to be 'of little use for our times' in comparison with the more frequently edifying *Satires* and *Epistles*. But the *Odes* came into their own at the dawn of the Renaissance. Its forerunner or founder, Petrarch, bought a manuscript of them in 1347. In his own writings he quotes Horace more often than any other poet with the single exception of Virgil. Since then, countless attempts have been made at the fascinatingly difficult task of translating these poems. Different aspects of them have attracted different ages and groups. In Britain the first man to be fully alive to the influence of Horace was Ben Jonson (1573–1637). Horace was his favourite poet—the Horace of the *Odes*, as well as of the *Satires* and *Epistles*. And Jonson's younger contemporary, Robert Herrick, is one of a number of men of that time who show a particular admiration for Horace's nature poetry. The *Odes* about life and death, too, were the models of countless seventeenth-century writers.

But meanwhile the turn of Horace's national *Odes* had come. Andrew Marvell (1621–78) recaptures Horace's grave fusion of ethics, religion and state affairs.

> 'Tis madness to resist or blame
> The force of angry heaven's flame;
>   And if we would speak true,
>   Much to the man is due,
> Who from his private gardens, where
> He lived reservèd and austere,
>   As if his highest plot
>   To plant the bergamot,
> Could by industrious valour climb
> To ruin the great work of Time,
>   And cast the kingdoms old
>   Into another mould.[1]

In the truly Horatian eighteenth century, too, the *Odes* which dealt with national matters were in favour with latter-day Augustuses such as Louis XIV and Frederick the Great. Not unnaturally, the same poems suffered a corresponding eclipse in the French Revolution. Horace's quiescence and acquiescence have sometimes caused impatience in progressive hearts. But William Wordsworth said that Horace was his favourite poet. This may be an unexpected choice; but both men were patriotic, both moralists, and both loved peace and quiet, and nature. And it seems that John Keats' *Ode to a Nightingale* owes much to Horace.

In our own day, the *Odes* are read less. For the artificial convention of this literary lyric is nowadays a hard obstacle to overcome. But controversy continues about the character and quality of Horace's poetic personality displayed in his poems. Yet his

---

[1] Andrew Marvell, *A Horatian Ode upon Cromwell's return from Ireland.*

personality is not enigmatic; but it is exceptionally many-sided. Together with Virgil, Horace represents the supreme efflorescence of classicism. He possesses that universality which Virgil also possessed—though Horace's gift, if less deep, spreads more widely. Horace's praise of the golden Mean does not indicate that his character was colourless. On the contrary, his character possessed great and rare qualities: but these illuminate and personify the Mean, for they are perfectly balanced and blended with each other.

Horace was satirist as well as lyric poet. But before anything can be said about his achievement in this field, some consideration must be given to the origins and character of this distinctive branch of Latin literature. 'Satire', says Quintilian, speaking from a national viewpoint, 'is all ours.'[1] He does not mean to imply by this that Greek Satire was non-existent, or that Roman Satire owed nothing to it. He means, rather, that this is a branch of literature and poetry in which Rome is pre-eminent; and that is true.

Moreover, the origins of Satire are, in part, Italian. Mention has already been made, in connection with Comedy, of Livy's record of a ceremony of 364 B.C. Now this ceremony, if Livy's description of it reflects part of the truth, had something to do with the origins not only of Comedy but of Satire as well. We are told that the ceremony started with Etruscan professional dancers; and that the Romans then imitated them, and added chanting, and later provided other refinements. And the more elaborate activity thus produced led the way both to drama and to this other literary form known to us as Satire, in which only the vocal content remains—the music and dancing have gone.

Indeed Livy actually uses the word 'Satire' for what developed quite early from these beginnings, while the music was still

[1] *Inst. Or.* x, i, 93.

there; he speaks of 'Satires set to music'. This chanting in time with a dance is not what we call satire today, but perhaps (though opinions differ) it is what Roman *satura* at first comprised. Later, however, *satura* became the description of a sort of poem—or a mixture of prose and verse. 'Mixture' is what it seems to mean; a mixture of different kinds of sketches of social life; of grave and gay, serious and comic. Nobody knows for certain what the origin of the word was. Some have argued that the meaning is related to food, to a kind of mixed salad. The root might be the same as that of *satis* = 'enough'; in which case a *satura* is a poem full of, 'stuffed' with, different materials, a 'hotch-potch'. But another theory rejects this derivation, and believes that the word comes from an Etruscan root *satr* 'to speak'. At all events, in Roman Satire, as it has come down to us, the vocal, verbal aspect finally excluded the dancing. Satire became a literary form, and not one intended for dramatic performance.

Like most literary forms, it owed a good deal of its impetus to Greek culture. As has been said, Quintilian's remark that Satire is 'all ours' must not be regarded as contradicting this assertion. Roman drama was overwhelmingly affected in the third century B.C. by Greek influence; and the same applies to Roman Satire. One significant ancestor of Roman Satire is the Athenian New Comedy of Menander. Other important Greek influences are those of popular philosophers. Typical of one group is Bion (fourth/third century B.C.). He was a kind of street-corner orator, who developed a witty and satirical, but crude, type of popular lectures which were called 'diatribes' (= leisure hours). Other Greeks of the Hellenistic period, for example Sotades (third century B.C.), carried on a tradition of moralising mixed with abuse, in iambic verse.

The Romans grafted these literary influences on to their native and primitive *satura*, and produced a literary form consisting of a 'mixture' of sketches with a moralising tone. As early as the second century B.C. there lived the 'founder of European Satire', Lucilius. Only 1,300 lines of his work have survived. But it is clear that John Dryden, Jonathan Swift and Alexander Pope stand in a line of succession which goes back to him. Literary *saturae* had started before him—Ennius in the days of Plautus had moralised in this *genre*—but it was Lucilius who made them what *we* call satirical, that is to say, critical of contemporary life and letters. Lucilius, like other distinguished writers of the day, was a friend of Scipio Aemilianus. But he risked the disapproval of other members of the governing class, with whom at least one dramatist (Naevius) had got into trouble for his criticisms. Lucilius, like contemporary politicians such as the Gracchi, sensed the democratic ideas that were in the air.

He was frank but not fanatical; he seems a genial amateur, whose standard was common sense. He owed a fair amount to men like Sotades and Bion, and adopted in Latin the vivid coarse style of utterance which Bion had employed in Greek. Lucilius regarded Satire as the 'mirror of life', and so wrote his hexameters in ordinary, popular language. He stamped his personality so strongly on the result that all later satirists have considered him their exemplar; no such claims have been made for Bion, Sotades and the like, of whom few people have heard. Lucilius possessed a peculiarly original talent. But his style was somewhat crude and slapdash in comparison with that of later masters. He naturally could not anticipate the artistry of the late Republic and Augustan Age, and Horace describes his writing as 'muddy'. Horace complains that Lucilius composed far too quickly: 'In an hour he often used to dictate 200 verses, as though this was a great achievement, "standing on one foot" [i.e. as an easy matter].' [1]

Lucilius wrote thirty books; at this rate the lines that have survived represent scarcely more than six hours' work! But Horace was prejudiced in his attitude to his predecessor, as is

[1] Horace, *Satires*, I, iv, 9.

shown by his comment that Lucilius was a mere imitator of Aristophanes and the classical Attic 'Old Comedy' of the fifth century B.C. This is a misleading observation, for there had been much Greek literature since then, and Lucilius' primary literary debt to Greece is rather concerned with the much later Hellenistic writers who have been mentioned.

Lucilius claimed that his criticism was for the good of society. This has always been said by every satirist and every critic of contemporary conditions. It is still said by every newspaper which tells of the seamy side of life. And the same traditional saying was often on the lips of the most famous of all the Roman writers who took to Satire, namely Horace. This idea fitted his general conception of the poet—a conception which he commended to his patron Augustus—as 'useful to the city', that is to say as educator and civiliser. Though he maintained much of his independence, he discussed the moral questions of the day with Maecenas and other people close to Augustus, and he felt he possessed a 'mission' to speak out on ethical problems. The Stoics had said that 'the good poet must first be a good man'. This was a widespread view among the ancients, and Horace, in his *Poetical Art* (*Ars Poetica*), similarly asserts that the first essential for a poet is moral philosophy.

So the hexameter poems which Horace called his *Talks* are of an ethical character. These comprise the *Satires* of his younger days, and the *Epistles* which followed them—the latter not professedly satirical, but in direct succession to his *Satires*. The *Satires* (Book I, c. 35 B.C.; Book II, c. 29 B.C.) are approximately contemporary with Virgil's *Georgics*—a little earlier than the *Cynthia* of Propertius. They were written by Horace in the youthful years which also produced his iambic *Epodes*; and the two collections of poems have something in common, since the subject-matter of both is largely critical and mordant. But the ancients would not have ranked the *Epodes* as Satire since their verse was iambic. According to the 'Doctrine of Kinds' the *genre* of iambic scurrilous verse was a distinct one; its ultimate Roman heritage is not Satire, but the epigram. True Roman Satire, a more important body of literature, was not in iambic verse but in another metre. Some satirists, it is true, strayed outside verse altogether on occasion, interlarding it with prose passages— such work was called 'Menippean' after the Greek Menippus of Gadara, imitated in Latin by Varro and Seneca—but the medium regarded as appropriate for Satire was the dactylic hexameter.

Horace, as has been said, disapproved of the hasty composition of Lucilius. Horace's hexameters, despite great debts to Virgil in details, do not aim at the latter's polished refinement, or at his subtlety or emotional effects. But they are rapid, vivid and graceful. They have an easy conversational fluency which is closer to the use of the same metre in Ovid's *Metamorphoses*; but Horace is the more colloquial and familiar, as befits the dialogue form of a number of his poems, and the superficial letter form of the *Epistles*.

The *Satires and Epistles* discuss questions of moral conduct. Here, for example, are some of the subjects of the *Satires*: the race for wealth and position; the folly of running to extremes; mutual forbearance; a defence of Satire; social and political ambition. Horace, for all his criticism of Lucilius' style, is using much the same sort of subject-matter as Lucilius had used. For example, the famous 'Journey to Brundusium'[1] with Maecenas is closely modelled on a Satire of Lucilius. But Horace's approach, with a few early exceptions, is closer to that of Lucilius' predecessor Ennius, whose treatment had tended to moralising rather than to severe criticism of society. Horace is also philosophical, closer than Lucilius to the moralising Hellenistic schools, and to Menander.

The maturest examples of such themes are to be found in Horace's *Epistles*, of which the greater part were published (shortly after *Odes* I–III) in 20–19 B.C.—not far from the publica-

[1] Horace, *Satires*, I, 5.

tion date of the *Aeneid*. Many people, especially in Britain, have regarded the *Epistles* as the best poems Horace wrote. He is called the 'poet of sanity', and they show him in this capacity. 'Idealised common sense' and 'the enthusiasm of moderation' are phrases used about the *Epistles*. Horace's *Epistles* are the expression of a highly civilised mind—of what the Romans called *urbanitas*. Their taste and their sense are both excellent. They are witty and charming, and they have a new grace of language and metre.

In the Middle Ages Horace's *Satires* and *Epistles* exercised much more influence than his *Odes* because of their moral tone. Their survival was owed to the initiative of Charlemagne and to the copying of Benedictine monks—though there was a strong tendency to copy out the more improving excerpts only. But in a single book of the eighth century we find no less than seventy-four citations of Horace. Half a millennium later it is still as 'satiro' that Dante values Horace. Three and four hundred more years passed, and in the seventeenth and eighteenth centuries these poems of Horace bore new and vigorous fruit; for they played their part in the Satire which is an ornament of English literature.[1] Ben Jonson and John Donne regarded Horace as their model. Much in Swift and Pope, as has been said, can be traced back ultimately to Lucilius. But so little of Lucilius was known to them, and Horace is an essential link in the chain—though both of the eighteenth-century writers (and Donne) lack his mildness, and their Satires are less philosophical and more contemporary. But Pope professes to be Horace's heir, and his brilliant *Imitations of Horace* keep fairly close to the original, while bringing his allusions up to date. In the same truly Horatian climate the essayists Addison and Goldsmith again reflect the spirit of the *Satires* and *Epistles*. But the appeal of Horace's friendly poems is permanent: 'in reading the *Satires* we all read our own minds and hearts'.

[1] Boileau is often the intermediary.

2. THE NEW ELEGY AND THE 'METAMORPHOSES': OVID

Ovid is the light of the middle and later years of Augustus. He was younger than the other leading elegists, and long outlived them. Much of his work belongs to a new era, and is of a new character. Virgil's *Aeneid* and Horace's *Secular Hymn* had not long been published when Roman society began to feel the inevitable reaction against their exalted imperialism. Love elegy had not long reached its summit under Propertius when a more blasé 'golden youth' began to feel a distaste for his strong expression of strong personal feeling—while equally deprecating the 'hearty', masculine double standard of feminine values displayed by Horace.

Ovid, like so many of his forerunners, was not a Roman; he came from Sulmo (Sulmona) in central Italy. But his father was a gentleman who gave him a fashionable Roman upbringing, and Ovid grew up to be the perfect representative of the less serious, more sophisticated smart society which now flourished at the capital. His diction reflects the new fashions of rhetorical education which he had experienced. Ovid's language moves rapidly, lightly and brilliantly. It unites perfectly with the elegiac metre. But this metre underwent a new interpretation at the hand of Ovid, in accordance with his talent and the spirit of the age. It became a more polished and refined medium than it had ever been before. Tibullus had pointed the path away from the passion and morbidity of Propertius. But with Ovid the flight becomes faster and lighter still, and there is little real seriousness left. He himself personifies the Elegiac Muse, no longer as 'tearful' according to the most familiar tradition, but as flippant and 'festive'. He develops this metre into a medium suited for the rapid production of satisfyingly neat effects of no very great profundity.

So a new era began, and was recognised to have begun, when soon after 16 B.C., Ovid published the first edition of his *Loves*

(*Amores*). At this time, Horace was setting his final signature to
the literary lyric by the preparation of his last *Odes*. The love-
elegies of Propertius and Tibullus had been known for more than
a decade. Ovid's *Amores* are love-poems too, as their title
indicates; but they are love-poetry of quite a new sort. Ovid is
not a poet of serious love. To him, love is as frivolous a subject as
it is to Horace. But Ovid, unlike Horace, has the Alexandrian
absorption in female psychology; Ovid understands the woman's
point of view. He 'possessed a...gift of sympathetic understanding often perceptible behind the gloss, the glitter, and the
cynicism of his society verse. A friend and a guide, he wants to
emancipate the fair sex from dullness and squalor.'[1]

The heroine of Ovid's verse is 'Corinna'. Twenty years later
he said that people were still asking who she was. Perhaps she
never existed. This is not subjective love-poetry, about passions
felt by Ovid himself. In case we did not notice this, he tells us so.
The *Amores* introduce us to the light-hearted Ovidian world, and
to the new, quick version of the elegiac metre which perfectly
reflects it. Only occasionally does Ovid show us what more he
could have done if he had wanted to. He is moving when he
writes of the death of Tibullus who had been his friend. More
often his regrets contain an element of mockery or humour—as
when he upbraids the tablets on which he had written an unfortunate love-letter:

> To these my love I foolishly committed,
> And then with sweet words to my mistress fitted.
> More fitly had they wrangling bonds contained
> From barbarous lips of some attorney strained.
> Among day-books and bills they had lain better,
> In which the merchant wails his bankrupt debtor.[2]

[1] R. Syme.
[2] Latin: 'in which the miser bewails his spent money'; and the 'attorney'
reads the bonds. Christopher Marlowe, after Ovid, *Amores*, I, xii, 21–6.

Ovid's second endeavour was called the *Heroides* ('heroines', i.e. legendary women). This is a collection of poetic letters. He himself describes them to us as letters (*epistulae*), recalling that Horace's first poetic *Epistles* were published a few years earlier. Most of these 'letters' of Ovid are ostensibly addressed by mythical ladies to their absent husbands or lovers. Unhappy love is the theme of the *Heroides*. Menander's Greek plays of the Athenian New Comedy had contained a love interest, but it is Ovid who handed down this permanently appealing theme to medieval and modern literature. His women's plaints are rhetorical and ingenious. They are presented with great vividness and modernity. Yet for literary purposes they are placed in the legendary epoch. This element of fantasy is an incentive to romance and adventurous excitement. It lends itself to an imaginative, lively vein, which foreshadows the romantics.

But Ovid often has his tongue in his cheek; and, even when he has not, this is not real, earnest love-poetry. The poet is almost feminine in his sensitiveness to his heroines, yet in writing of their passion he himself remains wholly dispassionate. He regards their psychological performances observantly and sympathetically, but with clinical objectivity. This interpretation of elegy was something new. So was Ovid's handling of the traditional myths. Quite gone is the reverence, the antique atmosphere with which Virgil had surrounded many old legends. Ovid's mythical heroines are entirely modernised, brought right up to date. They are, but for their names, ladies of the contemporary fashionable world.

They delighted the Middle Ages, and fostered the idea of knightly love—at times the letters were even believed to be real. They also delighted the Renaissance. Immediately after the invention of printing, editions of the *Heroides* were published in rapid succession: the first was printed at Rome in 1471, and there was a Venice edition twenty years later. An English translation appeared in 1567; and fifteen years later these poems engaged the attention of Christopher Marlowe, whose versions, however, were publicly burnt by order of the Church in 1599.

After the *Heroides*, Ovid hit on the idea of making fun—at one and the same time—of the love-elegy, of moralists, and of 'didactic' instructive poetry in general. He had already written in this vein 'On Painting the Face' (*Medicamina Faciei*). Soon after 1 B.C., he published his 'Art of Love' (*Ars Amatoria*). It pretends to treat of love didactically, as a science, and does so with a cynicism that is not typically Roman. At the same time this picture of Ovid as Professor of Love contains some of his maturest thoughts on life—for instance 'if you want to be loved, be lovable'. Macaulay described the *Ars Amatoria* as Ovid's best poem; and Goethe's *Roman Elegies* (1795) are prefaced by a motto from it, fittingly enough since Goethe knew Ovid better than he knew any other poet. In the intervals of ironic pedantry, the *Ars Amatoria* reverts to Ovid's prime talent of telling stories—to which his scintillating versification perfectly lent itself. These stories have won the fancy of many fine artists. Titian's 'Ariadne on Naxos' is said to be based, not on Catullus' famous poem on that subject, but on the version in Ovid's *Ars Amatoria*.

However, at the time of its publication, this poem flew against traditional respectability, and against the efforts of Augustus to revive the morals of Roman society. There was disapproval. Ovid himself bears witness to this by writing a conciliatory sequel, 'The Cures of Love' (*Remedia Amoris*). But this is too flippant to have reconciled any critics. Ovid did not at first experience imperial sanctions. But later, in A.D. 8, he was suddenly banished to a remote semi-barbarous frontier-post of the Empire, Tomis (Constanta in Roumania). During the remaining nine years of his life, including three under Augustus' successor Tiberius, he was never granted permission to return.

He himself describes the causes of his exile as two, 'a poem and a mistake'. The poem was presumably the *Art of Love*, but that had been published for quite a long time—perhaps eight years—before this bolt came from the blue. The 'mistake' was clearly regarded as the more serious reason for his downfall.

> The cause of this, too much to most revealed,
> Must be for ever by myself concealed.[1]

But Ovid suggests that he saw something he should not have seen. Now in A.D. 8, the year of Ovid's exile, it was disclosed that the emperor's grand-daughter Julia was involved in personal scandals. The emperor, with his official policy of moral improvement, did not tolerate this subversive activity in his own house; and she was disgraced—as her mother had been for similar reasons ten years earlier. Perhaps Ovid, banished in the same year, had seen misconduct by her, regarded as of political significance, which he ought to have reported.

For a townsman and a metropolitan like Ovid, the fate was a terrible one. At the time when it descended upon him, two important works were well under way. The *Metamorphoses*, in hexameters, were nearly ready. The *Fasti*, a calendar of the Roman year in elegiac verse, were about half finished; six out of the twelve books were complete. Ovid, having tried mock-didactic elegy in the *Ars Amatoria*, was now using the same metre for didactic that is more serious—though nothing written by Ovid can be wholly serious for long. This poetic calendar includes descriptions of festivals, religious rites, legends and historical events. The origins and antique customs of Rome were a time-hallowed subject for poetry, going back to Ennius. Ovid discusses them in something of the spirit of the Alexandrian master Callimachus, whose most famous poem had been his *Causes* (*Aitia*). The precedents of Callimachus and Ennius had likewise helped to inspire Virgil's talent for the antiquarian folk-lore of Italy.

But those three, the Greek and the two Romans, had written

---

[1] John Gower (*c.* 1635), after Ovid, *Tristia*, IV, x, 99 f.

in hexameters. The earliest surviving elegiac poetry dealing with such archaeological topics is from the hand of Propertius. In his later years, disappointed in love and encouraged by Maecenas, he had turned increasingly to the antiquities of Rome—but had retained his own elegiac metre, thus creating a new elegiac *genre* which Ovid now adapts to his own uses in the *Fasti*. Propertius had shown a profound insight into the romance of the legends, handling them with a power worthy of Virgil; Ovid is, rather, inclined to use these myths as a piquant source-book for his special gifts, including, now, an increased dexterity and neatness in his interpretation of the elegiac couplet.

Thus Ovid, too, became a national patriotic poet. He himself remarks what a strange thought this was. But it was evidently not enough for the emperor; or it was too late. It was sadly ironical that the patriotic *Fasti* should have been in progress when the order for his exile arrived. The poem was published, as far as it went, only after his death, with a dedication—added by him in his exile—to the heir presumptive Germanicus.

Ovid continued to write elegiac poetry from Tomis; and to express his grief at his banishment he had recourse to the epistolary form which he had used to such effect in the *Heroides*. The first collection published after his exile consisted of five books of *Lamentations* (*Tristia*), and they were followed by the *Letters from the Black Sea* (*Epistulae ex Ponto*). There is also the *Ibis*, a vigorous curse, and the *Nux*, a nut-tree's lamentation about the stones thrown at it. All these naturally lack the gaiety of earlier work, and Ovid grovels humiliatingly to the great. But the poems are of value for their personal and biographical indications; and his skill in handling the elegiac couplet is unimpaired.

His version of this couplet—not those of Catullus and Propertius—served as the model for successive generations. Rome never produced a rival to Ovid, though there are flashes of beauty in the elegies—four centuries later—of the last 'classical' poets, Ausonius and Claudian.

When Ovid was exiled, he had almost completed his most considerable and influential work, the *Metamorphoses* (*Transformations*). In disgust at his fate, he burnt the manuscript. But there were copies, and the work survived. Unlike all his poetry that has been mentioned, the *Metamorphoses* are in hexameters. They consist of fifteen books—the length of the major epic for which this metre was traditionally adapted. But this is not an epic. Ovid tells us that he did not attempt that *genre*, since he believed it to be beyond his powers—though he wrote a highly successful tragedy, the *Medea* (which is lost).

Instead of an epic, Ovid achieved something which the Latin language had never seen before, and he was aware that it was his most important work. This is a very long poem. It consists of over two hundred stories; they have one thing in common. They are all tales of magic changes of shape, a frequent theme from Homer onwards—they are about legendary people transformed into animals, or birds, or trees, or flowers, or stones.

> In all the world there is not that that standeth at a stay:
> Things ebb and flow, and every shape is made to pass away.[1]

The poet himself describes the theme by the simple phrase 'changed forms', which echoes the titles of Hellenistic didactic collections—though Ovid's poem is not didactic.[2] It might not be thought that such a collection as the *Metamorphoses* could possess sufficient unity to be a work of art. But the unity is there, just as there is unity in the *Arabian Nights*—or rather there is more unity in Ovid's poem, since the subjects of its stories are similar;

[1] Arthur Golding (1565-7), after Ovid, *Met.* xv, 177-8.
[2] He wrote a shorter didactic hexameter poem, the *Halieutica*, about Black Sea fishes.

and the same fabulous romantic atmosphere pervades them all. And Ovid did not want the resemblance to the epic to be any closer. He relied on his gift for narrative to carry him through.

Like other Roman masterpieces, the *Metamorphoses* owe much of their success to harmony between language and metre. Ovid does not make the mistake of emulating—for his very different subject—the grandeur of Lucretius. Nor, in spite of innumerable linguistic echoes, does he aim at the subtle, profound diction and rhythm of Virgil; nor are his verses conversational, like those of Horace's *Satires* and *Epistles*. Ovid adapts the hexameter to his own purposes, and makes something new of it. His verse races lightly along, with scintillations not very different from those of his elegies, though now displayed on a wider canvas lacking the limitations imposed by couplets. He does not attempt, or need, the architectural periods of Virgil, and their varieties of resonance. But the swift hexameter of Ovid takes its place next to Virgil's line as an unequalled interpretation of this greatest of ancient metres.

Like other Greek and Roman masters, Ovid achieves his success, and even—paradoxically it would seem to us—his originality, by a masterly use of partial precedents. In a sense, and in parts, this collection of stories recalls the technique of the miniature epics, which had come into fashion among certain 'Alexandrian' Greeks and had been cleverly attempted by Catullus and other Romans of the late Republic and Augustan Age.[1] A feature of these miniature epics had been their characteristically Alexandrian concern with psychology, and not least with feminine psychology. The *Heroides* had shown Ovid's keen interest in such themes; and his *Metamorphoses*, too, lent itself aptly to them. For the transformations which are their subject were caused by vicissitudes of love—such as the jealousy of gods or goddesses, and the vengeance of indignant lovers. Ovid shows great virtuosity

[1] The mock-heroic *Culex* ('Gnat') may belong to the later Augustan period.

in his portrayal of such crises, and he dwells with special insight on the temperaments of his heroines. These are particularly well displayed by set speeches, which give Ovid an opportunity to show the declamatory talents he had derived from a rhetorical education. But he aims less at elaborate, introspective analyses than at vivid pictures; and their vividness is unforgettable.

Ovid has shown in earlier works, and was showing again in his *Fasti*, something of what he could do with the tales of Greek mythology. Perhaps his greatest gift to literature is the vigorous life he gave to these myths in the *Metamorphoses*. Today the mythological allusions in ancient poetry seem to be one of its most difficult (and boring) features. But they were of vital importance, because they were the intellectual stock-in-trade of many educated Greeks and Romans. All of us have mental and verbal symbols which we use for the concise expression of our ideas; and the myths, which seem so elaborate and complicated to us, richly fulfilled this role for the ancients—and fulfilled it again, owing to Ovid's inspired handling, for the Middle Ages and Renaissance.

The great Athenian dramatists had seen and exploited the immense tragic—and even comic—potentialities of the myths, and the moral dilemmas latent in them. The Alexandrians had studied them with meticulous care. Ovid, like them, was learned; his knowledge and memory must have been portentous. But, unlike many of them, he did not make heavy weather of his learning. He gave the old legends new life, by the vigour of his imagination and fancy. He had always felt himself pulled in two directions, by the real world and by an imaginary world which he aspired to make his own. Here he conquers this imaginary world and makes it real to us—and real to his contemporaries, for this poem, like his elegies, was peopled by moderns whom they could see around them.

The legendary personages are divested of the grandeur of venerable antiquity. So are the gods. The parts that they play

are often unheroic: they are shady, seedy figures. This poem
deals with a vast range of the Roman religious background; yet
its general effect is irreligious. It could hardly have been welcomed by Augustus as an ally in his campaign to revive national
religion—though Ovid gracefully pictures Augustus, not indeed
in the central role, but as the last of the miracles. On the gods,
he has a neat but 'hard-boiled' comment: 'It is expedient that
there should be gods, and in accordance with expediency let us
suppose that there are gods.' This epigram belongs to the *Ars
Amatoria*, but the gods of the *Metamorphoses* are depicted in the
same spirit. Yet in other respects the latter is the least cynical of
all Ovid's poems. There is, it is true, a deficiency of heroics; there
is also perhaps a certain lack of depth. But there is an intuitive
and romantic quality. Ovid loves young people; and he loves
natural scenes and colours.

> O lovely Galatea, whiter far
> Than falling snows and rising lilies are;
> More flowery than the meads; as crystal bright;
> Erect as alders, and of equal height....
> Than apples fairer, when the boughs they lade;
> Pleasing as winter suns, or summer shade:
> More grateful to the sight than goodly planes,
> And softer to the touch than down of swans....
> More clear than ice, or running streams, that stray
> Through garden plots, but ah! more swift than they!
> Like sliding streams, impossible to hold;
> Like them fallacious—like their fountains, cold.[1]

This is 'Greek, though coloured by Italian vivacity, sensuousness
and love of Nature'.[2]

Ovid was the poet of a younger generation than that of

---

[1] Thomas Dryden, after Ovid, *Met.* XIII, 789–90, 793–7, 799, 801. In
the first and second lines Ovid wrote 'whiter than a snowy white shrub',
and in the last line 'more violent than a stream'.   [2] W. Y. Sellar.

Augustus—a generation which had not, like its forerunners, spent early manhood amid chaos and war. Ovid and his generation were well suited to each other. He was a modern, and was pleased to be. He tells us so: 'Let old-fashioned things please others. I am glad that I was not born until just when I was. *This* is the age which suits my ways.'[1] Critics of later generations, for example Quintilian, had severe things to say of Ovid's infatuation with his own cleverness, of his inability to leave well alone. But the influence of the *Metamorphoses* on medieval and later times has been immense. Its amorous, picturesque diversity, as interpreted by the medieval mind, opened the gate to romance. It is true that, when the idea of Romantic Love developed in about the twelfth century, its causes were in part Christian—the veneration of the Virgin Mary, and contempt of bodily hardship. But prominent among the other sources of inspiration was Ovid, with his quick and sensitive response to personal feeling and to nature. The poems which led the way were, to a lesser extent, the *Amores* and the *Heroides*, but in particular the *Metamorphoses*. In the thirteenth century this poem was translated into Greek and thus made accessible to the Eastern repository of culture, the Byzantine Empire. This was truly an 'Ovidian period' of the Middle Ages. And in the following century Chaucer knew Ovid much better than he knew any other Latin writer—he, again, was familiar with the *Metamorphoses*, to which he pays special tribute. It was an inexhaustible reservoir of stories—and of material for pictures, since the great word-pictures of this poem have been a major source of inspiration to Renaissance painters.

For wider reasons—for his wit and grace as well as his subjects—Ovid, far more than any other ancient poet, was the master and model of the Renaissance, and of the English Elizabethan Age. Edmund Spenser's *Faerie Queene* (1590–6) is steeped in Ovid. Moreover, the influence of the *Metamorphoses* on Shakespeare

[1] *Ars Amatoria*, III, 121–2.

himself—though he knew far less Latin than Spenser—is again so pervasive that it deserves a book to itself. This work of Ovid contains a treasure of poetic material from which Shakespeare—as well as a host of others—drew extensively. Like Christopher Marlowe's *Hero and Leander* before it, Shakespeare's youthful poem *Venus and Adonis* is wholeheartedly Ovidian. In his plays, too, critics have detected allusions to every one of the fifteen books of Ovid's poem. In Shakespeare's Cleopatra, for instance, scholars have claimed to see the influence of Ovid's Dido in the *Metamorphoses*—rather than the Dido of the *Aeneid*. It is Ovid, and particularly the Ovid of the *Metamorphoses*, who provided the mythological allusions which Shakespeare, in accordance with a contemporary taste alien from our own, so prodigally provided. Without going into the vexed question of his capacity (if any) to read Latin in the original, it may be pointed out that the whole of the *Metamorphoses* had, after a fashion, been translated into English by Arthur Golding in 1565–7; and thereby it made a great impact on Shakespeare's mind and poetry. Ovid's vivacious imagination, and preoccupation with love and the supernatural, appealed especially to that age—and to Shakespeare himself. 'Ovidius Naso was the man', is the sentiment ascribed to the schoolmaster in *Love's Labour's Lost*: 'and why indeed, Naso, but for smelling out the odoriferous flowers of fancy, the jerks of invention?'

His influence continued to be potent. At first sight there is a profound contrast between Ovid and the solemn Milton. Yet the latter's poetry shows a large number of detailed echoes of the *Metamorphoses*. Later, too, the heroic couplets of Dryden, Matthew Prior and Pope are Ovidian. In the nineteenth century, taste in love-poetry took a new and more 'lyrical' turn—using the word in the modern sense—but Ovid himself continued to receive praise. Wordsworth and Shelley reveal their debts to him; and Keats expressed the belief that a poet could have no more delightful material than the *Metamorphoses*.

3. POST-AUGUSTAN POETRY

The poetical events of the half-century after Augustus' death included new developments of the iambic metre. The climax of Roman iambic verse-writing had long passed, with the comic drama of Plautus and Terence. No great comedies were written after the latter's death; but the iambic still had an interesting and varied history ahead of it. Catullus and Horace (*Epodes*) had revived the traditional connection of this metre with personal attacks and ridicule, a tradition associated with the names of two early Greeks, Archilochus of Paros (eighth or seventh century B.C.) and Hipponax of Ephesus (sixth century B.C.). The iambic was also used for that semi-literary, topical form of stage sketch known as the 'mime'; it was appropriate to this colloquial, scarcely literary *genre*, since the ancients regarded the iambic as the metre nearest to conversation.

Soon after the death of Augustus, the Latin iambic was interestingly adapted to another popular, traditional form of literature, the Fable. In its most characteristic form, the kind of story which we know as a 'Fable' is a moral tale, about animals more often than not, though sometimes the subjects are human beings or even inanimate objects. The Latin master of the iambic Fable was a Thracian slave of the early Principate called Phaedrus. The Fable had been, occasionally and incidentally, employed by earlier writers—especially satirists—but as far as we know Phaedrus was the first Latin writer to concentrate on this form. He may have found it a useful convention at a time when it was imprudent to write too freely. But, even so, we hear that he suffered from the suspicions of Tiberius' chief minister Sejanus.

Phaedrus is unusual among Latin writers in that he wrote, not like most of them for educated people or for a clique, but for the general public. So he may be compared with Plautus, who had written for the people (in an earlier version of this same conversational metre) over two hundred years before. But this is a rare phenomenon in Latin literature, and it gives Phaedrus a special interest. Moreover, he was successful: his fables were evidently best-sellers. He was wholly ignored by the serious critics: less than ten years after his latest work, Seneca the Younger could even remark that the Fable was 'unattempted by Roman genius'. But influential best-sellers are often ignored by the critics; and neither circulation nor influence was lacking to Phaedrus, even in his own day. Nor has Seneca's neglect been endorsed by posterity.

Phaedrus was not, indeed, wholly original. His *Fables* were based on Greek collections of similar tales which went by the name of one Aesop, who was reported to have been a Phrygian slave and hunchback living in the sixth century B.C. But it was not until three hundred years after that date that the *Fables* bearing Aesop's name had been collected and published; so their actual authorship is, and will always be, obscure. At about the time of Phaedrus, a Greek named Babrius made another, revised, collection. In about the fifth century A.D. a much inferior Latin writer Avianus published a further book of *Fables*, deriving his material chiefly from Babrius; and in medieval times it was perhaps Avianus rather than Phaedrus who exercised the greatest influence.

This sort of literature became popular in the Middle Ages. Prose versions of the *Fables*, through one intermediary or another, were widely current. They enjoyed great vogue in France. In the fifteenth century, the Scottish Chaucerian Henryson published *Moral Fables of Aesop*. In many countries, stories such as 'The Wolf and the Lamb', 'The Fox and the Sour Grapes', have become classics. In 1690 it was remarked that Aesop was 'agreed by all ages since for the greatest master in his kind'.[1] But later writers and critics recognised the role of Phaedrus. The *Fables* of La Fontaine, in the early eighteenth century, have been described as 'mainly Phaedrus transmuted from silver to gold'.

[1] Sir William Temple.

It is to these post-Augustan years too—by an accident of survival—that we must postpone a brief consideration of another and very different use of the Roman iambic, for tragic drama. Of Roman tragedies intended for stage-production practically nothing has survived. In the third and second centuries B.C., Livius Andronicus, Naevius and Ennius had all written tragedies as well as comedies; a nephew of Ennius—Pacuvius—and his younger contemporary Accius specialised in the former. It is doubtful if we should have found them as interesting as Roman comic drama; certainly they were strange distortions of their Greek forerunners by Aeschylus, Sophocles and Euripides. The Romans liked in tragedy just what the twentieth century deplores—flamboyant melodrama, the incredible and violent, ghosts rattling their chains. Modern taste has different preferences. So had the Attic tragedians; though Euripides had relaxed their classical austerity, and Roman tragedy was nearer to Euripides than to the other Attic dramatists—but still not very near.

Lost, also, are two famous Augustan tragedies, the *Thyestes* of Varius (a friend of Virgil and Horace), and the *Medea* of Ovid. The latter no doubt showed the point and brilliance that Ovid owed to the newly fashionable rhetorical education. From a later date, nine plays of Seneca the Younger survive, in addition to his philosophical essays and letters (and a Satire). But these plays were evidently intended for recitation rather than production— except, possibly, in Nero's private theatre. The iambics in which all but the choruses are written are scarcely recognisable as the metre of Plautus. For centuries had elapsed between the two writers, and those centuries had witnessed the cultural changes described in the previous chapters of this book.

In particular, Ovid had shown the effect which rhetoric could exert on Latin poetry. And Seneca the Younger—like most imperial poets—is influenced by Ovid, and no doubt particularly by Ovid's famous lost tragedy. Seneca, son of the greatest imperial rhetorician, illustrates above all other writers—in his tragedies as in his prose works—the invasion of literature by rhetoric. These plays contain every possible antithesis, word-play, point and mannerism of Silver Latin. They are brilliantly epigrammatic. But the taste of today is likely to find them mechanical and tiring.

Rhetoric is here the servant of philosophy; Seneca the rhetorician is a Stoic moralist—and also a true 'eclectic' of his age, who can eloquently lay claim to rationalist Epicurean views concerning idle fears of death:

> We...to that mass of matter shall be swept
> Where things destroyed with things unborn are kept.
> Devouring Time swallows us whole,
> Impartial Death confounds body and soul.
> For Hell and the foul Fiend that rules
> The everlasting fiery goals,
> Devised by rogues, dreaded by fools,
> With his grim grisly dog that keeps the door,
> Are senseless stories, idle tales,
> Dreams, whimsies, and no more.[1]

Seneca stresses horrors, and his plays contain much that is morbid and blood-curdling, for such topics were excellently suited to the scintillations of rhetoric.

Many such horrors are echoed and imitated by dramatists of the sixteenth and seventeenth centuries. The influence of Seneca's tragedies on these is persistent and pervasive, and it is they—rather than the Athenian plays—which were the models for the classical French drama, and for the tragic poetry of Elizabethan and Jacobean Britain, when 'every schoolboy with a smattering of Latin had a verse or two of Seneca in his memory'.[2] His plays awoke an echo in the Elizabethan taste for bombast. Ben Jonson draws heavily on them; and they exercised a vast—direct or

---

[1] John Wilmot, Earl of Rochester (1647–80), after Seneca, *Troades*, ll. 400–8. This is a choral passage.   [2] T. S. Eliot.

indirect—influence on Shakespeare, who 'married the manner of Seneca to the matter of Plutarch'.[1]

But Shakespeare's matter, too, is often Senecan. Ghosts, revenge, treachery, bloodthirsty murder, blends of heroism and insanity, cruel tyrants, all show this ancestry—though the 'tragedy of blood' owes much to another of Seneca's progeny, the Italian Renaissance drama. There is a good deal of Seneca in *Julius Caesar* and *Macbeth*; *Hamlet* is quite like a Senecan play, only far better; and from Seneca, too, comes much of the hopeless fatalism in *King Lear*. 'Seneca was near enough to Renaissance exuberance to appeal to it as a model; classic enough, when taken as a model, to impose upon it a wholesome sense of structure and style...if you seek his memorial, look round on the tragic stage of England, France and Italy.'[2]

Two clever young men, Stoics like Seneca but some forty years junior to him, contributed in rhetorical but highly individual fashion to Roman hexameter poetry. One of these was Persius, who wrote six Satires in the reign of Nero and died at the age of twenty-eight. He was well-born, prosperous and a 'high-brow' who wrote for 'high-brows'. He owes a great deal to the earlier satirists Lucilius and Horace. But in Persius there is more Stoic philosophy and morality—a Stoicism more of the 'ivory tower' than that of Seneca, and learnt not only from him but from another contemporary philosopher, Cornutus. In Persius, too, there is a Stoic abruptness of phrase that was new to Satire. He is also capable of charming, natural descriptions. But often his terseness, though it makes arresting and vivid pictures, leads to contortion and obscurity.

Persius lacked humour. He 'was a poet of the closet, a student, a recluse, full of youthful enthusiasm, living in a retired atmosphere

[1] Through Sir Thomas North's translation of a French version.
[2] F. L. Lucas.

under the shelter of loving female relatives'.[1] Yet an ancient biography tells us that the slender book of his *Satires* enjoyed—no doubt in a circle of rarefied tastes—immediate admiration and success. Towards the end of the first century A.D., as we learn from the epigrammatist Martial, this reputation was still unimpaired: and Quintilian calls it an authentic one.

At that date Persius was already in the hands of scholars and commentators, who were challenged and attracted by his stylistic peculiarities. The early Christian Fathers admired him for another reason: his harsh, though impersonal, moral denunciation of current evils. In the Elizabethan period he was the model for young men in revolt against contemporary abuses.[2] For example John Donne published three *Satires* in 1593—but six years later the archbishop of Canterbury gave orders that no more 'satires or epigrams' should be printed. Thereafter, the satirical spirit seems at first to have flowed into drama; and it may be that the influence of Persius is apparent in Shakespeare's older contemporary, Ben Jonson.

Five years younger than Persius was another Stoic poet, Seneca's nephew Lucan (b. A.D. 39). Perhaps the two young poets shared the same master, Cornutus. But unlike Persius, who remained withdrawn from the public scene, Lucan became a friend (and expressed admiration) of his fellow-poet and senior by two years, the emperor Nero. All three men died young. Nero was killed in A.D. 68, when he was thirty-one; Persius had died at twenty-eight, six years earlier; and Lucan met his death midway between these two dates, at the age of twenty-six. Nero's friendship had turned—for reasons that are disputed—to an estrangement, which led Lucan to join a conspiracy against him; the plot was discovered, and Lucan was forced to commit suicide.

But this short life was full of poetical activity. Its surviving

[1] G. G. Ramsay.   [2] He influenced Rabelais and Montaigne.

monument is the ten-book hexameter poem *The Civil War* (*Bellum Civile*), often known to us as the *Pharsalia* after the battle of Pharsalus in Thessaly, in which Caesar overcame Pompey. Virgil's epic achievement might have seemed likely to put an end to epic poetry. But Lucan is trying something different. His epic deals with a historical subject—fairly recent history, the civil war between Pompey and Caesar, to which Virgil had devoted only a few poignant phrases.

Historical epic was as old as Ennius' *Annals*, and quite lately it had been attempted by several poets under rhetorical influences. Lucan, while setting himself this same difficult task, deliberately dispenses with the gods and their intervention in human affairs, which had formed the traditional machinery of the epic. His chief historical source was apparently Livy (whose own books relating to this period, however, are lost). Livy had written vividly; but, in Lucan's epic poem, the colour is heightened still further for purposes of drama and Stoic-Republican morality.

In particular, consecutive narrative is replaced by episodes, selected for their impressive and illustrative character (occasionally they are fictitious—for example, the speech before Pharsalus of Cicero, who was not there). These episodes are often depicted with a harrowing, morbid realism akin to the tragedies of Lucan's uncle Seneca. We are told of the nightmares of warriors before battle; and of the portents announcing fratricidal war.

> Lamenting Ghosts amidst their ashes mourn,
> And groanings echo from the marble urn.
> The rattling clank of arms is heard around,
> And voices loud in lonely woods resound....
> A Fury fierce about the city walks,
> Hell-born and horrible of size she stalks;
> A flaming pine she brandishes in air,
> And hissing loud uprise her snaky hair....[1]

[1] Lucan, *Bell. Civ.* I, 568–70, 572–4, tr. N. Rowe (1718).

From the first, critics observed that Lucan, who had a rhetorical upbringing, wrote poetry of a superlatively rhetorical quality. Quintilian seems to recognise that this had been welcome to contemporary taste, but he expresses the personal opinion that Lucan went too far—so far, indeed, that he should serve as a model for orators rather than poets. In the *Pharsalia* there is every rhetorical device—all the fireworks that Silver Latin culture could provide. Lucan is spectacular. Yet he has a very real flame of genius to display—a fervour which still burns vividly in many exciting and moving epigrams.

Caesar is by no means the hero of Lucan's poem. Indeed, as Lucan became less friendly with Nero, it seems that his dislike of Caesar increased. And, though the real Pompey was himself scarcely a heroic figure, there is passion and grandeur in Lucan's fierce contrast between his services to Rome and his miserable death on a distant shore.

> Perhaps, when flames their dreadful ravage make
> Or groaning earth shall from the centre shake;
> When blasting dews the rising harvest seize,
> Or nations sicken with some dire disease;
> The Gods, in mercy to us, shall command
> To fetch our Pompey from the accursed land....
> Perhaps Fate wills, in honour to thy fame,
> No marble shall record thy mighty name.
> So may thy dust, e'er long, be worn away,
> And all remembrance of thy wrongs decay:
> Perhaps a better Age shall come, when none
> Shall think thee ever laid beneath this stone....[1]

Such tragedy and pathos owe much to Seneca, though Lucan has a sense of the historic Roman community which Seneca, in his preoccupation with personal perfection, had hardly possessed. In this respect, as in others, Lucan's debt is to Virgil. Yet the spirit

[1] Lucan, *Bell. Civ.* VIII, 846–50, 865–70, tr. N. Rowe.

of the *Pharsalia* is not Virgil's. Since his day, there had been Ovid, and the coming of rhetoric to poetry; and the influence of Ovidian dexterity is apparent here.

Lucan's poem has been described as a 'magnificent failure'. But it had not been judged a failure throughout the intervening centuries. Roman poetry showed many debts to it; and then, in the Middle Ages, it enjoyed a great reputation, partly for the somewhat unexpected reason that it served as a historical source-book. Its vividness led to many imitations in early French heroic poetry—and to many more in the classical age of French drama. It contributed greatly also to the more elevated and grandiose forms of Elizabethan poetical diction.

In the nineteenth century, controversy raged about the merits of the *Pharsalia*. French opponents of Victor Hugo compared the two writers as distorters of literary standards. But, before that, Macaulay had spoken of Lucan in superlative terms; and Shelley wrote of his poem as showing genius transcending Virgil's. Shelley came to modify this opinion, but he remained an admirer of Lucan's burning poetical power—and also of his hatred for tyrants. But his rhetoric has not yet endeared him to the twentieth century.

Three epic poets slightly older than Lucan, or of about the same age, long outlived him—Silius Italicus, Valerius Flaccus and Statius. Silius' theme was the career of Hannibal, but the others reverted to mythological themes.[1]

To us it seems that a more interesting poetic achievement of the later first century A.D. lies in the field of epigram, in which one of these poets, Statius, was likewise active. Catullus had shown what skill and force the Roman epigram could achieve. Poets of the early Empire wrote short poems, again in various metres, which lack his epigrammatic 'sting' but possess a miniature

[1] Epic poetry was revived in the late fourth century by Claudian, 'the last of the classics', whom Coleridge preferred to Virgil.

beauty that reminds us of the Greek epigram. Among such poets are Petronius under Nero—his novel known to us as the *Satyricon* has been described—and the Neapolitan Statius under Domitian.

Statius wrote five books called the *Silvae*—lost in medieval times, until 1417—containing thirty-two fluent and polished poems, with debts to the Alexandrian 'miniature epic' as well as to epigrammatists. One of these, in hexameters, is about *Sleep*.

> Quiet are the brawling streams: the shuddering deep
> Sinks, and the rounded mountains feign to sleep.
> The high seas slumber pillowed on Earth's breast;
> All flocks and birds and beasts are stilled in rest.
> But my sad eyes their nightly vigil keep.[1]

The whole poem is nineteen lines long, and its brief, graceful completeness has suggested comparisons with a sonnet. It has something haunting and unfamiliar which has helped to inspire our own poets, such as the Scots humanist Drummond of Hawthornden, to compose sonnets on this same theme.

But these short poems of Statius are not epigrams in the modern sense, which demands wit or at least 'point'. The Latin writer who gave this meaning to the word was Statius' Spanish contemporary Martial. Despite poverty and the consequent need—for most of his life—for servility, he wrote twelve books of epigrams containing 1561 poems. A few are of hexameters, but most employ the metres (and some of the spirit) of Catullus.[2] Yet, despite its varied and borrowed metres, Martial deliberately differentiated the epigram from other literary *genres*. He claims that this form of poetry, for all its lightness and flippancy, is capable of quality and merit: 'Believe me, Flaccus, a man who calls epigrams mere jokes and frivolities does not know what they are.'[3]

[1] Statius, *Silvae*, v, iv, 3–8, tr. W. H. Fyfe.
[2] Some iambic, 77 'limping' iambic, 238 hendecasyllabic, 1,235 elegiac.
[3] Martial, IV, xlix.

Though the epigram was clearly suited to a time that loved 'point' as the Silver Age did—like our own eighteenth century— yet Martial is the only poet of that Age who is quite exempt from its rhetorical tendencies. His epigrams have a more direct sting. Like other writers of the day, he execrated Domitian (when that emperor was dead). It was hardly worth while, he says, to have had Domitian's good father Vespasian and brother Titus at the price of having Domitian:

> How much thy third has wronged thee, Flavian race!
> 'Twere better ne'er to have bred the other brace.[1]

Another couplet directed against a certain Sabidius has achieved a wide fame through adaptations in our own language.

> I do not love you, Dr Fell.
> But why I cannot tell.
> But this I know full well;
> I do not love you, Dr Fell.[2]

A number of other epigrams by Martial carry abuse too far to be printable.

But many more show the poet as a kind-hearted man with simple tastes, an appreciation of natural beauty, and a sensitive knowledge of the human soul. The pungency of many of his short poems is not unprofound. It is not enough to call him the 'laureate of triviality'; though a rather unworthy prince of the second century A.D., Aelius Caesar (Hadrian's heir), was either misguided or, more probably, joking when he described Martial as 'his Virgil'. Nearly seventeen hundred years later, Martial's thirteenth book, containing *Xenia* (= presents for guests—single couplets like cracker-mottoes), served as a model for Goethe and

[1] Anon., after Martial; scholiast to Juvenal, IV, 38.
[2] Tom Brown (1681), after Martial, I, xxxii. Tom Brown was an Oxford undergraduate, Dr Fell his Dean.

Schiller, who wrote similar *Xenien* to make fun of their literary opponents.

The epigram, like the iambic, is closely akin to Satire; the epigrammatist Martial influenced his younger friend, the satirist Juvenal. The origins and earlier history of Roman Satire have been described elsewhere. Juvenal is its most extraordinary exponent. He wrote sixteen Satires in the early second century A.D., under Trajan and Hadrian. Juvenal and the historian Tacitus are the men who prove that this was an age of literary genius, and that it is wrong indeed to suppose that great literature ended with Augustus.

Juvenal is forcible and impressive. He is realistic, unlike the cloistered Persius. He is violent, and the effect is remote from the urbane mockery of Horace. He himself was conscious that, in his hands, Satire had become different. He recognises that critics devoted to the Doctrine of Kinds will see in his work a grandeur appropriate to tragedy rather than to Satire. 'You say, this is a new invention, and Satire takes on the buskin of tragedy, and going beyond the limits and laws of those before me I mouth a grand theme in the tones of Sophocles...'[1]—or the tones of epic. For Juvenal not only, like satirists before him, borrows the metre of epic poetry, the hexameter, but, unlike them, invests it with a truly epic solemnity, an epic weight and magnificence. Each hexameter is a fresh hammer-blow, a whip-lash. He employs concisely, vigorously and with brevity the diction of the Silver Age. His language shows a careful study of Virgil; but his rhythm has a good deal in common with 'Silver' epic poetry, for instance that of Lucan.

Lucan had displayed the influence of rhetoric, but nowhere is this so dominant as in Juvenal, who is, 'first and last, a rhetorician'. His skill in this technique is one of his claims to genius. He uses

[1] Juvenal, *Satires*, VI, 634–5.

all the devices of rhetoric, and they lead him to fantastic exaggerations. Yet he has control, even of his exaggerations. It is not surprising to learn from an ancient biographer that he had for years been addicted to declamation and had practised his verses aloud. It has been observed that, while Horace had seemed to be talking to a friend, Juvenal always addresses an audience. And how violently he addresses them! The sixteen Satires which have come down to us—probably the bulk of what he wrote—are a torrent of relentless abuse, of crushing epigrams and cruel parodies. His tension never relaxes.

He was apparently poor—like his friend Martial. Juvenal emerges as a man with a fierce, hopeless sense of failure and injustice.

> What should I do at Rome? I have not learnt
> The art of lying. If a book be bad,
> I cannot praise and ask to take it home.
> I am ignorant of the movements of the stars.
> I neither will nor can promise a son
> His father's death. The entrails of a frog
> Never did I inspect. . . .
> From me no thief can expect aid; and so
> No Governor will appoint me to his staff:
> 'Tis just as though I were a poor maimed trunk
> With crippled hands, of no use any more.
> Who nowadays is courted, save a man
> Privy to some guilt, whose mind seethes and burns
> With things that must never be disclosed?[1]

Juvenal has no talent for arrangement or characterisation, but he has a gift for savage caricature. His mockery is not humorous, but stormy and grim; it is carried on the wings of rhetoric, but savage enough to give some plausibility to the satirist's traditional assertion that 'even if nature denies the gift, indignation brings

[1] Juvenal, *Satires*, III, 41–50, tr. R. C. Trevelyan (1940).

verse into being'.[1] And Juvenal claims, like many before and after him, that patriotic moral duty is his motive.

The themes of his Satires are as follows:

Book I

1. Reasons for writing satire.
2. Attack on men who cloak vice under an appearance of philosophy.
3. Miseries of poverty in Rome.
4. Mockery of the late emperor Domitian—his Council discuss his menu.
5. Humiliation of client at dinner with his patron.

Book II

6. Ruthless attack on the faults of women.

Book III

7. Wretched prospects of the literary profession without patrons.
8. Attack on pride of birth.
9. An obscene dialogue.

Book IV

10. Men's desire for the wrong things.
11. Contemporary extravagance.
12. True and false friendship.

Book V

13. To a friend who has been cheated of money.
14. The bad effect parents can have on their children.
15. A lynching—the brutality of men to each other.
16. The unfair privileges of soldiers.

In the first Satire there is an announcement which, at first sight, seems to rob these onslaughts of some of their vividness. Juvenal

[1] Juvenal, *Satires*, 1, 79.

states that it is not safe to attack the living, and that he is therefore only going to attack the dead. And such names as appear are those of dead people: for example, the emperors Nero (A.D. 54–68) and Domitian (A.D. 81–96). This is rather as if our Sunday papers denounced, as the most dangerous of influences among us today, Mr Gladstone. But Juvenal is apparently *thinking* of his own time, and using the names of the past as cloaks for men he had known. To us this may seem strange, since the Rome of Juvenal's day, though no doubt luxurious and vicious in parts, was on the whole well ruled. Yet, to a poor and embittered man living then, these merits may well have been less readily apparent than they are to us. However, it is possible that Juvenal (like Tacitus, whose history is at times equally savage) formed a good deal of his burning indignation in the days of Domitian, when it could not be openly expressed—and that its later expression was partly retrospective.

Juvenal's indignation was no doubt whipped up by personal disappointments. But it was the product of a profound moral sense. Its ideal is old-fashioned, narrow, and traditional: he has no sense of proportion. Nero, says Juvenal, murdered his mother and wife—and he acted on the stage! Here is the Stoic feeling that one fault is as bad as another, for all equally fall short of the theoretical Wise Man. So Juvenal 'uses the force of a steam-hammer to crack a nut'. But his morality was not exclusively Stoic. He was an eclectic: he speaks not as Stoic or Cynic or Epicurean alone, but with whatever speech the claims of moral rhetoric suggest. Some of his Satires, for instance the thirteenth, contain passages so noble that they seem to sum up the best in the Graeco-Roman philosophies, and to foreshadow the spread of Christianity in the Graeco-Roman world. The people of the Middle Ages noted this and were deeply interested in the moral value of Juvenal's *Satires*.

These poems, more than any others, have given Satire to the

world. On the whole, it has been Juvenal's eloquent bitterness rather than his moral tone which has impressed itself on posterity. His influence on seventeenth-century France was enormous.[1] And when John Donne said 'no poison's half so bad as Julia', he was writing in the spirit of Juvenal's remorseless description of womanhood in the sixth poem. In 1681-2 Dryden published three great Satires of his own, which—though they owe much to intermediate writers—provided vigorous adaptations of Juvenal (whom he later edited).

> A cook, a conjurer, a rhetorician,
> A painter, pedant, a geometrician,
> A dancer on the ropes and a physician;
> All things the hungry Greek exactly knows,
> And bid him go to heaven, to heaven he goes.
>
> But of all plagues the greatest is untold;
> The book-learned wife, in Greek and Latin bold;
> The critic dame, who at her table sits,
> Homer and Virgil quotes and weighs their wits
> And pities Dido's agonizing fits.
>
> Go, climb the rugged Alps, ambitious fool,
> To please the boys, and be a theme at school.[2]

Jonathan Swift is as ruthless as Juvenal but adds to his range. Pope's satirical portraits are not so vigorous as Juvenal's but are sharper. Later in the eighteenth century, it was Dr Johnson who reflected in our language the feature of Juvenal's poems which is perhaps of the deepest interest to us. This is his vivid description of daily life. For example, Juvenal's third Satire gives us an incomparable picture of the life of the capital, to which Johnson's *London* owes a very great deal (just as his *Vanity of Human Wishes* owes much to the tenth poem).

[1] It was spread by Boileau.

[2] John Dryden (1631–1700), after Juvenal, *Satires*, III, 76–8; VI, 434–7; X, 166–7.

For who would leave, unbrib'd, Hibernia's land,
Or change the rocks of Scotland for the Strand?
There none are swept by sudden fate away,
But all whom hunger spares with age decay:
Here malice, rapine, accident conspire,
And now a rabble rages, now a fire;
Their ambush here relentless ruffians lay,
And here the fell attorney prowls for prey;
Here falling houses thunder on your head,
And here a female atheist talks you dead.[1]

Juvenal is a unique figure: yet he has had many debtors. He also had many debts—among others, to Lucilius, Horace, Bion, and rhetoricians. By incorporating these influences into an intensely original creation he typifies the finest achievement of classicism.

[1] Samuel Johnson (1709–84), after Juvenal, *Satires*, III, 5–9.

THE SURVIVAL OF
ROMAN LITERATURE

THE SURVIVAL OF ROMAN LITERATURE

THIS book has been concerned with Latin literature while Roman was pagan. But even in so brief a survey something needs to be said of the great prose writings of the early Christians. During the first quarter of the fourth century A.D., under Constantine the Great, Christianity overcame its rivals in official favour, and overcame the traditional Roman religion itself. But important Christian writers in Latin had lived and written more than a century before this had happened; the first significant Christian writings in this language were beginning to appear before A.D. 200.

At first Christianity had been for the most part a sect among the poor and uneducated. But the challenge of extending Christianity among educated people was accepted eagerly by its thinkers. It was apparently for such men that the *Acts of the Apostles* were written in Greek, at a date not far removed from A.D. 100. About a century later, the same challenge was accepted by writers in Latin. The time-lag is not surprising when we recall that for a long time the Church consisted of men—mostly Greek and Jewish freedmen—who did not, even at Rome, use Latin as their first language. Gradually, however, the number of people in the West who spoke Latin increased. Moreover the Christian Latin writers, who are now encountered, were no longer half-educated men opposed to culture; nor were the audiences which they hoped to reach. So these writers tried to reinforce the arguments for Christianity by the eloquence and learning which they had derived from pagan civilisation. One of the first important Christian writers cast his work into the mould provided by Cicero. This was Minucius Felix, who lived in the late second or early third century A.D. and has left us a philosophical dialogue, set at Rome's port Ostia, called the *Octavius*.

Almost contemporary with Minucius—although the exact chronological relationship is disputed—was a more vigorous and peculiar Christian writer, Tertullian. It is characteristic of the age that Tertullian came from the Roman province of Africa (Tunisia and eastern Algeria); probably Minucius had also. Tertullian was a difficult character, often sarcastic and ill-tempered, rarely natural or simple. He was born a pagan (*c*. A.D. 160), and was brought up as a lawyer; he was converted to Christianity, and for ten years was one of its most prominent defenders. Then, soon after A.D. 200, he broke away from what was then regarded as orthodox Christianity and joined the heretical, rigorous sect of the Montanists. His finest surviving work is a speech of urgent persuasion, the *Apologeticus*—one of the very few Latin speeches of the first three centuries A.D. that have survived. It was addressed to Roman provincial governors, to whom it defends Christianity in language which they would be able to understand. But, in keeping with Tertullian's personality, its strength lies less in defence than in attack. Here is no marriage of Christianity with Ciceronian *humanitas*. Tertullian's uncompromising austerity points the way rather to the line of ascetics, monastics and martyrs who were soon to follow. In the end, he tried to break with pagan Greece and Rome. 'You are fond of spectacles,' Gibbon hears him say, 'expect the greatest of all spectacles, the last and eternal judgement of the universe!'

But the tradition had deep roots spreading back for a thousand years; and the greatest Christian writer of the fourth century is called 'the Christian Cicero'. This is Lactantius. His belief was that Christianity needed to draw on the pagan past for its formulation and enrichment. For this reason, he is important to those today who were brought up in a tradition which combines Christianity and the classics. Indeed, in the Renaissance, when this composite kind of upbringing first became possible, the earliest book to be printed in Italy, and one of the most popular, was by Lactantius.

He lived on for a decade or two into the fourth century A.D., the age in which Christianity survived its gravest persecutions to become the religion of the State. In this epoch, despite impoverishment and totalitarian government—the price at which survival had been bought—there were developments in education. It has been called a second 'Ciceronian Age'; and it witnessed the critical phase of Christianity's amalgamation with Graeco-Roman philosophy. There were still able pagan thinkers; one of them was the 'apostate' emperor Julian (A.D. 361–3), who wrote bitterly and extensively in Greek. But with a few such exceptions, the pagan prose writers were henceforward outshone by the Fathers of the Church, to whose brilliance the debt of Christianity is incalculable.

The greatest of them were the Saints Ambrose from Gaul, Jerome from Dalmatia and Augustine from North Africa. These were men profoundly differing in character, but alike in that they played substantial parts in the history of Latin literature as well as that of Christianity. The career of Ambrose, a Gaul, reveals the different position which Christianity enjoyed, now that it had become—as it had shortly before his birth—the established religion. He is an early example of the great Churchman who resists the civil power. He influenced successive emperors, even forcing the most formidable ruler of his day, Theodosius (A.D. 379–95), to make public repentance for murders carried out on his responsibility. 'In questions affecting the Faith', said Ambrose, 'it is the bishops who are judges of Christian emperors'—not the reverse. So the Church had, to a large extent, emancipated itself from the State. When, in the seventeenth century, Hobbes wished to enhance the authority of the State, it was chiefly against Ambrose that he argued.

Ambrose knew Greek well and was interested in philosophy;

so he carried further the interlocking of Christianity and the Graeco-Roman Stoic tradition. Like Tertullian, he was not a particularly original thinker. Unlike Tertullian, he was an impressive combination of mystic and man of affairs. He was vigorous and successful as a preacher, letter-writer and orator alike. But he was not a Ciceronian; like all the Latin Fathers, the rhythm and balance of his diction are closer to Seneca. In addition to his prose, Ambrose's hymns are of significance, since through them he is not only the heir of pagan hymn-writing, but the fore-runner and creator of the hymns and metrical psalms sung in our churches today.

But most important of all in the history of Latin literature and Christianity are the names of two younger contemporaries of Ambrose. One of these was Jerome (Eusebius Hieronymus), born in Dalmatia. An unusually, if not morbidly, inward-looking character led him to deliberate self-mortification, the prototype of the medieval monkish discipline. He has violent abuse for his enemies, many of them fellow clerics, about whom—in his lively letters—we read scathing accounts. But his greatest services were to the study of the Bible. His revised translation of the Bible, the Vulgate, has survived as the basis of the official Catholic version; and Jerome's Latin, as well as the substance of what he wrote, immensely influenced the Latinity of the Middle Ages. Of all the early Fathers he approaches most closely to Cicero's purity of style. In addition, his mind was impregnated with Virgil and Horace. He also incorporated in his work non-Latin elements (which he found in earlier Greek and Hebrew versions of the Bible)—and much of the Stoic philosophy, too, which he derived from the Greek writings of Origen (Origenes) of Alexandria (c. A.D. 185–254).

Jerome, then, was the greatest scholar of the early Christians. But as his impulse to monastic asceticism suggests, he was strongly aware of the distracting character of classical thought. Though he was deeply distressed by the sack of Rome by Alaric in A.D. 410, his whole object in life was to put his pagan scholarship at the disposal of the Christian Church. Like Tertullian, he made a determined attempt to free his ways of thinking from pagan influences. Jerome illustrates comprehensively the two currents pulling at Christian thought.

So does Jerome's even more distinguished contemporary Augustine. He was born at Thagaste in Numidia (N. Africa). Like the greater number of Latin Christian writers, Augustine was of the fertile and vigorous peoples of North Africa. His nature was friendly and sympathetic. Of this nature we learn very much from the predominantly autobiographical *Confessions*—as revealing a document in its way as Cicero's letters. Augustine's mind is imaginative and passionate, daring but sombre, poetical and romantic. He is introspective, with a ruthless self-criticism which stirred the admiration of Dante.

Augustine was a Bishop for forty years, and his activity as author was gigantic. Among the Early Fathers, he is the most vivid writer, as well as the most profound and subtle thinker. He was born of pagan parents, and studied the contemporary version of Platonism, under the influence—as a young man—of Cicero's philosophical dialogue the *Hortensius* (now lost). He continued to praise Cicero as well as Horace and Virgil—to whom he is closest in spirit—for the way they call men back to first principles. But Ambrose converted him to what was the orthodox Christian view of moral problems. This differed from the attitude of Cicero. Cicero had believed that virtue was the result of human effort, that human nature was naturally good, and that free will prevailed. Augustine came to feel otherwise: that virtue was the result of divine grace alone, that sin was original in human nature, and that the idea of free will was detestable.

On these as on other matters he writes with infinite variety and brilliance. The twenty-two books of his *City of God (De Civitate*

Dei) form a powerful exposition of the Christian Faith which dealt paganism its death-blow. He writes of the eclipse of worldly sovereignties, of the earthly city (founded by fallen angels) by the heavenly city—a 'Republic' not Ciceronian but divine. Why, with the coming of Christianity, had so many disasters overwhelmed the Empire? The *City of God* answers the question, arguing that the disasters were irrelevant, disasters that had happened to pagans—and could not touch Christians.

Augustine's influence on the Middle Ages was vast, though in its later centuries there was a move away from his directness and simplicity. But Luther and Calvin, too, admired Augustine most of all the Early Fathers; in the sixteenth and seventeenth centuries the Protestants were for him, many Catholics were against him. Today, his *City of God* is as poignantly relevant as ever: what are the possibilities of reconciling, in peace, the world of the spirit and the world in which we live? Augustine lived at the beginning of a new age and also at the end of an old one. The heritage which we have derived from Greece and Rome has come to us through him.

Roman literature is important not only because of its own quality and value but because of the influence that it has exerted on the successive generations between Roman times and our own. In the first place the most famous ancient writers vastly influenced the centuries which elapsed between their lifetimes and the final displacement of the Empire towards the East in the fourth and fifth centuries A.D. The process continued in the Middle Ages. The continuation of the Roman Empire, with its new capital Constantinople (Byzantium), was to last for a thousand years more. It kept Greek culture alive, and, through the Orthodox Church and other intermediaries, has immensely influenced the modern world. It was Byzantium that codified the Roman Law. But it was primarily in western Europe that the future of Latin studies lay.

There, however, the early part of this millennium is known

as the Dark Ages, because of its political chaos, and the rising illiteracy which this generated. But the view that Latin culture disappeared, only to be rediscovered in the Renaissance, is an over-simplification. There has been unbroken continuity in Latin culture; considerable parts of its legacy were transmitted direct throughout the Middle Ages without a break. This occurred in three main ways.

(1) Latin culture was to some extent transmitted by the works of the Early Christian Fathers, and by two learned men, Boethius (c. 480–524) and Cassiodorus (c. 487–583). The Latin in which they wrote, 'ecclesiastical Latin'—not Ciceronian, though recognisable as Cicero's heir—was employed for all learned subjects. It was the common language of scholars and men of science—it was a living tongue to the British scholar Bede (c. 672–735). Latin, of the literary but post-classical kind that these men used, was still the normal means of communication between educated men; it was authoritative and convenient (and helped to delay the growth of national languages).

(2) Yet much classical Latin literature also survived. By no means all of it survived; there were grave losses, temporary and permanent. But there was still much to be read; and a good deal of this was held in high honour.

One of the dominant features of medieval culture was the fabulous reputation of Virgil throughout its duration. Even in ancient times he had become not only a linguistic and spiritual model but an oracle. Constantine gave his official blessing to the interpretation of the Fourth Eclogue as Messianic prophecy; and 'When I should have been weeping for my own sins', said Augustine, 'I wept for Dido'. Learned men continued to revere Virgil until Dante—who chose him as his guide—and Chaucer:

> Glorie and honour, Virgile Mantuan,
> Be to thy name! and I shal as I kan
> Folowe thy lanterne as thou goste byforn.

But soon Virgil's fame also passed into the legends and folk-lore of thousands of superstitious people who knew nothing of Latin or any other letters. In popular story-telling the poet became a superhuman sage, an astrologer and a magician. At Rome he was said to have invented robots offering miraculous political intelligence reports, at Naples—where he was buried—a butcher's block which kept meat fresh for six weeks. The foundation of Naples itself was credited to him; and once an invading army could not be persuaded to demolish a gate under which Virgil was believed to have deposited a mass of serpents. Elsewhere, he becomes the son of King Gorgilius of Libya, and loves Julius Caesar's daughter; or it is the daughter of the Sultan of Babylon whom he abducts, while sorcerer at the court of Darius—or King Arthur; another story confers on him the headmastership of a school of necromancy. Truly here is 'one of the most extraordinary and bewildering vagaries of the human mind ever recorded'.

(3) This brings us to the third way in which Latin culture survived the Dark Ages. For now, in a more or less distorted form, it was affecting poor and uneducated people. The 'common man' had been relatively little heard of in the classical period. But it is he above all who transmitted Latin influence in the Middle Ages. He did so not only through his reverence for the great figures like Virgil. Much of the transmission was effected by more direct and simple means. The language lived on, in Italy, France, Spain and elsewhere, as the spoken tongue of the people. There were, it is true, many irruptions by external invaders. But these invaders often assimilated and accepted the speech of their new country with great speed. So the birth of Italian, as of other modern tongues, was still not at hand; at first, local dialects of Latin existed side by side, and no single one of them eliminated the others to become a national language.

Throughout the first half of the Middle Ages, Italy remained the hub of Latin-speaking civilisation, just as Constantinople had become the home and centre of the Greek tradition. In Italy as elsewhere education had declined, but there were a few important schools scattered about the country. There was a choir-school at Rome, the illiterate Lombards had a school for their Italian civil servants at Pavia, the Byzantines a law-school at Ravenna. In c. A.D. 613 an Irishman, St Columba, founded Bobbio (N.E. of Genoa), one of the monastic homes of learning that just managed to keep Latin literature from being forgotten. By the tenth century, the library of this monastery had collected one thousand manuscripts—a great achievement in those times of upheaval.

Gaul, too, before long became a centre of Latin learning again. After a century of darkness in which knowledge of Latin had sunk very low, there was a revival of letters at Aachen (Aix-la-Chapelle) and elsewhere, sponsored by Charlemagne and his educational adviser Alcuin of York. In A.D. 787 Charlemagne published an order that higher learning should be attained, and slipshod Latin avoided. The study of Virgil and other classical writers was encouraged on the grounds that only thus could the Scriptures, being Latin, be properly understood.

In the political sphere, too, Charlemagne's state even disputed, with the Papacy and Byzantium, the title of *Roman Empire*. The fact that the dispute took this form illustrates the whole trend of the Middle Ages. Most of the major movements were essentially dependent on the Roman heritage. The breaks in continuity were never complete. To avoid the worst horrors of a disturbed and wretched epoch, there were successive migrations of learned people, and transfers of learning itself, from one country to another. From the ninth century onwards, the break-up of Europe showed itself by the gradual evolution of Latin dialects into distinct languages resembling those spoken today. But the West European culture of the whole medieval millennium was pre-eminently Latin.

However, a system was built up which was very different from the old Ciceronian *humanitas*. Its balance of academic and wider studies, of mind and character, was lost. In the Middle Ages the normal course of education, despite its title 'The Seven Liberal Arts', was a narrower one. It had originated not with Cicero but in the educational reforms of the fourth century A.D. The Seven Arts included, first the *Trivium* (completed at school)— Grammar, Logic and Rhetoric; then the *Quadrivium*, Music, Arithmetic, Geometry and Astronomy. These seven studies were considered far more important than the actual study of classical authors.

From *c.* A.D. 1000 there was a gradual increase in political and economic stability; and, in these better conditions, attention to the classical past became stronger and more persistent. The twelfth century was the age of the first Universities; 'schools' at Chartres and Paris helped to create the movement known by the name of 'Scholasticism'. Its followers the 'Schoolmen', such as Albertus Magnus and St Thomas Aquinas, were no longer distressed, as Jerome and Augustine had been, by what seemed an implacable conflict between the classics and Christianity. The Schoolmen sought to revive the best in ancient thought, but they aimed to do so within the framework of the Church, and under its influence and control. So, in the face of opposition, they laid explicit stress on continuity: the system of Aquinas was based on both divine and human reason. The feeling was that truth was a treasure which had been handed down throughout the ages and could be added to by taking thought.

This was an age of a passionate devotion to Aristotle. The Arabs had long known Aristotle, and provided some of the leading Aristotelians of the age, such as Averroes of Cordova in the twelfth century and Avicenna of Baghdad 150 years earlier. But Italians, and other westerners, studied Aristotle in Latin; and Latin, again, is the language of the medieval prose chronicles of England. In this cultural efflorescence of the twelfth century, Latin still remained the chief medium of western culture; and it was the language of a charming lyric poetry.

> Sleep through the wearied brain
> Breathes a soft wind
> From field of ripening grain,
> The sound
> Of running water over clearest sand,
> A millwheel turning, turning slowly round,
> These steal the light
> From eyes weary of sight.[1]

Romantic Love was a new ideal, and Ovid, duly 'moralised', served as its model; and it was in Latin that songs were sung by generations of wandering scholars ('Vagantes'). However, there was now a powerful autonomous culture in Provence; and in Italian the oldest surviving document is a short song of *c.* 1150. But it is not until near the end of the 'Middle Ages', the early fourteenth century, that Dante writes at length in the 'Tuscan language'—and defends it as nobler than Latin, being natural instead of artificial. Yet he too was second to none in his admiration for Virgil; and thereby he sums up the whole medieval millennium, of which the culture was predominantly Latin.

The 'Renaissance' in fifteenth-century Italy was the age of two sorts of discovery—geographical, the discovery of the world by explorers; and spiritual, the discovery of man. The spiritual advance came about because of an increase of *individualism*— a new consciousness of the dignity of human beings, of the potentialities of their will, and of their part in the universe. This

[1] Carmina Burana, 37 [from Benediktbeuern in Bavaria], tr. Helen Waddell.

was felt, not as a burdensome responsibility, but as freedom—as an exciting liberation from medieval restriction.

It was in many ways an unfamiliar idea that man was some good in himself; that he was worth studying and believing in for his own sake—and not only as part of medieval theology, as a powerless instrument of Divine Will. It is because of this new conception that the chief studies of the Renaissance came to be known as the 'Humanities'; this is the age of Humanism and the Humanists. There was a gay, joyful spirit, a fresh response to beautiful things. The active, secular States of North Italy took the lead; life in them was stimulating and relatively unhampered.

This intensified consciousness was linked with, indeed based on, a study of the *past*. It was felt that only a study of past writers and thinkers could show what humanity had achieved—and so what humanity *could* achieve. And, to these men of the Renaissance, the study of the past was the study of the ancient classics: for it is these which illuminated past epochs and cultures. But at first a knowledge of Greek was scarce, so very often classical literature meant Latin literature. Now it is true that in the Middle Ages, too, the basis of civilisation had been Latin. But the men of the Renaissance, though they were the heirs of the Middle Ages, 'the brilliant climax of the process of a thousand years',[1] were not content with the Seven medieval Liberal Arts. They wanted to go back to the classical literature itself, to the source—to the Greek and Roman originators of this culture, and to the finest exponents of its thought. That is why the Renaissance, and the Humanities, have a classical tone: because their exponents found in ancient literature everything that they wanted and idealised—including classical precision of form, which became a Renaissance ideal, in literature as in the arts. Thus classical, and particularly Latin, literature was the basis of this Renaissance, the beginning of an epoch which lasted from the end of the Middle Ages until nearly

[1] D. Bush.

1900—if not later. The thinkers of the fourteenth and fifteenth centuries turned with enthusiasm to the renewed study of those Latin writings which had survived from the ancient world, and to the discovery, in old libraries, of other Latin works which had been lost and forgotten.

The first, or forerunner, of the Renaissance Humanists was Petrarch (Francesco di Petracco). He was a Florentine, born in exile near Arezzo (thirty miles south-east of Florence) in 1304; he died in 1374 near Padua. He was educated in France and Italy, and travelled constantly in those countries and in Germany. Petrarch was the first man to attach this increased significance to the classical writers. He led the way to the Renaissance; he was a medieval who possessed the Renaissance spirit. Even as a boy he was engrossed in ancient Latin literature. His father, it is said, caught him reading it when he ought to have been reading law, and threw the books in the fire, saving only, at his son's earnest entreaty, Cicero's rhetorical treatises and Virgil. Whether that is true or not, Petrarch's mind was largely moulded by these two writers. But his devotion to Virgil was not that of the Middle Ages. Petrarch no longer regarded him as distant and supernatural, but as a friendly guide and model. However, his greatest admiration of all was for Cicero—as philosopher and orator alike.

And perhaps next to Cicero, in his veneration, was St Augustine, whom he quotes many times. Petrarch was a loyal churchman, who regarded the study of the classics not as an enemy of Christianity, but as one of its most valuable auxiliaries. Nevertheless, like Cicero, he was essentially an individualist. He could not, like the Schoolmen, accept Aristotle as the last word on all subjects; he wrote a treatise *On his own Ignorance and that of other people*. And he could not merge his individuality in the Church with the same wholeheartedness as a medieval thinker. Petrarch has been described as 'the first modern man', and 'the Columbus of a new spiritual hemisphere'; and he was fully conscious of living in a transitional age.

His discovery of a new attitude and way of life was accompanied and symbolised by the actual dramatic discovery of long-lost manuscripts. Successive finds enlarged and altered men's view of the ancient world. When Petrarch discovered a manuscript he would 'publish' it by copying it and urging his friends to do the same, and would give it added circulation by discussion. In 1333, he initiated a century of such discoveries by finding two forgotten speeches of Cicero at Liége. He at once copied them, with the help of a friend—using yellow ink, since no other was available. Twelve years later he discovered half the letters of Cicero, and again at once went to great pains to transcribe them. He wrote an essay, in the classical form of a 'letter' addressed to Cicero, recording the discovery. From this we learn how Petrarch was shocked to read of the political and personal vacillations of the man whose oratory and philosophy had contributed more than anyone else to the standards which were now being revived. But Petrarch partly overcame these feelings; and, after him, Cicero's public life itself became part of the Renaissance ideal, as an example of an active life of civic responsibility appropriate to the Italian city-states—in reaction from the medieval view that the only place for virtue was the cloister. Cicero was also admired as an Italian patriot and Republican, by an age in which those attitudes were popular.

Petrarch wrote fine Italian poetry, but—characteristically— was prouder of his Latin verse (especially an epic poem called *Africa*) and Latin prose. He hardly knew any Greek. He started learning it from an Italian monk called Baarlam. But then a bishopric became vacant, and Petrarch recommended his tutor for it. So he never learnt more than the Greek capital letters. His culture was Latin.

The first Renaissance scholar to know Greek, the first Greek scholar of the modern western world, was another Florentine, Giovanni Boccaccio, author of the *Decameron* in his native Italian. Boccaccio knew Tacitus, and with him the 'Silver Age' of Latin letters began to play a large part in the Renaissance. Thus, early in the fifteenth century, a further Florentine scholar, Poggio Bracciolini, found—in a disused tower at St Gallen in Switzerland—a complete manuscript of Quintilian; then others translated it into Italian and wrote influential educational treatises based on its doctrines. Then, in *c.* 1465, began the earliest printing of classical authors—again in Italy; though printing was introduced to that country by German monks from Mainz.

In the sixteenth century another epoch of the Renaissance may be said to have begun. This was an epoch in which, for the first time, outstanding talent in classical studies is apparent on a considerable scale in countries other than Italy. Among the great scholars of the early sixteenth century was a Spaniard, Vives (1492–1540), who lived in the Low Countries and died at Bruges. Erasmus (1466–1536) was born at Rotterdam, died at Basle, and brought the flower of Renaissance classical scholarship to northern countries including England. But the centre of classical research, in this epoch, belongs rather to France. Greek and Roman studies were at their height in France before the time of its classic, classically inspired dramatists. An important date is 1530, when King Francis I founded a college called the Corporation of Royal Readers; among its first students were such widely divergent theologians as Ignatius de Loyola and Calvin. The Corporation inaugurated a phase of many-sided, encyclopaedic scholarship, and of voluminous learning. Perhaps the greatest exponent of French learning was J. J. Scaliger, jun. (1540–1609), a Frenchman of Italian descent who died at Leiden; and a monument of the age was the series of sixty-four Delphin (Dauphin) Classics, editions of the ancient writers, mostly published between 1674 and 1698.

Another land which was prominent in the earlier part (at least) of this period was Scotland. George Buchanan (1506–82) wrote a twenty-volume history of his country in Latin. This was read for many generations, and was held by a number of scholars to be superior to the works of the great Roman historians themselves. But his contemporary fame was chiefly due to his poetry—again in Latin: poems, plays and a famous version of the Psalms, dedicated to Mary Queen of Scots. It was still as it had been in the days of Petrarch: to write good Latin verses was reckoned more valuable than a gift for the vernacular tongue. So it was a high compliment when Scaliger himself said that Buchanan's Latin poetry was the finest in Europe. Yet, though Buchanan is the greatest Scottish classic, it was after his death, between 1604 and 1640, that Scotland enjoyed its golden age of humanistic studies.

But then later on, from about 1700 for a hundred years, classical studies were no longer centred in France, and were no longer so prominently represented in Scotland. This was a century in which the attention of the learned world was, rather, directed to England, and to the Netherlands. The first of our 'modern' periods (the Italian period, c. 1330–1530) may be called the Age of the first Humanists, our second, French period (c. 1530–1770) the Age of many-sided Scholarship, and this third period the Age of Criticism.[1]

In this third epoch lived Richard Bentley (1662–1742), Master of Trinity College, Cambridge. He was a figure of fabulous repute and eccentricity, overbearing and sarcastic, but with a mighty devotion to the truth. This showed itself in his insistence on sound classical texts. Ancient manuscripts often left room for doubt, and by the eighteenth century the texts in use were often uncertain and corrupt. Bentley's achievement was to emphasise, with vigour and indeed violence, the fundamental necessity of

[1] J. E. Sandys.

establishing the best possible readings. This had, at the time, an enlivening effect on the classics. For, in order to reconstruct faulty texts, it is necessary to grapple with fundamental questions of linguistic usage; and this cannot be done without an intimate understanding of the ancient languages. So Bentley's quest spurred the scholars of his day to a strenuous discipline that almost constituted a new Renaissance of Greek and Latin literary studies; though at the same time he set such a high standard that men of letters—amateur classics—could no longer compete, and tended to drop out of scholarly investigation.

The eighteenth century witnessed a stimulation of the classics in other respects also. Travelling was frequent and widespread, and here again the English were in the forefront. Their tours and voyages produced and encouraged interest in archaeology. Another study which came into its own was comparative philology. It started with the recognition by English scholars in India that Sanskrit was of importance owing to its link with Greek and Latin. This recognition is usually dated to 1786; and two years later came another landmark in the history of the classics, the completion of the great *Decline and Fall of the Roman Empire* by Edward Gibbon. 'His whole genius was pre-eminently classical; order, lucidity, balance, precision—the great classical qualities—dominate his work; and his History is chiefly remarkable as one of the supreme monuments of Classical Art in European literature.'[1]

But already at this time a new movement was beginning. Despite the influence of ancient writings on the American and French Revolutions, the centre of the fourth great period of modern classical learning is Germany. If the foregoing century, in which England and the Netherlands supplied the impetus, can be described as the Age of Criticism, this predominantly German period, roughly corresponding with the nineteenth century, is

[1] G. Highet.

the Age of *Systematic* Scholarship. One of many names at the beginning of this period is that of F. A. Wolf, who was Professor at Halle University until Napoleon closed it down. One of Wolf's contributions is Greek (and Greece and its products received the warmest admiration of all time in this romantic century). It was he who roused into life the permanent controversy about the authorship of Homer's *Iliad* and *Odyssey*. But another achievement with which Wolf's name deserves to be associated is of more general character. He was the first, or one of the first, to try to combine in his teaching all the different fields of classical studies. He refused to regard them as separate hermetically sealed compartments. Instead he aimed at presenting to his pupils the whole, many-sided structure of ancient life. It is characteristic, however, of the beginnings of this German movement that Wolf's greatest work is to be found not in books but in his teaching—in the pupils whom he stimulated to be the future leaders of classical scholarship. Germany encouraged the formation of 'schools' of thought and scholarship, transmitting subjects and methods of study from one generation to the next— from teachers to their graduate-pupils, whom they collected around themselves to engage in joint projects of research. This is known as the 'seminar-system', which is one of the most characteristic features of German nineteenth-century scholarship and culture.

Of the twentieth century, though it is more than half over, it is still, perhaps, too early to generalise. Classical research has gained in extent and in intricacy, and has become increasingly scientific and systematic; and, though the total number of pupils in these subjects has decreased, the number of specialists with a serious interest has become greater. It becomes continually clearer that the task of research even on the central subjects is infinitely far from complete. There is need of people who, with admiration for the achievements of previous scholars but without automatic acceptance of everything they have said, will attack the engrossing problems which confront Latin literature at this present day. The quest is worth while, since its reward is that enriched knowledge of past thought which can help us to face the future with experience, and so with a measure of confidence.

APPENDICES

GREEK PHILOSOPHY LEARNT BY
THE ROMANS

THE Romans, with very few exceptions, were not capable of those speculations about the universe which had been the characteristic activity of Greek philosophers until Socrates (469–399 B.C.). But Rome keenly followed the ethical preoccupations which Hellenistic philosophers inherited from Plato (c. 429–347 B.C.) and Aristotle (384–322 B.C.). What, it was asked, is the supreme Good?—in particular, what will make a man impervious to the hazards of Fortune? The pupils of Diogenes the Cynic (c. 400–c. 325 B.C.) said this could be done by renouncing all material possessions. But other Hellenistic answers had more influence on Roman thought:

(1) *Epicureanism* ('The Garden'), founded by Epicurus of Samos (341–270 B.C.). Epicurus believed in the guidance of the senses, and believed that they teach the supreme Good to be *Happiness*, which he identified with *ataraxia* = the absence of pain or disturbance. Like Democritus of Abdera (c. 460–370 B.C.) (following Leucippus of Miletus, fifth century B.C.), Epicurus believed that sensation contacts objects by 'effluences' thrown off by them through the movement of *atoms*, of which everything (except the void) was held to consist.

Epicurus departed from fatalism by allowing that some arbitrary factor makes these atoms *swerve* from their straight movement: thus he left room for free will. He believed that 'gods' live between the worlds, but have no concern with worlds or men, and that there is no after-life of the soul: so that fears of the gods or of death are vain. This doctrine and his non-moral and antisocial beliefs gave Epicureanism a hard passage in Republican Rome; yet in the first century B.C. it was given its finest expression by Lucretius.

(2) *Stoicism* ('The Porch') was founded, again in *c.* 300 B.C., by Zeno of Citium in Cyprus (335–263 B.C.). He taught belief in Divine Providence, and in Virtue as the supreme Good—a creed of a new ethical urgency. Panaetius of Cos (*c.* 185–109 B.C.) adjusted this doctrine to Roman society and public life by modifying its rigidity so as to leave room for imperfect virtue, 'progression *towards* virtue'. This idea was adopted in Cicero's *De Officiis* and implied in Virgil's conception of his hero Aeneas, who gradually wins his way towards the virtue of the Stoic Sage. A further Stoic idea, that of the Law of Nature by which all men are Brothers in the 'world-state' (*cosmopolis*), was adapted to Rome by Posidonius of Apamea (*c.* 135–50 B.C.), who identified the 'world-state' with the Roman empire.

These Stoic ideas were propagated by Seneca the Younger, and by the poor man's philosopher Epictetus (*c.* A.D. 55–*c.* 135) who wrote in Greek. The early emperors paid much lip-service to Stoicism, but gradually, during the first century A.D., its opposition to *bad* monarchy came to be confused with the Cynics' opposition to *any* monarchy, and Stoics were persecuted. However from A.D. 161 to 180 the Empire was ruled by a convinced Stoic, Marcus Aurelius, whose philosophical *Meditations* (written in Greek) have come down to us. He and Seneca, as well as opponents of the temporal power, were admired by the Christians, in whom a great deal of Stoic thought reappeared.

Epicureans and Stoics owed much to two schools depending directly on Plato and Aristotle:

(3) *The Peripatetics* (Peripatos = 'Covered Arcade'), the followers of Aristotle, expounded his science and philosophy, developed historical studies such as biography, and propagated Aristotle's belief in the typically Greek concept 'the Mean'.

This doctrine of moderation is constantly echoed by Cicero and Horace.

(4) *The Academy*, founded in *c.* 385 B.C. by Plato. Influenced by the Sceptic Pyrrho (*c.* 360–*c.* 270 B.C.), who refused to admit that real knowledge could be acquired, Carneades of the Academy (*c.* 214–*c.* 129 B.C.) introduced Rome to criticisms of the Stoic and Epicurean dogmatism about life and philosophy. More positive was the *eclectic* approach of Cicero's teacher Antiochus of Ascalon (*c.* 130–*c.* 68 B.C.), who sought to select and blend together the good points of various schools—in the spirit of Aristotle's 'Mean'. Eclecticism prevailed: the ethics of the Academic Cicero are largely Stoic, but he too, as has been said, believed in the 'Mean'; so did Horace, who adds an Epicurean belief in friendliness and moderate good living.

Two other schools left little imprint on surviving Latin literature: the *Neo-Pythagoreans*—including P. Nigidius Figulus (first century B.C.) and the ascetic miracle-worker Apollonius of Tyana (first century A.D.)—who revived in Rome and Alexandria the theological number-symbolism of Pythagoras of Samos (sixth century B.C.); and the school which absorbed them, the *Neo-Platonists*. The *Enneads* of Plotinus (A.D. 205–*c.* 269), in Greek, were published by Porphyry (*c.* A.D. 300–3). The last important synthesis of ancient philosophy in the Latin tongue was that of Boethius (*c.* A.D. 480–524), who profoundly influenced medieval thought.

METRE

NEARLY all English poetry is scanned according to stress-accent:
that is, the syllables receiving metrical weight (*ictus*) are those
emphasised in ordinary speech. Nearly all Latin poetry, however,
is scanned according to *quantity*, each line consisting of a fixed, or
narrowly variable, system of quantitatively long and short syllables: metrical *ictus* can fall only on the former (syllables can
be long either by nature (*aciēs*) or by position, i.e. after a double
consonant (*ērrānt*)); *ictus* and stress-accent may fall on different
syllables. When a word beginning with a vowel or 'h' follows
a word ending with a vowel or 'm', the initial syllable of the
second word is *elided* with the final syllable of the first word.
Latin lines normally contain a rhythmical break (*caesura*).

Metrical technique plays a very great part in the achievement of
the principal Roman poets.

(1) Plautus admitted scansion by quantity, in accordance with
Greek metrical practice. (Ennius, however, was the first to impose
scansion by quantity *alone*.) The portions of Plautus' plays
intended for intonation, the *cantica*, are usually based on trochees
(– ◡), or cretics (– ◡ –), or bacchiacs (◡ – –). Outside the *cantica*,
his main metre is the iambic *senarius* = six *iambi* (◡ –), often
'resolved' into tribrachs (◡ ◡ ◡) or spondees (– –) or anapaests
(◡ ◡ –) or dactyls (– ◡ ◡). Longer iambic lines, up to 7½ feet, are
also not uncommon.

(2) Catullus: (i) *the elegiac couplet*, consisting of a hexameter
and a pentameter. (*a*) hexameter: six feet, dactyls (– ◡ ◡) or
spondees (– –), the fifth normally a dactyl, the sixth a spondee

(or a trochee). (The hexameter—unaccompanied by the penta-meter which completes the elegiac couplet—was wrought to a new grandeur by Lucretius and a new subtlety by Virgil.) (*b*) *penta-meter* (five feet, 2½ in each half of the line, those in the second half being always dactyls). The elegiac metre was developed by Propertius, Tibullus and Ovid. Tibullus (usually) and Ovid required the pentameter to end with a dissyllabic word; Catullus and Propertius (in his earlier days) did not. In both hexameter and pentameter the metrical *ictus* falls on the first syllable of each foot, whether dactyl or spondee.

(ii) the 'limping iambic' (*scazon*): an iambic *senarius* with a spondee instead of an *iambus* in the last foot.

(iii) the hendecasyllabic (= line of eleven syllables), a more delicate Greek metre of which Catullus discovered the Latin possibilities (*āt nōbīs mălă mūltă dī dĕaēqŭe*).

(3) Virgil. See above, Catullus (i *a*). Virgil varies caesuras and pauses with masterly refinement. The sense now begins regularly to overflow the single line, thus permitting great variety and complexity of structure. While adhering to the rules of *ictus*, Virgil simultaneously exploits the emphases of stress accents (still valid, in Latin, as they had been in pre-literary times before the days of quantity), bringing about deliberate oppositions or coin-cidences of these two kinds of stress in order to produce a great range of different rhythmical movements. Alliteration and as-sonance contribute to the creation of sound-effects of unprece-dented delicacy and power.

The hexameters of Horace's *Epistles* and *Satires* are conversa-tional and fluent. The rapid verses of Ovid's *Metamorphoses* have debts both to Virgil and Horace.

(4) Horace's lyric metres (*Odes*).

(i) *Alcaic* stanza, often for grand themes, with three types of line (the first repeated), and strongly moving close (| = *caesura*):

281

līnquēndǎ tēllūs | ēt dǒmǔs ēt plǎcēns
ūxōr, nēque hǎrūm | quās cǒlǐs ārbǒrūm
   tē praētěr īnuīsās cǔprēssōs
      ūllǎ brěuēm dǒmǐnūm sěquēntǔr.

(ii) *Sapphic* stanza, light and delicate. The usual form of the stanza has two types of line (the first twice repeated, and the last very short).

dīc ět ārgūtaē | prǒpěrēt Něaēraē
mūrrěūm nōdō | cǒhǐběrě crīnēm:
sī pěr īnuīsūm | mǒrǎ iānǐtōrēm
   fīět, ǎbītō.

(iii) *Asclepiad*, pithy and incisive. The principal form of this metre uses three different types of line. They do not always appear together, but in some stanzas all three are found (the first being repeated):

nūpēr sōllǐcǐtūm | quae mǐhǐ taēdǐūm
nūnc dēsīděrǐūm | cūrǎquě nōn lěuǐs
   īntērfūsǎ nǐtēntēs
      uītēs aēquǒrǎ Cÿclǎdǎs.

Horace uses various other metres also. His metrical accomplishment is linked with his concise manipulation of word-order, rhythm and syntax.

LIST OF ROMAN EMPERORS

Julio-Claudian Dynasty

Augustus   31 B.C.–A.D. 14 (sole rule)

From 43 B.C. until shortly before the battle of Actium (31) he formed one of the Second Triumvirate, with Antony and Lepidus (who was expelled from it in 36). Born C. Octavius (of a family from Velletri [Velitrae], near Rome), he assumed the name C. Julius Caesar in 44, and Augustus in 27 B.C.; before 27 he is known to us as 'Octavian'.

	A.D.
Tiberius	14–37
Caligula	37–41
Claudius	41–54
Nero	54–68
Civil Wars (Galba, Otho, Vitellius)	68–69

Flavian Dynasty

Vespasian; b. Rieti (Reate), central Italy	69–79
Titus	79–81
Domitian	81–96
Nerva	96–98

The Spanish Emperors

Trajan; b. Santiponce (Italica) near Seville, S. Spain	98–117
Hadrian; b. Cadiz (Gades), S. Spain	117–138

The Antonines

A.D.

Antoninus Pius; b. Lanuvio (Lanuvium) near
Rome (family from Nîmes) — 138–161

Marcus Aurelius (family from Spain) — 161–180

Commodus — 180–192

Civil Wars (Pertinax, Didius Julianus) — 193

The North African and Syrian Emperors (*Severi*)

Septimius Severus; b. Zliten (Lepcis
Magna), Libya — 193–211

Caracalla — 211–217

Macrinus — 217–218

Elagabalus; b. Homs (Emesa), Syria — 218–222

Severus Alexander — 222–235

Among later emperors, reference may be made to the Illyrians Aurelian (270–5), Diocletian (284–305; d. 313), and Constantine I 'the Great' (306–37; b. Niš [Naissus], Yugoslavia; edict in favour of the Christians 313; sole rule from 323; Constantinople built as new capital 324–30); Theodosius I (379–395; b. Spain; sole rule from 392); Justinian I (Emperor of East, 527–65; reconquered Italy 553); Constantine XII (last Emperor of East, 1448–53).

WHO'S WHO

This includes the names of some of the numerous Roman writers whose works have not survived (dealt with briefly or not at all in the text). The writers are listed in alphabetical order of their most familiar names.

ACCIUS, L., 170–c. 85 B.C.; b. Pesaro (Pisaurum), Marche, Italy. Tragic poet (fragments survive).

AFRANIUS, L., b. c. 150 B.C. Writer of comedies 'in Roman dress' (fragments survive).

ALBINOVANUS PEDO, wrote under Tiberius. Epic poet and epigrammatist (fragments survive).

AMBROSE (AURELIUS AMBROSIUS), c. A.D. 337–97; b. France. Christian writer (Saint); works include ninety-one letters and hymns.

AMMIANUS MARCELLINUS, b. c. A.D. 330 at Antakya (Antioch), S. Turkey. Wrote history of years A.D. 96–378 (Books 14–31 survive).

ANTONIUS, M., 143–87 B.C. Speeches (lost).

APULEIUS, L., b. c. A.D. 123, at Mdaourouch (Madaurus), Algeria. Writings include only Latin novel surviving complete (*Metamorphoses*, or 'The Golden Ass', including *Cupid and Psyche*); speech *Apologia*, etc.

AUFIDIUS BASSUS, first century A.D. Historian and Epicurean (works lost).

AUGUSTINE (AURELIUS AUGUSTINUS), A.D. 354–430; b. Souk-Ahras (Thagaste), Algeria. Christian writer (Saint); many surviving works, including *Confessions* (13 books) and *De Civitate Dei* (22 books).

AUSONIUS, DECIMUS MAGNUS, c. A.D. 310–c. 395; b. Bordeaux (Burdigala). Poet (descriptive poem *Mosella*, etc.); Christian.

AVIANUS, wrote c. A.D. 400. Fables in elegiac verse.

APPENDICES

BOETHIUS, ANICIUS MANLIUS SEVERINUS, *c.* A.D. 480–524. Christian philosopher: *De Consolatione Philosophiae*, etc.

CAECILIUS STATIUS, *c.* 219–*c.* 166 B.C., a Gaul born in N. Italy. Comic dramatist (fragments survive).

CAESAR, C. JULIUS, dictator, 102/100–44 B.C. Seven books of 'Commentaries' on Gallic War, three on Civil War. Speeches have not survived.

CALPURNIUS SICULUS, T. Wrote *c.* A.D. 50–60. Pastoral poet.

CALVUS, C. LICINIUS MACER, 82–47 B.C. Attic orator and poet (works lost).

CATO, M. PORCIUS, 'the Censor', 234–149 B.C.; b. Tusculum (near Frascati), Lazio, Italy. Seven books of *Origines* (fragments); *De Agri Cultura*; first Latin text-book on rhetoric, and scientific studies (as part of an encyclopaedia), etc.

CATO, *see also* Valerius.

CATULLUS, C. VALERIUS, *c.* 84–*c.* 54 B.C.; b. Verona. Lyric poet, writer of miniature epics, and epigrammatist.

CATULUS, Q. LUTATIUS, consul 102 B.C. Philosophy, speeches, myths, epigrams (lost).

CELSUS, A. CORNELIUS. Wrote under Tiberius, A.D. 14–37. Encyclopaedist (medical sections survive).

CICERO, M. TULLIUS, 106–43 B.C.; b. Arpino (Arpinum), Lazio, Italy. Speeches: *Pro Quinctio, Pro Sex. Roscio Amerino, Pro Roscio Comoedo, In Caecilium Divinatio, In Verrem (Act.* I–II*), Pro Tullio, Pro Fonteio, Pro Caecina, Pro Lege Manilia, Pro Cluentio, Contra Rullum* (III), *Pro C. Rabirio, In Catilinam* (IV), *Pro Murena, Pro Sulla, Pro Archia, Pro Flacco, Post Reditum ad Quirites, Post Reditum in Senatu, De Domo Sua, De Haruspicum Responso, Pro Sestio, In Vatinium, Pro Caelio, De Provinciis Consularibus, Pro Balbo, In Pisonem, Pro Plancio, Pro Rabirio Postumo, Pro Milone, Pro Marcello, Pro Ligario, Pro Rege Deiotaro, Philippics* (XIV). Rhetorical Works: *De Inventione, De Oratore, Oratoriae Partitiones, De Optimo Genere Oratorum, Brutus, Orator, Topica.* Philosophical Works: *De Republica* (VI), *De Legibus* (I–III survive), *De Consolatione* and *Hortensius* (both lost), *Academica* (two versions, parts lost), *De Finibus Bonorum*

et Malorum (V), *Tusculanae Disputationes* (V), *De Natura Deorum*
(III), *De Divinatione* (II), *De Fato*, *De Senectute* (*Cato Major*),
De Amicitia (*Laelius*), *Paradoxa Stoicorum*, *De Officiis* (III),
Cato and *De Gloria* (both lost). Letters: sixteen books each
To Friends and *To Atticus*, three to *Quintus*, nine (two surviving)
to *Brutus*. Poetry (fragments).

CLAUDIAN (CLAUDIUS CLAUDIANUS). Wrote *c.* A.D. 395–404; b.
probably at Alexandria. Pagan poet.

CLUVIUS RUFUS, first century A.D. Histories of early Principate (lost).

COLUMELLA, L. JUNIUS MODERATUS, b. Cadiz (Gades), Spain. Wrote
c. A.D. 65, on agriculture, in prose and verse.

COMMODIANUS, fifth century A.D.; b. Arles (Arelate). Wrote poetry
(largely based on stress-accent).

CORNELIUS SEVERUS, Augustan poet (Sicilian War, etc.; lost).

CRASSUS, L. LICINIUS, consul 95 B.C. Speeches (lost).

CREMUTIUS CORDUS, A., d. A.D. 25. Histories of Republican tendency
(lost).

CYPRIAN (CAECILIUS CYPRIANUS), *c.* A.D. 200–58; b. N. Africa.
Christian writer (Saint).

DONATUS, AELIUS, fourth century A.D. Grammarian. Wrote commentaries on Terence and Virgil, of which parts survive (including *Life of Virgil*).

ENNIUS, Q., 239–169 B.C.; b. Rudiae (near Lecce), S.E. Italy. 'Father
of Roman Poetry.' Epic poem: *Annals* (550 lines out of eighteen
books survive). Tragic and comic dramatist, didactic poet
(fragments).

FESTUS, SEX. POMPEIUS, late second century A.D. Epitomiser of
Verrius Flaccus (*q.v.*).

FRONTINUS, SEX. JULIUS, *c.* A.D. 30–104. Writer on military subjects
and engineering.

FRONTO, M. CORNELIUS, *c.* A.D. 100–66; b. Constantine (Cirta),
Algeria. Chief orator of his day, developed 'New Speech'.

GAIUS, second century A.D. Writer on Law (*Institutes*).

GALLUS, C. CORNELIUS, *c.* 69–26 B.C.; b. Fréjus (Forum Julii),
S. France. Elegiac poetry (lost).

GELLIUS, A., *c.* A.D. 123–65. Twenty books of *Noctes Atticae* in prose.

HIRTIUS, A., d. 43 B.C.; b. Ferentino (?) (Ferentinum), Lazio, Italy. Wrote eighth book of Caesar's *Gallic War*, and *Alexandrine War*.

HORACE (Q. HORATIUS FLACCUS), 65–8 B.C.; b. Venusia (near Rionero), S.E. Italy. Lyric poetry: four books of *Odes*, *Secular Hymn*. Hexameter poetry: two books of *Satires*, two of *Epistles*, *Ars Poetica*. Iambic poetry: *Epodes*.

HORTENSIUS (Q. HORTENSIUS HORTALUS), 114–50 B.C. Leading orator (speeches lost).

JEROME (EUSEBIUS HIERONYMUS), *c.* A.D. 348–420; b. Stridon in Dalmatia, Yugoslavia. Christian writer (Saint); Latin Bible (Vulgate), *Chronicle*, etc.

JUVENAL (DEC. JUNIUS JUVENALIS), *c.* A.D. 50–after 127; b. Aquino (Aquinum), Lazio, Italy. Sixteen Satires.

LACTANTIUS, CAECILIUS FIRMIANUS, *c.* A.D. 250–317 (?); b. N. Africa. Christian writer (*Divinae Institutiones*).

LAEVIUS, MELISSUS (?), wrote *c.* 100 B.C. Erotic and mythological poetry (fragments).

LIVIUS ANDRONICUS, L., *c.* 284–204 B.C.; b. Taranto (Tarentum), S. Italy. Wrote first Latin comedy and tragedy.

LIVY (T. LIVIUS), 59 B.C.–A.D. 17; b. Padua (Patavium), N.E. Italy. History of Rome (*Ab Vrbe Condita*) in 142 books (35 survive).

LUCAN (M. ANNAEUS LUCANUS), A.D. 39–65; b. Cordova (Corduba), Spain. Epic poem: *Bellum Civile* ('Pharsalia') in ten books.

LUCILIUS, C., *c.* 180–102 B.C.; b. Suessa Aurunca, Lazio-Campania border, W. Italy. Thirty books of *Satires* (1,300 lines survive).

LUCRETIUS (T. LUCRETIUS CARUS), *c.* 94–55 (?) B.C. Philosophical poem: *De Rerum Natura* in six books.

MACROBIUS, AMBROSIUS THEODOSIUS, wrote *c.* A.D. 400. *Saturnalia* (Symposium in seven books).

MANILIUS, M., wrote under Augustus and Tiberius. Poem on science and astronomy: *Astronomica*, five books survive.

MARTIAL (M. VALERIUS MARTIALIS), *c.* A.D. 40–104; b. Calatayud (Bilbilis), Spain. Twelve books of *Epigrams*.

MARTIANUS CAPELLA, wrote *c.* A.D. 420. Allegory of Seven Liberal Arts (prose and verse).

MELA, POMPONIUS, wrote under Caligula (A.D. 37–41) or Claudius; b. Tingentera (near Gibraltar). Geographical writer: *De Chorographia*, three books.

MINUCIUS FELIX, second or third century A.D.; b. N. Africa (?), Christian philosopher (dialogue *Octavius*).

NAEVIUS, CNAEUS, c. 270–201 B.C. Comic dramatist and epic poet (*Bellum Poenicum*) (fragments survive).

NEMESIANUS, M. AURELIUS OLYMPIUS, late third century A.D.; b. Carthage. Pastoral and didactic poet.

NEPOS, CORNELIUS, c. 99–24 B.C.; b. N. Italy. Biographer (*De Viris Illustribus*, parts survive).

NIGIDIUS FIGULUS, P., first century B.C. Scholar, scientist, philosopher (fragments).

OVID (P. OVIDIUS NASO), 43 B.C.–A.D. 17 (?); b. Sulmona (Sulmo), Abruzzi, Central Italy. Elegiac poetry: *Amores* (3 books), *Heroides*, *Medicamina Faciei*, *Ars Amatoria* (3 books), *Remedia Amoris*, *Fasti* (6 books), *Tristia* (5 books), *Epistulae ex Ponto* (4 books), *Ibis*, *Nux*, others lost. Hexameter poetry: *Metamorphoses* (15 books), *Halieutica*. Tragedy: *Medea* (2 lines survive).

PACUVIUS, M., 220–c. 130 B.C. Tragic dramatist (works lost).

PAPINIAN (AEMILIUS PAPINIANUS), d. A.D. 212. Writer on Law.

PERSIUS (A. PERSIUS FLACCUS), A.D. 34–62. Philosophical satirist.

PETRONIUS ARBITER, C. (?), d. A.D. 65. Novelist: 'Satyricon'; large part lost, but *Dinner of Trimalchio*, poems, etc., survive.

PHAEDRUS, c. 15 B.C.–A.D. 50; b. Macedonia. Fables in iambic verse.

PLAUTUS, T. MACC(I)US, c. 254–184 B.C.; b. Mercato Saraceno (Sarsina), Emilia (Umbria), Italy. Comic dramatist: *Amphitruo*, *Asinaria*, *Aulularia*, *Bacchides*, *Captivi*, *Casina*, *Cistellaria*, *Curculio*, *Epidicus*, *Menaechmi*, *Mercator*, *Miles Gloriosus*, *Mostellaria*, *Persa*, *Poenulus*, *Pseudolus*, *Rudens*, *Stichus*, *Trinummus*, *Truculentus* and fragments of *Vidularia*.

PLINY THE ELDER (C. PLINIUS SECUNDUS), A.D. 23/4–79; b. Como (Comum), Lombardy, N. Italy. *Naturalis Historia* (37 books). Lost works: on military science, language, history (20 books on German wars, 31 on recent Roman history).

PLINY THE YOUNGER (P. CAECILIUS SECUNDUS, then—after adoption
by his uncle Pliny the Elder—C. Plinius Caecilius Secundus),
A.D. 61/2–before 114; b. Como (Comum), Lombardy, N. Italy.
Ten books of literary *Letters*. Speech: *Panegyricus* to Trajan.

POLLIO, C. ASINIUS, 76 B.C.–A.D. 5. Histories, Atticist speeches,
letters, writings on grammar and literary criticism, tragedies
(lost).

PROPERTIUS, SEX., 54/48–after 16 B.C., probably b. Assisi (Assisium),
Umbria, Central Italy. *Cynthia* and three other books of elegiac
poetry.

PRUDENTIUS, AURELIUS CLEMENS, A.D. 348–after 405; b. Spain,
Christian poet.

PUBLILIUS SYRUS, first century B.C.; b. Syria, writer of mimes, including maxims.

QUINTILIAN (M. FABIUS QUINTILIANUS), *c.* A.D. 35–after *c.* 95;
b. Calahorra (Calagurris), Spain. Educationalist: *Institutio Oratoria* (12 books, literary criticism in Book x).

SALLUST (C. SALLUSTIUS CRISPUS), 86–*c.* 34 B.C.; b. San Vittorno (Ami-
ternum), Abruzzi, Central Italy. Historian: *Histories* (5 books,
lost), *Bellum Catilinae, Bellum Jugurthinum*.

SCAEVOLA, Q. MUCIUS, 'Pontifex', d. 82 B.C. Writer of first systematic treatise on Civil Law (lost).

SENECA THE ELDER, L. (?) ANNAEUS, *c.* 55 B.C.–A.D. 37; b. Cordova
(Corduba), Spain. *History* (lost). Writer on rhetoric: *Controversiae* (5 out of 10 books survive), *Suasoriae* (1 book survives).

SENECA THE YOUNGER, L. ANNAEUS (= 'Seneca'), *c.* 5/4 B.C.—A.D. 65;
b. Cordova (Corduba), Spain. Speeches (lost). Ethical treatises:
*De Providentia, De Constantia Sapientis, De Ira, De Vita Beata,
De Otio, De Tranquillitate Animi, De Brevitate Vitae, De Cle-
mentia* (3 books, 1 and part of a second survive), *De Beneficiis,*
and three *Consolations*: *Ad Marciam, Ad Polybium, Ad Helviam
Matrem*. Scientific writings: *Naturales Questiones*. Ethical,
literary letters: *Epistulae Morales* (124). Satire in prose and
verse: *Apocolocyntosis*. Tragedies: *Agamemnon, Hercules, Hercules
Oetaeus, Medea, Oedipus, Phaedra, Phoenissae, Thyestes,
Troades.*

SERVIUS (MARIUS (?) HONORATUS), fourth/fifth century A.D. Grammarian; commentary on Virgil.

SIDONIUS APOLLINARIS (C. SOLLIUS MODESTUS (?) APOLLINARIS SIDONIUS), *c.* A.D. 430–soon after 479; b. Lyon (Lugdunum). Christian poet (Saint). Also nine books of *Epistulae*.

SILIUS ITALICUS, A.D. 25/6–101, probably b. Padua (Patavium), N.E. Italy. Epic poet: *Punica* (17 books).

SISENNA, L. CORNELIUS, d. 67 B.C. *Histories* (12 books, lost). Translations of Greek 'Milesian Tales' (lost).

STATIUS, P. PAPINIUS, *c.* A.D. 45–96; b. Naples (Neapolis). Poet. Epics: *Thebais* (12 books), *Achilleis* (2 books). Lyric and occasional poems: *Silvae* (5 books).

SUETONIUS (C. SUETONIUS TRANQUILLUS), *c.* A.D. 69–140; probably b. Rome. Biographer: *De Vita Caesarum* (12 Caesars), *De Viris Illustribus*, including *De Grammaticis et Rhetoribus*, *De Poetis* (at least 3 survive), *De Oratoribus* (15, summary of 1 survives), *De Historicis* (1 out of 6 survives). Many other works (only fragments survive).

SULPICIA, late first century B.C., elegiac poetess (6 short poems survive).

TACITUS, CORNELIUS, *c.* A.D. 55–after 115; possibly b. N. Italy. Historian: *Histories* (12 or 14 books; 4 and part of a fifth survive), *Annals* (18 or 16 books; 11 and part of a twelfth survive). Biographer of *Agricola*. Descriptive work: *Germania* (*De Origine et Situ Germanorum*).

TERENCE (P. TERENTIUS AFER), *c.* 195–159 B.C.; b. Carthage (?). Comic dramatist: *Andria*, *Adelphi*, *Eunuchus*, *Heautontimorumenus*, *Hecyra*, *Phormio*.

TERTULLIAN (Q. SEPTIMIUS FLORENS TERTULLIANUS), *c.* A.D. 160–225; b. N. Africa. Christian writer, latterly of Montanist sect. Over thirty surviving works including *Apologeticus* (speech).

TITINIUS, second century B.C. (?). Earliest known writer of comedies 'in Roman dress'.

TRIBONIAN, d. A.D. 543–5; probably b. Manavgat (Side), S. Anatolia. Chief collaborator of Byzantine Emperor Justinian in codification of laws.

ULPIAN (DOMITIUS ULPIANUS), d. A.D. 228; b. Sur (Tyre), Lebanon. Writer on Law.

VALERIUS ANTIAS, early first century B.C. Historian ('annalist') (at least 75 books, lost).

VALERIUS CATO, P., b. *c.* 100 B.C., N. Italy. Poet, leader of 'younger' ('Neoteric') school (works lost).

VALERIUS FLACCUS BALBUS SETINUS, C., d. A.D. 90/3. Epic poet: *Argonautica* (8 books survive).

VALERIUS MAXIMUS, wrote under Tiberius (A.D. 14–37). Moral and rhetorical historian: *Facta ac Dicta Memorabilia* (9 books).

VARIUS RUFUS, wrote under Augustus. Epic poet: *De Morte* and *Panegyric* of Augustus (both lost). Tragic dramatist: *Thyestes* (lost). Helped to edit *Aeneid.*

VARRO, M. TERENTIUS, 116–27 B.C.; b. Rieti (Reate), Lazio, Italy (or Rome?). Greatest Roman scholar. *De Lingua Latina* (25 books, 2 and parts of 4 more survive), *Res Rusticae* (3 books); *Saturae Menippeae* (prose and verse; 150 books, fragments survive), *Antiquitates* (25 books on *res humanae*, 16 on *res divinae*; lost); *Disciplinae* (9 books, encyclopaedia; lost), *De Vita Populi Romani* (lost), *De Iure Civili* (15 books; lost), and many other works, all lost.

VELLEIUS PATERCULUS, C., *c.* 19 B.C.–after A.D. 31, b. Campania. Amateur historian: *Historiae Romanae.*

VERRIUS FLACCUS, wrote under Augustus. Scholar. *Res Memoria Dignae* (lost), *De Significatu Verborum* (epitomised by Festus), etc.

VIRGIL (P. VERGILIUS MARO), 70–19 B.C.; b. Andes, near Mantua, Lombardy, North Italy. Earliest poems of doubtful attribution: at least parts of *Catalepton* (14 short poems) are by him. Pastoral poetry: *Eclogues* (10 poems). Descriptive, quasi-didactic poetry: *Georgics* (4 books). Romantic epic poetry: *Aeneid* (12 books).

VITRUVIUS POLLIO, wrote under Augustus. Writer on architecture and engineering: *De Architectura* (10 books).

INDEX

*The principal references to authors are printed in bold type. See also
Who's Who (Appendix 4, p. 285).*

Academy 65, 279

Accius 237

Acts of the Apostles 255

Aelius Caesar 245

Aeschylus 22, 192, 237

Aesop 236

Agricola 108, 118

Agrippa 142, 204, 211

Agrippina (junior) 118

Alaric 259

Alcaeus 184, 207 f.

Alexander the Great 120, 148, 151

Alexandrian School 118, 120, 144, **148–
52**, 153 f., 157–61, 163, 165, 167 f.,
170 f., 175 f., 186 f., 191 f., 208–
10, 223, 230 f., 244

Ambrose, St 138, 161, 215, **257 f.**, 259

Ammianus Marcellinus 116

Annales Maximi 92

Antiochus of Ascalon 66, 279

Antoninus Pius 12, 284

Antony (Marcus Antonius) 41, 49,
77, 181, 199, 283

Aper 59

Apollonius of Rhodes **192–8**

Apollonius of Tyana 279

Apuleius 12 f., **125–9**, 147

Aratus of Soli 186

Archilochus 165, 235

Aristides of Miletus 121

Aristophanes 20, 22

Aristophontes of Athens 128, 220

Aristotle 51, 65, 84 f., 118, 134, 141,
145, 191, 213, 264, 267, 277 f.

Atellan Fables 17 f.

Atticus 43, 76–9, 85

Attius, *see* Accius

Augustine, St 13, 126, 138, 257, **259 f.**,
261, 264, 267

Augustus 10 f., 41, 56, 58, 68, 77,
101–3, 105–9, 113, 134 f., 170,
172–4, 181, 183–5, 189, 199 f.,
204 f., 207, 210 f., 220, 223, 226 f.,
232 f., 235, 283

Aurelian 13, 284

Aurelius, Marcus 12, 126, 278, 284

Ausonius 229

Avianus 236

Babrius 236

Bion 218 f., 251

Boethius 14, 261, 279

Brutus 41, 53, 76, 79, 94, 105, 211

Caelius 78

Caesar, Julius 9, 17, 29, 39 f., 53,
77 f., **94–7**, 99–102, 105, 108, 113,
117, 199, 239, 241 f., 262, 283

Caligula 57, 70, 104, 108 f., 119, 283

Callimachus 150, 158, 167 f., 171,
176, 192, 227

Camillus 105

Carneades 279

Carvilius, Spurius 37

Cassiodorus 261

Cassius 41, 105

Catalepton, see Virgilian Appendix

Catiline 39, 89, 98–100

Cato the Elder (Censor) 51, 91 f., 187

Cato the Younger 9, 95 f., 99 f.

INDEX

Catullus 10, 151, **159–69**, 170, 177, 205, 208, 226, 228, 230, 235, 243 f., 280 f.

Catulus, *see* Lutatius

Christians, Christianity 13 f., 66, 68 f., 75, 83, 161, 181 f., 198, 215, 240, 249, **255–60**, 261, 278

Chrysogonus 38

Cicero, in general 10, 14, 27, 31, 268
letters **76–80**, 85, 89 f., 157, 268
literary and rhetorical criticism **50–5**, 56, 63 f., 84–6, 88–90, 92, 136 f., 157, 194, 267
philosophical works **66–8**, 71 f., 75, 79, 93, 259 f., 278 f.
poetry 159, 186
reputation 47–50, 255–61, 264
speeches **35–50**, 57 f., 60–3, 79, 126, 268
style 12, 29, 44–8, 62, 70, 79 f., 107, 110, 125, 258, 261

Cicero, Quintus 76, 79, 157

Ciris, see Virgilian Appendix

Claudian 229, 243

Claudius 11, 69 f., 109, 119, 283

Cleopatra 78, 198 f., 234

Clitarchus 120

Clodia 161

Clodius 40

Cluentius, Aulus 42

Constantine the Great 13, 182, 261, 284

Copa, see Virgilian Appendix

Cornutus 239 f.

Crassus 40, 172

Culex, see Virgilian Appendix

Curio 79

Cynics 249, 277 f.

Democritus 154

Demosthenes 35, 44 f.

Diocletian 13, 284

Diogenes 277

Dolabella 79

Domitian 12, 61–3, 108, 111, 245, 249, 283

Elocutio Novella, see New Speech

Empedocles 153

Ennius 9, 123, 153 f., **193 f.**, 195, 198, 219, 221, 227, 237, 241, 280

Epictetus 278

Epicurus, Epicureans 65, 80, 135, 154–7, 213 f., 238, 249, **277 f.**, 279

Euphorion 158

Euripides 22, 147, 192, 237

Fabius Pictor 90

Fescennine Verses 15–17

Fronto 126

Gaius, emperor, *see* Caligula

Gaius, lawyer 73

Gallus 169 f., 175, 177, 180

Germanicus 186, 228

Granius Licinianus 99

Hadrian 12, 73, 113 f., 118, 245 f., 283

Hannibal 243

Hebrews 182, 255

Herennius 52

Herodotus 107

Hesiod 153, 184, 186

Hieronymus, *see* Jerome

Hippolochus 123

Hipponax 165, 235

Hirtius, Aulus 97

Homer 129, 134, 137, 146, 153, 160, 191–5, 197, 199–201, 229, 272

Horace, in general 10, 82, 105, 151, 172, 179, 211, 216 f., 224, 237, 258 f., 279
Epodes 166, 211, 220 f., 235
literary criticism 3, 21, 28, 60, 134 f., **137–42**, 144, 146 f., 177, 185, 219 f.
Odes (and *Secular Hymn*) **205–17**, 221–3, 281 f.

294

Horace (*cont.*)
   Satires and *Epistles* (*see also* literary
      criticism) 80, 206, 215, 217, **220–
      2**, 225, 239, 246 f., 251
   style and metre 21, 141, 160, 162,
      166, 208–10, 220 f., 281 f.
Hortensius 39, 53, 259

Isaiah, *see* Hebrews
Isocrates 44 f., 51, 85 f.

Jerome, St 13, 182, 257, **258 f.**, 264
Jews, *see* Hebrews
Jugurtha 98 f.
Julia 227
Julian 'the Apostate' 257
Justinian I 14, 74, 284
Juvenal 12, 245, **246–51**

Lactantius **256 f.**
Laevius 151
Lepidus (triumvir) 41, 283
Leucippus 154
Livius Andronicus 18 f., 27, 161, 193,
   237
Livy 10, 16, **103–7**, 108, 113, 217, 241
'Longinus' 44 f., 59
Lucan 122, **240–3**, 246
Lucceius 89 f.
Lucian 125
Lucilius 9, **219 f.**, 221 f., 239
Lucius of Patrae 125
Lucretius 10, 65 f., 135, **153–8**, 185 f.,
   188, 194, 202, 230, 278, 281
Lutatius Catulus, Quintus 151
Lysias 53

Maecenas 10, 173 f., 185, 206, 211,
   215, 220 f., 228
Marius 9, 38, 98 f.
Martial 98, 107, 240, **244–6**, 247
Maternus 59 f.
Meleager 163, 176
Menander 20, 22 f., 29 f., 218, 221, 225

Menippus, Menippean satire 121 f.,
   129, 165, 221
Messalla (Corvinus) 174
Metellus (Numidicus) 99
Milesian Tales 121 f.
Minucius Felix 13, **255 f.**
Molon 53
Moretum, see Virgilian Appendix

Naevius 28, 193–5, 198, 237
Neoptolemus 137
Neo-Pythagoreans, *see* Pythagoreans
Neoterics 158 f., 170 f.
Nepos 118
Nero 11, 61, 68 f., 108–10, 118–21,
   182, 237, 239 f., 242, 244, 249,
   283
Nerva 81, 114, 283
New Speech 12, 126
Nicander 186
Nigidius Figulus, Publius 279

Octavian, *see* Augustus
Oppianicus senior and junior 42
Origen 258
Ovid 10, 80, 125, 168, 170, 173 f.,
   221, **223–34**, 237, 243, 281

Pacuvius 237
Panaetius 9, 278
Papinian 13, 74 f.
Paul, St 69
Peripatetics 65, 213 f., 278 f.
Persius **239 f.**, 246
Pervigilium Veneris 161, 215
Petrarch 47, 64, 79, 115, 215, **267 f.**
Petronius 11, **121–5**, 126, 129, 141,
   209, 244
Phaedrus **235 f.**
Philip of Macedon 148
Phlyax Farces 18
Piso 137
Plato 44, 59, 80, 123, 134, 259, 277,
   279

Plautus 8 f., **19–29**, 30 f., 141, 144, 152, 235, 237
Pliny the Elder 81 f.
Pliny the Younger **80–3**, 112
Plotinus 279
Plotius Gallus 37
Plutarch 118, 239
Pollio 97, 105, 181
Polybius 87, 90, 93
Pompey 9, 25, 40, 96, 105, 199, 241 f.
Porphyry 279
Posidonius 278
Propertius 169, **170–3**, 174, 179, 184, 220, 223 f., 228, 281
Prudentius 14, 215
Publilius Syrus 17
Pyrrho 279
Pythagoreans 279

Quintilian 4, 44–7, 57, **60–4**, 68, 84–6, 101 f., 107, 134, 136, 162, 165–70, 173, 194, 205, 209, 217 f., 233, 240, 242, 269

Roscius, Sextus 38

Sallust **97–101**, 103, 107 f., 110
Salvius Julianus 73, 75
Sappho 160, 171, 207 f.
Sassia 42
Sceptics 279
Scipio Aemilianus 9, 30, 51, 219
Sejanus 235
Seneca the Elder **57–9**, 61, 64, 237 f.
Seneca the Younger, in general 11, 39, 61, 120
   letters **80**, 81, 237
   literary criticism 31, 62, 188, 236
   philosophy 31, 61–3, **68–71**, 75, 80, 237 f., 242, 278
   reputation 11, 61 f., 69, 238 f.
   satire 70, 221, 237
   speeches 57, 120
   style 48, 61 f., 69–71, 82, 238
   tragedies 70, 122, **237–9**, 241 f.
Severus, Septimius 13, 74, 284
Silius Italicus 243
Simonides 163
Sisenna 121
Socrates 277
Sophocles 22, 192, 237
Sotades 218 f.
Statius 157, **243 f.**
Stesichorus 175
Stoics 11, 31, 65–72, 75, 80, 85, 99, 113, 135, 196–8, 201, 212–14, 220, 238–41, 249, 258, **278**, 279
Suetonius **117–20**
Sulla 9, 38 f., 42, 99
Sulpicia 174

Tabulae Pontificum 91
Tacitus 12, 57, **59–60**, 61, 81, 87, **108–17**, 118, 246, 249, 269
Terence 8 f., 26, **29–31**, 152, 235
Tertullian 13, **256**, 258 f.
Theocritus 175 f., 178 f., 182 f.
Theodosius I 257, 284
Thucydides 101
Tiberius 57, 109–11, 114, 226, 235, 283
Tibullus 169, **173–4**, 179, 223 f., 281
Tiro 76
Titus 12, 61, 245, 283
Trajan 12, 81, 83, 114, 246, 283
Trebonius 77
Tribonian 74 f.
Tucca 199
Tullia 43
Twelve Tables 71, 75

Ulpian 13, 74

Valerius Flaccus 243
Varius Rufus 199, 237
Varro 20, 36, 118, 121, 165, 187 f., 221

INDEX

Verres 39

Vespasian 12, 61, 245, 283

Virgil, in general 10, 82, 137, 151, 174, 210 f., 214, 217, 225, 227 f., 237, 243, 245

    Aeneid 104, 112, 138, 172, 183, **190–204**, 205, 223, 234, 241, 278

    early poems attributed to, *see* Virgilian Appendix

    Eclogues 170, **175–83**, 184, 186 f., 199, 202

    Georgics 157, 177, 183, **184–90**, 202, 220

    reputation 181–3, 190, 215, 258 f., 261–3, 265, 267

    style and metre 142, 183, 188, 191, 202–4, 209, 221, 230, 246, 281

Virgilian Appendix 123, 160, 169, 175, 230

Zeno 278

In this survey of the literature of the Romans and the Latin-speaking peoples and their empire, Professor Grant writes for the reader outside the ranks of classical specialists as well as for those who know Latin. He writes especially about works that have clearly helped to form our civilization.

CONTENTS:

Introductory sections summarize the main periods of Roman literary activity, its historical background, and its relation to Greek authors. Then follows a description of its beginnings, leading to the great comic dramatists.

In the main portion of the book, Part I gives an account of Latin prose writings and Part II of poetry. When he discusses poetry, oratory and history, Professor Grant explains the difficulties that we have to overcome before we can appreciate and enjoy the Roman achievement.

The last chapter suggests how the great early Christian writers made use of this Roman heritage and passed it on to us, and finally something is said of the preservation and handing down of Latin literature and thought during the past 1500 years.

TRANSLATIONS:

Passages quoted from Latin writers are given in English translations, including a number by well-known living poets; care has been taken to choose versions which avoid boring conventions of language and which best convey the spirit or quality of their originals.

NOTES AND REFERENCES:

For the convenience of students, explanatory notes and discussions are added at the end of the book. A 'Who's Who' gives a list of leading Roman writers, their dates and the names of their principal works.

THE AUTHOR

Michael Grant after occupying a Fellowship at Trinity College, Cambridge, became in 1948 Professor of Humanity in the University of Edinburgh. He is President of the Royal Numismatic Society. His previous books include: *From Imperium to Auctoritas* (Cambridge University Press, 1946); *Roman Anniversary Issues* (Cambridge University Press, 1950); *Aspects of the Principate of Tiberius* (American Numismatic Society, New York, 1950); *Ancient History* (Methuen, 1952); *The Six Main Aes Coinages of Augustus* (Edinburgh University Press, 1953); *Roman Imperial Money* (Nelson, 1954).

	Comedy	Oratory	Literary criticism	
3rd/2nd CENT. B.C.	Plautus Terence			
MID 1st. CENT. B.C. *Ciceronian Age*		Cicero	Cicero	
LATE 1st CENT. B.C./ **EARLY 1st CENT. A.D.** *Augustan Age*			Horace	
1st CENT. A.D. *Post-Augustans*			*Seneca the elder* Tacitus Quintilian	th
EARLY 2nd CENT. A.D. *Climax of Silver Age*				
2nd/3rd CENT. A.D. *The Africans*				
4th/5th CENT. A.D. *The Fathers*			*Servius*	